Farm
Journal's
BEST-EVER
PIES

Farm Journal's BEST-EVER

PIES

By Patricia A. Ward

Farm Journal, Inc.
Philadelphia, Pennsylvania

Distributed to the trade by
Doubleday & Company, Inc.
Garden City, New York

Other Farm Journal Cookbooks

Farm Journal's Country Cookbook
Homemade Bread
America's Best Vegetable Recipes
Homemade Candy
Homemade Ice Cream and Cake
Country Fair Cookbook
Great Home Cooking in America
Farm Journal's Homemade Snacks
Farm Journal's Best-Ever Recipes
Farm Journal's Great Dishes from the Oven
Farm Journal's Freezing and Canning Cookbook
Farm Journal's Friendly Food Gifts from your Kitchen
Farm Journal's Choice Chocolate Recipes
Farm Journal's Cook It Your Way
Farm Journal's Complete Home Baking Book
Farm Journal's Meal & Menu Planner
Farm Journal's Speedy Skillet Meals
Farm Journal's Best-Ever Cookies

Book Design by Michael P. Durning

Color photographs by William Hazzard/
Hazzard Studios; Hoedt Studios (facing
p. 54); and Bruce Harlow (facing p. 151).

Library of Congress Cataloging in Publication Data
Main entry under title:
Farm journal's best-ever pies.
Includes index.
1. Pastry. I. Ward, Patricia A.
II. Farm journal (Philadelphia, 1956-)
III. Title: Best-ever pies.
TX773.F328   641.8'652   81-12455
ISBN 0-385-17729-1   AACR2

Contents

Color Photographs

following page 54

Decorative Pie Edges
Lemon Velvet Pie
A Trio of Chiffon Pies
Fruit and Cream Tart

following page 150

Chocolate Cheese Swirl Pie
Apple Pie in Cheddar Crust
Savannah Pecan Pie
Cheese-Spinach Quiche

Foreword

You can *like* cake, you can be *fond* of ice cream... but *pie* is dessert. You agree? Then let me tell you of the piece of pie that stands first among all the succulent wedges served me in farm kitchens over many years.

Doris Thompson's sweet-cream raisin pie. She presented it modestly at the close of a simple noon dinner. Oh, for more such simple meals prepared by a truly fine country cook. Home-raised beef, slow-cooked, fork-tender, dressed in its own juices. A small cloud of whipped potatoes, topped with smoking brown gravy that distilled the flavor of the meat. And the vegetable! Corn frozen fresh from the farm garden, now brought to life in a casserole, combined with eggs, milk, cracker crumbs and a hint of onion—a common dish raised to gourmet taste.

Such undeniably good food deserved appreciative palates. And we came to the table ready, her husband and I, spirits and appetites braced by an autumn morning tangy as a Jonathan apple. We ate in the kitchen, surrounded by cooking smells, warm, relaxed.

But the pie! *Sweet*-cream raisin—she accented the sweet to distinguish it from the sour-cream variety. And to compare it with the raisin-cream pies common to café menus—raisin-studded vanilla pudding—would do it a grave injustice.

She brought the pie from her work counter, and cut it in our view. A double-crust pie, the crust a bit pale. But I later learned the reason for that.

Her knife slipped easily through the tender pastry. She worked pieces gently from the tin and settled them on plates with care. And now I had the pie before me, still faintly warm from the oven.

I dipped my head to first enjoy the fragrance of this master cook's creation. Delicate, yet with an underlying richness, it moved my hand to my fork almost unconsciously. Yet I paused a second, sharpening desire with anticipation. The filling, the pale gold of freshly-churned natural butter, had set into a custard just firm enough to support the crust and stand without spreading.

When I could wait no longer, I pressed my fork through the flaky crust and tender filling, and lifted the first bite to my mouth. And smiled. Even as I swallowed that introductory sample, I turned to express my delight to my hostess. She had watched my face, and I saw her eyes warm with pleasure at my reaction. I asked for details of the ingredients even as I raised another bite. Although automatically I chewed, my tongue alone could have blended that airy mixture of crust and custard. And the flavor! Sunny and sweet as a finch's song, with the raisins adding warm brown notes.

What magic a skilled cook can work with a simple combination of fresh heavy cream, sugar, eggs and in this pie, raisins. Yes, those ingredients made up Doris Thompson's sweet-cream raisin pie. But the exact recipe. . . ah! I can't reveal that. A cook should retain the privilege of sharing a recipe individually with friends, bestowing it as a gift from a treasury of experience and skill.

I savored the pie, bite by bite, then shamelessly burnished the plate with my fork, recovering every crumb of the pale, delicious crust. (Why pale? The filling, in large part cream, fares best with a lower-than-usual oven temperature.)

Finished, I praised the pie again, and the dinner as well. Mrs. Thompson, predictably, turned my compliments aside. "Oh, I'm sure you were just extra-hungry," she protested. I smiled and shook my head, and she smiled, too, as she cleared away the dishes.

Doris Thompson's sweet-cream raisin pie. It became my new standard for measuring *desserts*. I don't expect to find its equal. But I do feel a duty to continue the search.

Dick Seim
Associate Editor, Farm Journal

Introduction

We have good reason for believing that these pie recipes are the best ever, because they were created by the finest pie-bakers anywhere—the women who live on farms and ranches all over America.

Much has changed in American agriculture and in American cooking over the last few generations: the "pie safes" once used for food storage have become collector's items, and since the publication in 1965 of Farm Journal's original *Complete Pie Cookbook*, the food processor has joined the rolling pin as basic equipment in many a farm kitchen. Yet the values and basic know-how of good country cooks have been preserved—in a legacy of wonderful recipes and the belief that a little extra effort in the kitchen reaps abundant rewards at the dinner table.

Recently we asked the readers of Farm Journal Magazine to once again share their favorite pie recipes, and their enthusiastic response proved that pies are as popular as ever. After reading hundreds of recipes, our home economists sampled the most tempting-sounding and refined each recipe in our own Farm Journal Test Kitchens. Then we adapted 60 of the most popular dessert and main-dish recipes from our first pie book, plus scores of other Farm Journal recipes, updating ingredients and techniques.

At the same time, we made sure to keep all the old-fashioned good taste as well as a bountiful variety of flavors. No matter which pie you think of whenever you think of pie, you're sure to find a reliable recipe for it in the pages that follow—and you won't have to look far if you're like the Oregon farmer who told me that he likes only two kinds of pie: one-crust and two-crust.

Whatever your preference, I hope you'll enjoy preparing and savoring these pies just as much as we did.

Basic Pie-making Utensils

All these utensils are handy to have, but you can get along fine without some of them (and we'll tell you how). Many recipes also call for such basic kitchen equipment as a mixer or saucepan, and if you're lucky enough to own a microwave oven or a food processor, you'll be able to put those appliances to use with some of the recipes, too.

Cooling Racks: One or two wire racks are needed. Every baked pie should be cooled on a rack so that air can circulate underneath.

Flour Sifter: You'll need a sifter to sift flour before measuring and to help mix dry ingredients. A large sieve will do the job, too.

Kitchen Shears: Kitchen shears are useful for trimming the pastry overhang. You also can use regular scissors or a sharp knife.

Measuring Cups: Two types of cups are needed for measuring dry and liquid ingredients. To be accurate, never substitute one type of measuring cup for the other.

For measuring dry ingredients, nested-type metal or plastic cups are available, in sets of four: ¼ cup, ⅓ cup, ½ cup and 1 cup.

For measuring liquids, use glass or plastic measuring cups with ounce measurements marked on the sides. Liquid measuring cups are available in 1-cup, 1-pint and 1-quart sizes.

Measuring Spoons: You'll need a set of four in these sizes: ¼ teaspoon, ½ teaspoon, 1 teaspoon and 1 tablespoon.

Metal Spatula: A flat metal spatula is handy for leveling dry ingredients and shortening in measuring cups. (You also can use a knife.)

Oven Thermometer: It's a good idea to check the temperature of your oven each time you use it.

Pastry Blender: If you don't have this wire utensil to cut solid fat into dry ingredients, you can use two table knives.

Pastry Cloth: Well worth the small investment if you plan to bake lots of pies, a pastry cloth makes quick work of rolling out pie dough. You also can roll out pie dough on a lightly floured countertop or board, but use as little flour as possible.

Pie Plates: Heat-resistant glass pie plates help turn out well-baked pie crusts because they absorb heat, ensuring beautifully browned crusts. We use "glass" pie plates in our Test Kitchens because they give consistent results. Dull anodized aluminum, enamel or darkened metal pans work well, too. Don't use shiny metal pans because they reflect the heat. All our recipes call for 8″, 9″ or 10″ pie plates.

Rolling Pin and Cover: Choose a heavy rolling pin that fits comfortably in your hands. A stockinet cover for the rolling pin helps keep the dough from sticking to the rolling pin.

Rubber Spatula: A rubber or plastic spatula is useful for folding ingredients into beaten egg whites or whipped cream or for scraping out mixing bowls.

1   All About Pie

It's America's favorite dessert—more pie is consumed in the United States than anywhere else in the world!

Our love of pie dates back to colonial days when pies were more crust than filling, an ingenious way to stretch scarce ingredients. Those first pies usually were main-dish pies, simple meat-and-potato combinations much like those served in Europe.

Before long, the fruits and vegetables so abundant in the New World were baked into sweet dessert pies, and the first rhubarb and pumpkin pies appeared. Soon inventive cooks were turning out all kinds of new fruit pies to celebrate the seasons—luscious berry and peach pies in the summertime and juicy pear and apple pies in the fall—and regional specialties evolved, made with such ingredients as molasses, pecans and the yellow limes of the Florida Keys. As each generation created new recipes, the variety and popularity of pies increased.

Everyone has a favorite pie, and there are recipes in this collection to suit every taste: fruit pies, turnovers and tarts; custard pies, cream pies and refrigerated pies, including some spectacular ice cream pies; and savory main-dish pies, from creamy quiches to spicy pizza pies.

In the pages that follow, you'll find all the traditional favorites plus new flavor combinations and recipes designed for today's technology. You'll also find step-by-step directions for making conventional pastry, cream pies, meringues, custard pies and chiffon pies—guaranteed to help you turn out beautiful, great-tasting pies every time.

For a refresher on the basics of pie-making, you'll find all the information you need, starting with a list of Basic Pie-making Utensils on page x as well as tips on how to measure ingredients. We've also compiled some simple baking tips on page 3 that will be useful whether you're a novice or a blue-ribbon winner.

Everyone knows that pie tastes best on the day it's made, but if it's stored properly, it will be almost as good the next day. This chapter concludes with a few reminders on storage and freezing, so that you can enjoy the fresh taste of homemade pie tomorrow or even next month—if you can wait that long!

How to Measure Ingredients

Dry Ingredients

Baking powder, baking soda, salt: Scoop directly into container with measuring spoon and level the top with the edge of a metal spatula or knife.

Flour (all-purpose): Sift the flour even if it's sold as presifted. Carefully spoon the flour into a nested-type measuring cup; don't shake or pack down. Level the top with a metal spatula or knife.

Flour (whole-grain): Don't sift; just stir. Carefully spoon the flour into a nested-type measuring cup without shaking or packing down. Level the top with a metal spatula or knife.

Sugar (brown): Spoon into a nested-type measuring cup, pack firmly and level the top with a metal spatula or knife.

Sugar (confectioners'): Sift the sugar, then spoon it lightly into a nested-type measuring cup. Level the top with a metal spatula or knife.

Sugar (white): Scoop into a nested-type measuring cup and level the top with a metal spatula or knife.

Liquids

Honey, juices, milk, oil, syrups and water: Place a liquid measuring cup on a level surface, fill to desired mark, and check at eye level, keeping the cup on a level surface.

Vanilla and other extracts: Pour into a measuring spoon.

Eggs: We used large eggs to test each recipe.

Shortenings

Spoon into a nested-type measuring cup and press firmly into the cup. Level the top with a metal spatula or knife. Butter and margarine packed in ¼-pound (½-cup) units usually have tablespoon measurements marked on the package; simply cut off the amount needed.

Ten Tips for Baking Perfect Pies

1. Use the ingredients specified in the recipe; don't make changes or substitutions.

2. Measure ingredients carefully.

3. Use iced water in making pastry unless the recipe specifies otherwise. (Just add ice to water and let stand a few minutes; then measure the amount of water needed.)

4. For best results, use a pastry blender to cut in the shortening, a rolling pin with a stockinet cover to roll out the dough and a pastry cloth to keep the dough from sticking.

5. For baking, use heat-resistant glass, ceramic or dull metal pans; these absorb heat so that crusts brown perfectly. (We tested each recipe in a "glass" pie plate.) Shiny metal pans reflect heat and will produce a soggy crust.

6. Use the size pie plate or pan recommended in the recipe so that the filling and crust will fit. If the size isn't marked on the bottom of the pie plate or pan, you can check by measuring the top inside diameter.

7. Preheat your oven according to manufacturer's directions, allowing 10 to 15 minutes. Be sure the oven temperature is correct before putting in the pie.

8. For more even baking, bake pies on the center rack of the oven. You can bake more than one pie at a time—just leave enough space between the pies and the sides of the oven to let air circulate.

9. If the crust begins to brown too soon during baking, cover loosely with foil. (For single-crust pies, use a narrow strip of foil to cover the rim of the pie.)

10. Cool baked pies on a wire cooling rack so that air can circulate under the pie and prevent sogginess.

Keeping Pies at Their Freshest

Most fruit pies can be stored at room temperature overnight—just cover with foil or plastic wrap. Any pie containing dairy products or eggs should be refrigerated as soon as possible after cooling to avoid spoilage, particularly in warm, humid weather. Meringue-topped pies are best served as soon as they're cool because refrigeration toughens the meringue. Main-dish pies containing meat or fish should be refrigerated immediately after serving.

Some pies can be frozen as long as 6 months with no loss of flavor if they're wrapped properly in moisture-vapor-proof materials such as plastic wrap, heavy-duty aluminum foil or polyethylene bags. Be sure to label and date each pie.

To Freeze Pie Dough

Form dough into a ball. Or roll out pastry to size needed and place on freezer paper or aluminum foil (several can be stacked with a layer of paper or foil between each layer). Wrap, label and freeze.

To Defrost: Thaw wrapped ball of dough at room temperature, about 3 hours, before using. Rolled-out pastry will thaw in about 15 minutes. Use as directed in recipe.

Storage Time: 3 months.

To Freeze Pie Shells

Both baked and unbaked shells can be frozen. (If baked, cool thoroughly first.) Wrap, label and freeze.

To Defrost: Unwrap baked shells and thaw at room temperature 15 minutes or in a 350° oven for 8 minutes.

Unwrap unbaked shells, place directly in 475° oven and bake 8 to 10 minutes or until golden brown.

Storage Time: For baked shells, 4 to 6 months; unbaked shells, 2 to 3 months.

To Freeze Two-Crust Pies

All baked pies should be thoroughly cooled before freezing. It's best to bake fruit pies before freezing because unbaked, frozen fruit pies tend to have soggy crusts. However, if you wish to freeze an unbaked fruit pie, be sure to increase the thickener in the filling by 1 to 3 tablespoons. When the pie has cooled, wrap, label and freeze.

To Defrost: Let wrapped, baked pies stand at room temperature 30 minutes. Unwrap and heat in 350° oven 30 minutes. Remove from oven and let stand about 15 minutes before serving.

For unbaked pies, unwrap and bake as directed in recipe, adding 15 minutes to baking time. (Pie should bubble in center when done.)

Storage Time: For baked pies, 4 to 6 months; for unbaked pies, 2 to 3 months.

To Freeze Chiffon Pies

Prepare chiffon pies as directed in recipe. Freeze, label and wrap.

To Defrost: Unwrap and thaw at room temperature about 3 hours or in the refrigerator overnight.

Storage Time: 1 month.

Secrets
of Successful
2 Pastry-making

Country cooks know that you can't have a good pie with-out a good crust—the crust can make the difference be-tween an ordinary pie and a prizewinner. If you've ever had trouble making pie crust, you're not alone; many farm and ranch women who specialize in homemade breads, cookies and cakes feel that they just don't have the knack for turning out light, flaky pie crusts.

There's nothing mysterious about making a good pie crust—it's just a matter of being exact. More than any other type of baking, pie-making is a precision operation. Certain basic techniques must be followed, whether you're making your first pie or your 500th.

The secret of making perfect pastry is in the way you handle the dough. The step-by-step directions that follow aren't difficult, and if you follow them exactly, you'll get a perfect pie crust every time. In this chapter we also tell how to finish off the crust with a flourish by adding a dec-orative edge, and each recipe yields enough dough to let you do this easily.

The recipes in this chapter offer a choice of methods and ingredients. New recipes are designed to take advan-tage of the food processor and microwave oven, and there are also easy recipes for no-roll crusts made with margarine, vegetable oil and buttermilk baking mix as well as conventional pastries made with shortening, lard or margarine. Quiche pastry, sweet graham cracker crusts, crunchy cookie crusts and crisp meringue shells are in-cluded in this chapter, too.

Once you've mastered the basic crusts, try some of the variations: more than a cupful of shredded cheese gives our new Cheddar Cheese Pastry a wonderful flavor and color, and a little less shortening produces a Calorie-reduced Pie Shell. You can experiment with flavors, too—complement a filling by adding a pinch of cinnamon, marjoram or grated orange rind to a basic pastry.

Additional recipes for pie crusts that were especially developed for specific pies are found in each chapter throughout the book (and listed in the Index). Many of these crusts adapt well to different fillings. You can be really creative with combinations of textures, flavors and even colors; the Chocolate Pie Shell from Chapter 6 might be just the thing for the Peanut Butter Meringue Pie from Chapter 4.

Even if your pies have been winning blue ribbons for years, you'll probably find some helpful information in the basic directions that follow. If you want to teach someone else to make pastry—or are just learning yourself—this chapter will tell you how.

How to Make Perfect Pie Crust

Because flaky pie crust needs a certain balance of flour, shortening and liquid, the first important step is to measure the ingredients accurately. If you're not sure how to do this, turn to How to Measure Ingredients, page 2. It's also essential to have the right tools; the kitchen equipment you'll need is described in Basic Pie-making Utensils, page x.

When you're ready to begin, follow these steps to make perfect pastry.

1. **Mixing:** Combine the flour and salt in a mixing bowl. Then cut in the shortening with a pastry blender until the mixture forms coarse crumbs.

Be sure that the shortening is distributed evenly throughout the flour—this is what produces a flaky crust. Do not overhandle the dough at this stage, because the particles of shortening may melt and blend with the flour into a solid mass, making the baked crust hard and tough.

2. **Adding Water:** Always use iced water because it helps to keep the shortening cold. Sprinkle the water over the crumb mixture a tablespoon at a time, tossing quickly with a fork. Mix lightly; a strong stirring or mixing motion will blend the shortening and the flour into a solid mass.

Push the moistened portion to one side of the bowl before adding more water. You'll need to add a little more or a little less water to the flour mixture, depending upon the humidity; on a humid day, the flour will absorb moisture from the air as it's mixed, so you'll need to add less water than usual. Too much water will make the baked crust brittle; if you add too little water, the dough will crack at the edges as you roll it out.

When the mixture still looks crumbly, but is moist enough to hold together under slight pressure, stop tossing. Too much handling of the dough after the water has been added will produce a tough crust with a very pale, smooth surface. Gently gather the dough together with your hands and shape it into a ball.

If you feel that you've added too much or too little water at this stage, it's too late to remedy the mistake. Just throw away the dough and start over.

3. **Rolling:** To prevent sticking, place the ball of dough on a lightly floured surface; a pastry cloth rubbed with flour is ideal. (If you are making a double-crust pie, divide the ball of dough nearly in half and roll out the larger half as follows.) Try to use as little flour as possible; the less flour on the surface, the flakier the pastry will be.

Flatten the ball of dough with your hands. Roll out the dough from center to edge, using light, even strokes with a stockinet-covered rolling pin. As the rolling pin approaches the edge of the dough on each stroke, lift up instead of rolling over the edge to keep the edge from becoming too thin. Try to keep the dough in the shape of a circle as you roll it out.

If the dough sticks to the pastry cloth, lift up the dough with a metal spatula and sprinkle a little flour on the spot. The dough should be lifted frequently during rolling, but it should never be turned over. If bits of dough gather on the rolling pin, remove them immediately so they won't tear holes in the dough. Roll out the dough to the size specified in your recipe.

4. **Fitting:** Run a metal spatula carefully under the circle of dough to loosen it. Be very gentle so as not to tear the dough.

To transfer the circle of dough to the pie plate, fold it in half and lift carefully into the pie plate, placing the fold in the center; unfold it and fit loosely into the plate. Or, wrap the dough loosely around the rolling pin and then unroll it over the pie plate. Don't stretch or pull the dough because it will shrink as it bakes.

To repair tears, moisten the edges with water and press together. Pat the dough over its entire surface to ease out air pockets underneath, using your fingers.

For a single-crust pie with a simple edge, trim the dough even with the rim of the pie plate, using a sharp knife, and finish with one of the simple edges described on the next page.

For a single-crust pie with a fluted edge, trim the dough 1" from the rim of the pie plate, using kitchen shears or a sharp knife. Fold the edge under, even with the edge of the pie plate. Press dough gently with your fingers to form a stand-up ridge and finish with one of the fluted edges described on the next page.

If the pie shell is to be baked without a filling, prick the bottom and sides all over with a fork. Be sure the holes are made all the way through so that steam can escape during baking to prevent the crust from puffing up. Don't prick the pie shell if the filling is to be baked in it.

For a double-crust pie with a simple edge, add the filling. Roll the other half of the dough to the size specified in recipe and fold in half. Cut several slits in the dough, using a sharp knife, to allow steam to escape during baking. Or, if you wish, cut slits after the dough is placed on top of the filling. (You can make a variety of decorative designs if the slits are made before the crust is placed over the filling.)

Moisten the edge of the bottom crust with water, using your fingertips. Carefully center the folded circle on top of the filling and unfold it. Do not stretch. Pat the top and bottom crusts together along the rim of the pie plate. Trim the top and bottom crusts even with the rim of the pie plate, using a sharp knife, and finish with one of the simple edges described on the next page.

For a double-crust pie with a fluted edge, add the filling and trim the bottom crust ½" beyond the edge of the pie plate, using kitchen shears or a sharp knife. Add the top crust and join as described above. Then trim the top crust to 1" beyond the rim of the pie plate, using kitchen shears or a sharp knife. Fold the top crust under the edge of the bottom crust, even with the rim of the pie plate. Press dough gently with your fingers to form a stand-up ridge and finish with one of the fluted edges described on the next page.

Decorative Pie Edges

Simple Edges

These edges are quickly and easily made—great for novice cooks or for days when you're in a hurry. The decorative edge lies flat along the rim of the pie plate and works well for all kinds of pie except those requiring a high fluted edge. (Our recipes tell which pies need a fluted crust.)

To make these edges, press the dough down along the edge of the pie plate and trim it even with the rim, using a sharp knife.

Fork: Press the rim with a floured fork. For variety, use a floured teaspoon, curved side down.

Coin: Cut ¾" rounds from pastry scraps. Moisten the rim and place the rounds on it, overlapping them slightly. Press lightly into place. For variety, use other small cutouts such as leaves, stars or hearts.

Spoon Scallop: Cut a scalloped edge around the rim, using the tip of a regular teaspoon. If you wish, mark each scallop with a floured fork.

Fluted Edges

These edges require a bit of practice, but if you follow the directions carefully, you'll be making perfect fluted edges in no time. If a recipe requires a pie shell with a fluted edge, the directions will note this.

To make a fluted edge, you must first trim dough 1" from rim of pie plate, using kitchen shears or a sharp knife. Then press the edge gently with your fingers into a stand-up ridge, and proceed as follows.

Conventional: Press the stand-up ridge with your index finger (keeping your hand outside the pie plate) against the thumb and index finger of your other hand (placed inside the pie plate), making V shapes ½" apart. Continue until the entire ridge is fluted. Sharpen points by going around the ridge again.

Scalloped: Place a measuring tablespoon inside the stand-up ridge, curved side down. Press the dough around the spoon, using your other thumb and index finger. Continue until the entire ridge is fluted. Sharpen edges by going around the ridge again.

Rope: Place your thumb on the edge of the stand-up ridge at an angle. Pinch the dough between your index finger and thumb by pressing your thumb against the knuckle of your index finger and twisting your hand to make a curved flute. Continue until the entire ridge is fluted. Sharpen edges by going around the ridge again.

Fluted Fork: Press the stand-up ridge at ½" intervals, using a floured fork. Continue until the entire ridge is fluted.

Fluted Coin: Make a conventional fluted edge. Cut ¾" rounds from pastry scraps. Moisten the outside edges of fluting and press a round into each flute.

Scalloped Fork: Make a scalloped fluted edge and press a floured fork in each scallop.

Lattice Tops

Prepare dough as directed for a two-crust pie and line the pie plate, trimming dough to 1" beyond the rim. Roll out remaining dough and proceed as follows.

Basic: Cut dough into ½" strips and place 5 to 7 strips (depending upon size of pie) over filling, about 1" apart. Repeat with remaining strips, placing them in the opposite direction to form diamonds or squares. Trim strips even with pie edge. Turn the bottom crust up over the ends of strips and press firmly all around to seal.

Woven: Cut dough into ½" strips and place 5 to 7 strips (depending upon size of pie) over filling, about 1" apart. Weave a cross strip through the center by first folding back every other strip in the row. Continue adding strips until the lattice is complete, folding back alternate strips each time you add a cross strip. Trim strips even with pie edge. Turn the bottom crust up over the ends of strips and press firmly all around to seal.

Twisted: Follow directions for basic lattice, but twist the strips as you place them over the filling.

Spiral: Cut dough into ¾" strips and fasten them into a single strip by moistening the ends with water and pressing them together. Twist the strip and swirl it in a spiral, starting at the pie's center, covering the filling.

Wedge: Cut dough into ½" strips and place over the filling in as many V shapes as you plan to cut pieces of pie. Use more pastry strips to make smaller V shapes inside the larger ones (see photo facing page 54). Trim strips even with pie edge. Turn the bottom crust up over the ends of strips and press firmly all around to seal.

Flaky Pastry for 2-Crust Pie

Once you've tasted this pastry, you'll want to make it for all kinds of double-crust pies. Ingredients for a big 10" pie are listed separately.

2 c. sifted flour	¾ c. shortening or ⅔ c. lard
1 tsp. salt	4 to 5 tblsp. iced water

Combine flour and salt in bowl. Cut in shortening until coarse crumbs form, using a pastry blender.

Sprinkle iced water over crumb mixture a little at a time, tossing with a fork until dough forms. Press dough firmly into a ball.

Use as directed in recipe. Makes pastry for 1 (2-crust) 8" or 9" pie.

2-Crust 10" Pie: Follow directions for basic pastry, but use 3 c. sifted flour, 1½ tsp. salt, 1 c. plus 2 tblsp. shortening or 1 c. lard and 8 tblsp. iced water.

Margarine Pastry for 2-Crust Pie

The key ingredient gives this pastry a rich golden hue and enriches the flavor. Margarine makes the dough pliable and easy to work with, too.

2 c. sifted flour	⅔ c. regular margarine
¾ tsp. salt	4 to 5 tblsp. iced water

Combine flour and salt in bowl. Cut in margarine until coarse crumbs form, using a pastry blender.

Sprinkle iced water over crumb mixture a little at a time, tossing with a fork until dough forms. Press dough firmly into a ball.

Use as directed in recipe. Makes pastry for 1 (2-crust) 8" or 9" pie.

Oil Pastry for 2-Crust Pie

Roll out this pastry between sheets of waxed paper.
To prevent it from slipping, wipe the counter with a damp cloth.

2 c. sifted flour	½ c. cooking oil
1 tsp. salt	3 tblsp. iced water

Combine flour and salt in bowl. Add oil and mix well with a fork.

Sprinkle iced water over flour mixture a little at a time, tossing with a fork until dough forms. Divide dough almost in half. Press each half firmly into a ball.

Use as directed in recipe, rolling out dough between 2 sheets of waxed paper. Makes pastry for 1 (2-crust) 8" or 9" pie.

Electric Mixer Pastry for 2-Crust Pie

Here's a simplified method of making a basic double-crust pastry; it takes less than a minute of mixing, and the water is added all at once.

1¾ c. sifted flour
1 tsp. salt

⅔ c. shortening
¼ c. iced water

Combine flour, salt and shortening in bowl. Mix 30 seconds, or until coarse crumbs form, using an electric mixer at low speed.

Add iced water all at once and mix at low speed 15 seconds, or until dough forms. Press dough firmly into a ball.

Use as directed in recipe. Makes pastry for 1 (2-crust) 8″ or 9″ pie.

Food Processor Pastry for 2-Crust Pie

Don't be tempted to overmix the dough—it takes just 35 seconds in a food processor. Longer processing will only make the pastry tough.

½ c. regular margarine
2 c. sifted flour

1 tsp. salt
⅓ c. iced water

Freeze margarine until firm.

Fit food processor with steel blade.

Cut frozen margarine into 6 pieces. Combine margarine, flour and salt in processor bowl.

Process until coarse crumbs form, about 15 seconds. Add iced water all at once through food chute. Process until dough forms a ball, but for no longer than 20 seconds. If ball has not formed, press dough firmly into a ball with your hands.

Use as directed in recipe. Makes pastry for 1 (2-crust) 8″ or 9″ pie.

Never-Fail Pie Pastry

The Kansas farm woman who shared this recipe says she uses it whenever she makes a cherry pie—her family won't settle for anything less!

4 c. sifted flour
1 tblsp. sugar
1 tsp. salt
1¼ c. shortening

1 egg, beaten
1 tblsp. vinegar
½ c. iced water

Combine flour, sugar and salt in bowl. Cut in shortening until coarse crumbs form, using a pastry blender.

Blend together egg, vinegar and iced water in another bowl. Sprinkle egg mixture over crumb mixture a little at a time, tossing with a fork until dough forms. Divide dough in half. Press each half firmly into a ball.

Use as directed in recipe. Makes pastry for 2 (2-crust) 8" or 9" pies.

Rich Pastry

Egg yolk, milk and just a tablespoon of sugar make this pastry rich and tender. There's a tablespoon of lemon juice, too, to liven up the flavor.

2¼ c. sifted flour
1 tblsp. sugar
1 tsp. salt
¾ c. shortening

1 egg yolk, beaten
¼ c. milk
1 tblsp. lemon juice

Combine flour, sugar and salt in bowl. Cut in shortening until fine crumbs form, using a pastry blender.

Blend together egg yolk, milk and lemon juice in small bowl. Add egg yolk mixture to dry ingredients, tossing with a fork until dough forms. Press dough firmly into a ball.

Use as directed in recipe. Makes pastry for 1 (2-crust) 8" or 9" pie.

Lard Pastry

Lots of country cooks wouldn't dream of making a pie crust using anything but lard—nothing else gives pastry quite the same flakiness.

3 c. sifted flour
1 tblsp. confectioners'
    sugar
1 tsp. salt

1¼ c. lard
Milk
1 egg, beaten

Sift together flour, confectioners' sugar and salt into bowl. Cut in lard until coarse crumbs form, using a pastry blender.

Add enough milk to egg to make ½ c.; blend well. Sprinkle milk-egg mixture over crumb mixture, tossing with a fork until soft dough forms. Press dough firmly into a ball.

Use as directed in recipe. Makes pastry for 1 (2-crust) 8" or 9" pie.

Country Lard Pastry

A Minnesota homemaker who recently sent us this recipe
says she always uses it to bake a mincemeat pie at Christmas.

2 c. sifted flour	¼ c. boiling water
¾ tsp. salt	¾ c. lard
½ tsp. baking powder	1 tblsp. milk

Combine flour, salt and baking powder in bowl.

Pour boiling water over lard in another bowl. Stir until blended, using a
fork. Stir in milk. Add dry ingredients to lard mixture, stirring until soft
dough forms.

Chill in refrigerator at least 30 minutes.

Use as directed in recipe. Makes pastry for 1 (2-crust) 8″ or 9″ pie.

Extra-Flaky Pastry

This recipe is extra-generous, too, because it makes enough pastry
for two double-crust pies. Use it next time you have an abundance of fruit.

4 c. sifted flour	2 eggs, beaten
2 tsp. salt	¼ c. iced water
1½ c. lard	

Combine flour and salt in bowl. Cut in lard until coarse crumbs form,
using a pastry blender.

Blend together eggs and iced water in small bowl. Sprinkle egg mixture
over crumb mixture a little at a time, tossing with a fork until dough forms.
Divide dough in half. Press each half firmly into a ball.

Use as directed in recipe. Makes pastry for 2 (2-crust) 8″ or 9″ pies.

Cheddar Cheese Pastry

Adds a delicious contrast to main-dish pies as well as fruit desserts. Use
either sharp or mild cheese, depending upon how much flavor you like.

2 c. sifted flour	½ tsp. salt
1¼ c. shredded Cheddar	⅔ c. shortening
cheese	5 to 6 tblsp. iced water

Combine flour, cheese and salt in bowl. Cut in shortening until coarse
crumbs form, using a pastry blender.

Sprinkle iced water over crumb mixture a little at a time, tossing with a
fork until dough forms. Press dough firmly into a ball.

Use as directed in recipe. Makes pastry for 1 (2-crust) 8″ or 9″ pie.

Homemade Pastry Mix

If you make lots of pies, you'll find that this lard pastry mix
is a real timesaver. It makes enough pastry for five 9″ pie shells.

> 7 c. sifted flour   2 c. lard
> 4 tsp. salt

Combine flour and salt in bowl. Cut in lard until coarse crumbs form,
using a pastry blender.

Cover tightly and store in refrigerator up to 4 weeks. Makes 8¾ c.

8″ Pie Shell: Place 1½ c. Homemade Pastry Mix in bowl. Sprinkle 2 to
4 tblsp. iced water over mix a little at a time, tossing with a fork until
dough forms. Press dough firmly into a ball.

Roll out dough on floured surface to 12″ circle. Fit loosely into 8″ pie
plate. Gently press out air pockets, using your fingertips. Trim edge to 1″
beyond rim of pie plate. Fold under edge of crust and form a ridge. Flute
edge.

Use as directed in recipe.

For a baked pie shell, chill in refrigerator 30 minutes. Prick entire surface of pie shell with a fork.

Bake in 425° oven 10 to 15 minutes, or until crust is golden brown.
Cool on rack. Fill as directed in recipe.

9″ Pie Shell: Follow directions for 8″ pie shell, but use 1¾ c. Homemade Pastry Mix. Roll out dough to 13″ circle and fit into 9″ pie plate.
Use as directed in recipe.

Pastry for 2-crust 8″ Pie: Place 2⅓ c. Homemade Pastry Mix in bowl.
Sprinkle 4 to 6 tblsp. iced water over mix a little at a time, tossing with a
fork until dough forms. Press dough firmly into a ball. Use as directed in
recipe.

Pastry for 2-crust 9″ Pie: Follow directions for 2-crust 8″ pie, but use
2¾ c. Homemade Pastry Mix. Use as directed in recipe.

Basic Pie Shell

With this recipe, even a first-time pie-baker will have enough pastry
to make a pretty fluted edge. (For directions on fluting, see page 9.)

> 1⅓ c. sifted flour   ½ c. shortening or ½ c. lard
> ½ tsp. salt   3 tblsp. iced water

Combine flour and salt in bowl. Cut in shortening until coarse crumbs
form, using a pastry blender.

Sprinkle iced water over crumb mixture a little at a time, tossing with a fork until dough forms. Press dough firmly into a ball.

Roll out dough on floured surface to 13" circle. Fit loosely into 8" or 9" pie plate. Gently press out air pockets, using your fingertips. Trim edge to 1" beyond rim of pie plate. Fold under edge of crust and form a ridge. Flute edge.

Use as directed in recipe.

For a baked pie shell, chill in refrigerator 30 minutes. Prick entire surface of pie shell with a fork.

Bake in 425° oven 10 to 15 minutes, or until crust is golden brown. Cool on rack.

Fill as directed in recipe. Makes 1 (8" or 9") pie shell.

10" Pie Shell: Follow directions for basic recipe, but use 2 c. sifted flour, 1 tsp. salt, ¾ c. shortening or ⅔ c. lard and 4 to 5 tblsp. iced water. Roll out dough to 14" circle and fit loosely into 10" pie plate.

Margarine Pie Shell

This pastry is a little more pliable and doesn't dry out as quickly as some others, so it's easier to form it into a decorative fluted edge.

1⅓ c. sifted flour	½ c. regular margarine
½ tsp. salt	3 tblsp. iced water

Combine flour and salt in bowl. Cut in margarine until coarse crumbs form, using a pastry blender.

Sprinkle iced water over crumb mixture a little at a time, tossing with a fork until dough forms. Press dough firmly into a ball.

Roll out dough on floured surface to 13" circle. Fit loosely into 8" or 9" pie plate. Gently press out air pockets, using your fingertips. Trim edge to 1" beyond rim of pie plate. Fold under edge of crust and form a ridge. Flute edge.

Use as directed in recipe.

For a baked pie shell, chill in refrigerator 30 minutes. Prick entire surface of pie shell with a fork.

Bake in 425° oven 10 to 15 minutes, or until crust is golden brown. Cool on rack. Fill as directed in recipe. Makes 1 (8" or 9") pie shell.

Calorie-reduced Pie Shell

If you're counting calories or want to cut down on saturated fats,
try this new pastry; your taste buds will never miss the extra shortening.

1⅓ c. sifted flour	⅓ c. shortening
½ tsp. salt	3 to 4 tblsp. iced water

Combine flour and salt in bowl. Cut in shortening until coarse crumbs form, using a pastry blender.

Sprinkle iced water over crumb mixture a little at a time, tossing with a fork until dough forms. Press dough firmly into a ball.

Roll out dough on floured surface to 13" circle. Fit loosely into 9" pie plate. Gently press out air pockets, using your fingertips. Trim edge to 1" beyond rim of pie plate. Fold under edge of crust and form a ridge. Flute edge.

Use as directed in recipe.

For a baked pie shell, chill in refrigerator 30 minutes. Prick entire surface of pie shell with a fork.

Bake in 425° oven 10 to 15 minutes, or until crust is golden brown. Cool on rack.

Fill as directed in recipe. Makes 1 (9") pie shell.

Butter Crust Pie Shell

This buttery, cookie-like pie crust fits a 10" pie plate;
use it for just about any recipe that calls for a baked pie shell.

1¾ c. sifted flour	¾ c. butter or
1 tblsp. sugar	regular margarine
1 tsp. baking powder	1 egg yolk, beaten
¼ tsp. salt	1 tblsp. iced water

Combine flour, sugar, baking powder and salt in bowl. Cut in butter until coarse crumbs form, using a pastry blender.

Blend together egg yolk and iced water in small bowl. Sprinkle egg mixture over crumb mixture, tossing with a fork until dough forms. Press mixture into bottom and up sides of 10" pie plate.

Bake in 375° oven 20 minutes, or until golden brown. Cool on rack.

Fill as directed in recipe. Makes 1 (10") pie shell.

Electric Mixer Pie Shell

A basic recipe that can be used to make an 8″ and a 9″ pie shell. The electric mixer makes quick work of the job of cutting in the shortening.

> 1⅓ c. sifted flour
> ½ tsp. salt
>
> ½ c. shortening
> 3 tblsp. iced water

Combine flour, salt and shortening in bowl. Mix 30 seconds, or until coarse crumbs form, using an electric mixer at low speed.

Add iced water all at once, and mix at low speed 15 seconds, or until dough forms. Press dough firmly into a ball.

Roll out dough on floured surface to 13″ circle. Fit loosely into 8″ or 9″ pie plate. Gently press out air pockets, using your fingertips. Trim edge to 1″ beyond rim of pie plate. Fold under edge of crust and form a ridge. Flute edge.

Use as directed in recipe.

For a baked pie shell, chill in refrigerator 30 minutes. Prick entire surface of pie shell with a fork.

Bake in 425° oven 10 to 15 minutes, or until crust is golden brown. Cool on rack. Fill as directed in recipe. Makes 1 (8″ or 9″) pie shell.

Egg Pastry Pie Shell

Especially good for any recipe that calls for baking the filling
and the shell together, because the egg helps the pastry shell stay crisp.

> 1½ c. sifted flour
> ½ tsp. salt
> ½ c. shortening
>
> 1 egg, beaten
> Iced water

Combine flour and salt in bowl. Cut in shortening until coarse crumbs form, using a pastry blender.

Blend together egg and 1 tblsp. iced water in small bowl. Add egg mixture to crumb mixture, tossing with a fork until dough forms, adding 1 tblsp. additional iced water, if necessary. Press dough firmly into a ball.

Roll out dough on floured surface to 13″ circle. Fit loosely into 8″ or 9″ pie plate. Fold under edge of crust and form a ridge. Flute edge.

Use as directed in recipe.

For a baked pie shell, chill in refrigerator 30 minutes. Prick entire surface of pie shell with a fork.

Bake in 375° oven 12 minutes, or until crust is golden brown. Cool on rack.

Fill as directed in recipe. Makes 1 (9″) pie shell.

Golden Egg Pie Shell

Rich-looking and rich-tasting, this golden pie shell is a terrific match for tart, colorful fruit; use it for an open-face rhubarb or cranberry pie.

> *1 c. sifted flour*
> *1 tsp. baking powder*
> *½ tsp. salt*
> *2 tblsp. butter or*
> *regular margarine*
>
> *1 egg, beaten*
> *2 tblsp. milk*

Sift together flour, baking powder and salt into bowl. Cut in butter until coarse crumbs form, using a pastry blender.

Blend together egg and milk in another bowl. Sprinkle egg-milk mixture over crumb mixture, tossing with a fork to mix. Press mixture into bottom and up sides of greased 9" pie plate.

Use as directed in recipe.

For a baked pie shell, prick entire surface of pie shell with a fork.

Bake in 375° oven 12 minutes, or until crust is golden brown. Cool on rack.

Fill as directed in recipe. Makes 1 (9") pie shell.

No-Roll Margarine Pie Shell

A sweet pie shell that's super-simple to make; use your electric mixer to blend the ingredients, and just press the dough into a 9" pie plate.

> *⅓ c. regular margarine*
> *¼ c. sugar*
>
> *1 egg yolk*
> *1 c. unsifted flour*

Cream together margarine and sugar in bowl until light and fluffy, using an electric mixer at medium speed. Add egg yolk; beat well.

Gradually stir flour into cream mixture. Press mixture into bottom and up sides of 9" pie plate.

Use as directed in recipe.

For a baked pie shell, prick entire surface of pie shell with a fork.

Bake in 375° oven 10 minutes, or until crust is golden brown. Cool on rack.

Fill as directed in recipe. Makes 1 (9") pie shell.

Quick-Mix Pie Shell

This shortcut recipe takes advantage of buttermilk baking mix, so it saves several steps. Baking powder in the mix makes the pastry light.

6 tblsp. regular margarine
1½ c. buttermilk baking mix

2 tblsp. boiling water

Cut margarine into baking mix in bowl until coarse crumbs form, using a pastry blender. Add water, stirring until dough forms, using a fork.

Press dough into bottom and up sides of 9" pie plate, forming ½"-high ridge. Flute edge. Use as directed in recipe.

For a baked pie shell, chill in refrigerator 30 minutes. Prick entire surface with a fork.

Bake in 425° oven 8 to 10 minutes, or until golden. Cool on rack.

Fill as directed in recipe. Makes 1 (9") pie shell.

No-Roll Oil Pie Shell

Even novice cooks turn out tender crusts with this recipe.
Just stir up the dough with a fork and press it into a pie plate.

1½ c. sifted flour
2 tsp. sugar
1 tsp. salt

½ c. cooking oil
2 tblsp. milk

Combine flour, sugar and salt in bowl.

Combine oil and milk in another bowl. Add oil mixture all at once to flour mixture. Stir with a fork until dough forms.

Press dough evenly into bottom and up sides of 9" pie plate. Press dough above rim of pie plate, forming ½"-high ridge. Flute edge.

Use as directed in recipe.

For a baked pie shell, chill in refrigerator 30 minutes. Prick entire surface of pie shell with a fork.

Bake in 425° oven 10 to 15 minutes, or until crust is golden brown. Cool on rack.

Fill as directed in recipe. Makes 1 (9") pie shell.

Microwaved Pie Shell

Because pastry doesn't brown when it's cooked in a microwave oven, we've used margarine in this recipe to give the pie shell a golden color.

1¼ c. unsifted flour
Dash of salt

½ c. regular margarine
2 to 3 tblsp. iced water

Combine flour and salt in bowl. Cut in margarine until coarse crumbs form, using a pastry blender. Sprinkle iced water over crumb mixture a little at a time, tossing with a fork until dough forms. Press firmly into a ball. Roll out dough on floured surface to 13″ circle. Fit loosely into 9″ pie plate. Gently press out air pockets, using your fingertips. Trim edge to 1″ beyond rim of pie plate. Fold under edge and form a ridge. Flute edge. Chill in refrigerator 30 minutes. Prick surface of pie shell with a fork.

Microwave (high setting) 3 minutes. Rotate plate one-half turn. Microwave 3 to 4 minutes more, or until pastry is dry and opaque. Cover any brown spots that appear with small pieces of aluminum foil. Cool on rack.

Fill as directed in recipe. Makes 1 (9″) baked pie shell.

Quiche Pastry Shell

This simple, classic pastry is made with margarine
and can be used to line either a 9″ pie plate or 10″ quiche pan.

1½ c. sifted flour	½ c. regular margarine
½ tsp. salt	4 to 5 tblsp. iced water

Combine flour and salt in bowl. Cut in margarine until coarse crumbs form, using a pastry blender.

Sprinkle iced water over crumb mixture a little at a time, tossing with a fork until dough forms. Press dough firmly into a ball.

Roll out dough on floured surface to 13″ circle. Fit loosely into 10″ quiche pan. Trim edge even with rim of pan.

Use as directed in recipe. Makes 1 (10″) quiche shell.

Rich Quiche Pastry Shell

A buttery crust that's appropriate for any quiche, whether you're serving it as a main dish or as an appetizer. An egg adds the richness.

1½ c. sifted flour	½ c. butter
¼ tsp. salt	1 egg, beaten

Combine flour and salt in bowl. Cut in butter until coarse crumbs form, using a pastry blender.

Add egg to crumb mixture, tossing with a fork until dough forms. Press dough firmly into a ball.

Roll out dough on floured surface to 13″ circle. Fit loosely into 10″ quiche pan. Trim edge even with rim of pan.

Use as directed in recipe. Makes 1 (10″) quiche shell.

Baked Tart Shells

So attractive for a company meal, and so easy to serve. Once they're baked, they can be frozen; just wrap in foil and pop them into the freezer.

> 1⅓ c. sifted flour
> ¼ tsp. salt

> ½ c. shortening
> 3 to 4 tblsp. iced water

Combine flour and salt in bowl. Cut in shortening until coarse crumbs form, using a pastry blender.

Sprinkle iced water over crumb mixture a little at a time, tossing with a fork until dough forms. Press dough firmly into a ball.

Roll out dough on floured surface to ⅛" thickness. Cut 8 rounds, using floured 4½" round cookie cutter, rerolling dough as needed. Line 6-oz. custard cups with rounds. Prick entire surface of each with a fork.

Bake in 400° oven 12 minutes, or until golden brown. Cool on rack.

Fill as directed in recipe. Makes 8 (3½") baked tart shells.

Golden Tart Shells

These buttery, cookie-like tart shells can be used in many ways; pour in a cream or chiffon filling to make two dozen delicious little pies.

> 1 c. butter or regular
>   margarine
> ½ c. sugar

> ⅛ tsp. salt
> 2 c. sifted flour

Cream together butter, sugar and salt in bowl until light and fluffy, using an electric mixer at medium speed. Stir in flour. Press dough firmly into a ball.

Divide dough in half. Roll out half of dough on floured surface to ⅛" thickness. Cut 12 rounds with floured 3" round cookie cutter with scalloped edge, rerolling dough as needed. Line 2½" muffin-pan cups with rounds. Repeat with remaining dough.

Bake in 325° oven 15 minutes, or until lightly browned. Cool on racks. Remove from pans.

Fill as directed in recipe. Makes 24 (2½") tart shells.

Graham Cracker Crust

Easy to make, and good with so many different kinds of pies. For a slightly different flavor, try adding half a teaspoon of cinnamon.

> 1¼ c. graham cracker
>   crumbs
> ¼ c. sugar

> 6 tblsp. butter or regular
>   margarine, melted

Combine graham cracker crumbs, sugar and butter in bowl. Mix until crumbly, using a fork. Press mixture firmly into bottom and up sides of 9″ pie plate. Chill in refrigerator 30 minutes.

Fill as directed in recipe.

For a baked Graham Cracker Crust, bake in 375° oven 6 to 8 minutes, or until edges are brown. Cool on rack. Makes 1 (9″) pie crust.

10″ Graham Cracker Crust: Follow directions for basic recipe, but use 1¾ c. graham cracker crumbs, ⅓ c. sugar and ½ c. butter or regular margarine (melted).

Graham Cracker Tart Shells: Follow directions for basic recipe, but use 2 c. graham cracker crumbs, ½ c. sugar and ½ c. butter or regular margarine (melted). Press mixture into bottom and up sides of 18 paper-lined 3″ muffin-pan cups.

Vanilla Wafer Crumb Crust

This crumb crust pairs well with any cream or chiffon filling because it's mildly flavored and adds a crunchy contrast. It's easy, too!

1½ c. vanilla wafer crumbs

⅓ c. butter or regular margarine, melted

Combine vanilla wafer crumbs and butter in bowl; mix well. Press crumb mixture into bottom and up sides of 9″ pie plate.

Bake in 350° oven 10 minutes, or until golden brown. Cool on rack.

Fill as directed in recipe. Makes 1 (9″) pie shell.

Chocolate Cookie Crust

Show your children how to make this one. The creamy vanilla filling in the centers of the cookies sweetens the flavor of this no-roll crust.

18 chocolate sandwich cookies

3 tblsp. butter or regular margarine, melted

Finely crush chocolate sandwich cookies in plastic bag, using a rolling pin. (You should have about 1⅔ c. crumbs.)

Combine cookie crumbs and butter in bowl; mix well. Press crumb mixture into bottom and up sides of 9″ pie plate.

Fill as directed in recipe. Makes 1 (9″) pie shell.

3-Egg White Meringue Pie Shell

Crackly-crisp, tender, and ever so lightly browned, a meringue shell is the perfect complement to a cream filling. This is our basic recipe.

3 egg whites	⅛ tsp. salt
¼ tsp. cream of tartar	¾ c. sugar

Beat together egg whites, cream of tartar and salt in bowl until foamy, using an electric mixer at high speed. Gradually add sugar, 1 tblsp. at a time, beating well after each addition. Continue beating until stiff, glossy peaks form. Spread meringue mixture over bottom and up sides of well-greased 9″ pie plate.

Bake in 275° oven 1 hour, or until crisp and lightly browned. Cool on rack.

Fill as directed in recipe. Makes 1 (9″) pie shell.

2-Egg White Meringue Pie Shell

Just as you'd expect, this meringue shell bakes a little crisper and a little thinner than our basic recipe, made with three egg whites.

2 egg whites	½ c. sugar
⅛ tsp. cream of tartar	

Beat together egg whites and cream of tartar in bowl until foamy, using an electric mixer at high speed. Gradually add sugar, 1 tblsp. at a time, beating well after each addition. Continue beating until stiff, glossy peaks form. Spread meringue mixture over bottom and up sides of well-greased 9″ pie plate.

Bake in 275° oven 50 to 60 minutes, or until crisp and lightly browned. Cool on rack.

Fill as directed in recipe. Makes 1 (9″) pie shell.

3 Fabulous Fruit Pies

From the first hint of spring through the full blaze of autumn, fresh fruits are bountiful. Country cooks pick each fruit as it ripens, celebrating the gradual change of seasons with a succession of freshly baked pies, made first with strawberries and rhubarb, then blueberries, raspberries, blackberries and gooseberries, followed by cherries and plums and peaches and pears—until at last the apples ripen, green and red and golden.

The fresh flavors of these just-ripened fruits have become widely available year 'round, thanks to good transportation and improved techniques for freezing, canning and storage. In this chapter you'll find more than a hundred ways to enjoy them, including microwave versions of traditional favorites and some new combinations such as Blueberry-Peach Pie and a plump double-crust pie made with sweet green grapes and tart apples.

To start, we've chosen three dozen versions of America's all-time favorite dessert—apple pie. There are recipes for double-crust, single-crust and no-crust apple pies; old-time upside-down pies; miniature apple pies fried to a golden crisp; and a microwaved pie with a crunchy crumb topping. Some are spicy and some are tart; some are topped with caramel or maple glaze, and one is wrapped in an extra-flaky crust made with sharp Cheddar cheese. You'll find a sheet apple pie that serves 16, and an elegant apple tart. And, of course, we've included our own favorite recipe for Old-fashioned Apple Pie.

We've tested each of these apple pie recipes with all-purpose apples—Winesap, Jonathan or McIntosh. If you prefer a tart cooking apple such as Rhode Island, Greening or Rome Beauty, you'll need to increase the baking time because these varieties take longer to cook.

All the luscious summertime fruit pies are here, too—cherry, peach, pear, nectarine, Concord grape and purple plum. Because cherry pie is so popular, we've included seven super versions, including Crisscross Cherry Pie, a lattice-topped pie with an extra-rich pastry, and Regal Cherry Pie, made with a no-roll cookie crust and crowned with billows of meringue. (If you need to sharpen your meringue-making techniques, see How to Make Perfect Meringue on page 99.)

The best of the berry pies are here, too—two of the simplest and the best are Double-good Blueberry Pie and our new Glazed Fresh Strawberry Pie. Each one is made with whole fresh berries lightly glazed with a fruit purée, folded into a baked pie shell and chilled, then topped with a cloud of whipped cream. Each forkful is absolute heaven—you'll want to serve these pies often during their short season.

Celebrate the arrival of spring as many farm families do with a classic rhubarb pie. A favorite in one Wisconsin family, Grandmother's Superb Rhubarb Pie, has a delicate custard filling interlaced with diced rhubarb and spread with crunchy-crisp meringue.

Old-fashioned raisin pies are as popular as ever in farm kitchens, especially at harvest time, so we've chosen six, including a walnut-studded Raisin-Nut Pie and a Minnesota farm woman's recipe for Sour Cream-Raisin Pie.

If you own a microwave oven, you can use it to "bake" a homemade fruit pie from scratch. In half the time it takes to bake a pie in the oven, you can microwave an apple, blueberry, strawberry, orange-rhubarb or even a mince pie. Each has a rich, flaky crust developed in our Farm Journal Test Kitchens especially for microwaving.

Company coming? For a sumptuous selection of both large and small fruit tarts, turn to the end of this chapter. Fruit and Cream Tart is an exquisite round of flaky pie crust spread with a cream cheese filling and topped with circles of glazed strawberries, mandarin oranges and sliced bananas. If you prefer petite, individual-sized tarts, try our new recipes for Peach Melba Tarts or Ambrosia Tarts; they're among several varieties that can be made a day in advance and refrigerated until serving time.

Best of all, you needn't put off your pie baking until your favorite fruits are in season. Many of these recipes are especially suited for fruits that are canned, frozen or dried, so you can enjoy fresh-tasting fruit pies all year.

Old-fashioned Apple Pie

Farm Journal's classic apple pie—plump and juicy
with lots of apples, and lightly spiced with cinnamon and nutmeg.

Pastry for 2-crust 9" pie
7 c. sliced, pared apples
¾ c. sugar
2 tblsp. flour
½ tsp. ground cinnamon

⅛ tsp. ground nutmeg
¼ tsp. salt
2 tblsp. butter or
* regular margarine*

Divide pastry almost in half. Roll out larger half on floured surface to 13" circle. Line 9" pie plate with pastry. Trim edge to ½" beyond rim of pie plate.

Combine apples, sugar, flour, cinnamon, nutmeg and salt in bowl; mix well. Arrange apple mixture in pastry-lined pie plate. Dot with butter.

Roll out remaining pastry to 11" circle. Cut slits. Place top crust over filling and trim edge to 1" beyond rim of pie plate. Fold top crust under lower crust and form a ridge. Flute edge.

Bake in 400° oven 1 hour 10 minutes, or until apples are tender. Cover loosely with foil if top becomes too brown. Cool on rack. Makes 6 to 8 servings.

Spicy Apple Pie

If you like spicy apple pies, this recipe
is bound to be a favorite at your house. Terrific served warm.

Pastry for 2-crust 9" pie
6 c. sliced, pared apples
1 c. sugar
¼ c. flour

1 tsp. ground cinnamon
½ tsp. ground nutmeg
3 tblsp. butter or
* regular margarine*

Divide pastry almost in half. Roll out larger half on floured surface to 13" circle. Line 9" pie plate with pastry. Trim pastry to ½" beyond rim of pie plate.

Combine apples, sugar, flour, cinnamon and nutmeg in bowl; mix well. Arrange apple mixture in pastry-lined pie plate. Dot with butter.

Roll out remaining pastry to 11" circle. Cut slits. Place top crust over filling and trim edge to 1" beyond rim of pie plate. Fold top crust under lower crust and form a ridge. Flute edge.

Bake in 400° oven 45 minutes, or until apples are tender. Cool on rack. Makes 6 to 8 servings.

Old-fashioned Apple Cider Pie

This country-style recipe guarantees good eating—
apple cider enriches the delicate flavor of the filling.

Pastry for 2-crust 9" pie
6 c. sliced, pared apples
1 c. apple cider or apple
   juice
⅔ c. sugar
Apple cider or apple juice

2 tblsp. cornstarch
2 tblsp. water
½ tsp. ground cinnamon
1 tblsp. butter or
   regular margarine

Divide pastry almost in half. Roll out larger half on floured surface to 13" circle. Line 9" pie plate with pastry. Trim edge to ½" beyond rim of pie plate.

Combine apples, 1 c. apple cider and sugar in 3-qt. saucepan. Cook over high heat until mixture comes to a boil. Reduce heat to low and simmer 8 minutes, or until apples are tender. Drain apples, reserving syrup. Add enough additional apple cider to syrup to make 1⅓ c. Return syrup and apples to saucepan.

Combine cornstarch and water in small bowl; stir until blended. Stir cornstarch mixture and cinnamon into apple mixture. Cook over medium heat, stirring constantly, until mixture comes to a boil. Remove from heat. Stir in butter. Pour mixture into pastry-lined pie plate.

Roll out remaining pastry to 11" circle. Cut slits. Place top crust over filling and trim edge to 1" beyond rim of pie plate. Fold top crust under lower crust and form a ridge. Flute edge.

Bake in 400° oven 40 to 45 minutes, or until golden brown. Cool on rack. Makes 6 to 8 servings.

All-American Apple Pie

The crust is extra-tender and extra-flaky because it's made
with lard. Many folks feel that a lard pastry just can't be beat.

Lard Pastry (see
  Index)
6 c. thinly sliced, pared
  tart apples
⅔ c. sugar
2 tblsp. flour

1 tsp. ground cinnamon
¼ tsp. ground nutmeg
¼ tsp. salt
1 tblsp. lemon juice
2 tblsp. butter or
  regular margarine

Prepare Lard Pastry and divide pastry almost in half. Roll out larger
half on floured surface to 13" circle. Line 9" pie plate with pastry. Trim
edge to ½" beyond rim of pie plate.

Combine apples, sugar, flour, cinnamon, nutmeg, salt and lemon juice
in bowl; mix well. Arrange half of the apple mixture in pastry-lined pie
plate. Dot with butter. Top with remaining apple mixture.

Roll out remaining pastry to 11" circle. Cut slits. Place top crust over
filling and trim edge to 1" beyond rim of pie plate. Fold top crust under
lower crust and form a ridge. Flute edge.

Bake in 400° oven 55 minutes, or until apples are tender. Cool on
rack. Makes 6 to 8 servings.

Apple Pie in Cheddar Crust

What a combination! The Cheddar cheese for this
apple pie is baked right into the rich, golden crust.

Cheddar Cheese Pastry
  (see Index)
7 c. sliced, pared apples
½ c. sugar
2 tblsp. flour

½ tsp. ground cinnamon
2 tblsp. butter or
  regular margarine
1 egg yolk, beaten
1 tblsp. water

Prepare Cheddar Cheese Pastry and divide pastry almost in half. Roll
out larger half on floured surface to 13" circle. Line 9" pie plate with pastry. Trim edge to ½" beyond rim of pie plate.

Combine apples, sugar, flour and cinnamon in bowl; mix well. Arrange
apple mixture in pastry-lined pie plate. Dot with butter.

Roll out remaining pastry to 11" circle. Cut slits. Place top crust over
filling and trim edge to 1" beyond rim of pie plate. Fold top crust under
lower crust and form a ridge. Flute edge. Combine egg yolk and water.
Brush over crust.

Bake in 400° oven 45 to 50 minutes, or until apples are tender and
crust is golden brown. Cool on rack. Makes 6 to 8 servings.

Orange-glazed Apple Pie

A double-crust pie topped with an orange glaze;
the filling is dotted with plump sweet raisins. Delicious!

Pastry for 2-crust 9" pie
6 c. sliced, pared tart
*   apples*
½ c. raisins
¾ c. sugar
2 tblsp. flour
½ tsp. ground cinnamon

⅛ tsp. salt
2 tblsp. orange juice
3 tblsp. butter or
*   regular margarine*
Orange Glaze
*   (recipe follows)*

Divide pastry almost in half. Roll out larger half on floured surface to 13" circle. Line 9" pie plate with pastry. Trim edge to ½" beyond rim of pie plate.

Combine apples, raisins, sugar, flour, cinnamon and salt in bowl; mix well. Arrange apple mixture in pastry-lined pie plate. Sprinkle with orange juice and dot with butter.

Roll out remaining pastry to 11" circle. Cut slits. Place top crust over filling and trim edge to 1" beyond rim of pie plate. Fold top crust under lower crust and form a ridge. Flute edge.

Bake in 400° oven 50 minutes, or until apples are tender.

Prepare Orange Glaze and pour over hot pie. Cool on rack. Makes 6 to 8 servings.

Orange Glaze: Combine 1 c. sifted confectioners' sugar, 3 tblsp. orange juice and 1 tsp. grated orange rind in bowl. Beat until smooth, using a spoon.

Caramel-topped Apple Pie

After this apple pie is baked to golden perfection,
a caramel topping is poured over the top crust. Scrumptious!

Pastry for 2-crust 9" pie
4 c. diced, pared tart
*   apples*
½ c. sugar
2 tblsp. flour
¼ c. water

¼ c. butter or
*   regular margarine*
½ c. sugar
¼ c. butter or
*   regular margarine*
¼ c. milk

Divide pastry almost in half. Roll out larger half on floured surface to 13" circle. Line 9" pie plate with pastry. Trim edge to ½" beyond rim of pie plate.

Combine apples, ½ c. sugar and flour in bowl; mix well. Arrange apple mixture in pastry-lined pie plate. Pour water over apples. Dot with ¼ c. butter.

Roll out remaining pastry to 11″ circle. Cut slits. Place top crust over filling and trim edge to 1″ beyond rim of pie plate. Fold top crust under lower crust and form a ridge. Flute edge.

Bake in 400° oven 10 minutes. Reduce temperature to 350° and bake 40 minutes more, or until apples are tender. Place on rack.

Combine ½ c. sugar, ¼ c. butter and milk in 2-qt. saucepan; mix well. Cook over medium heat, stirring constantly, until mixture comes to a boil. Reduce heat to low and simmer 3 minutes. Remove from heat. Beat until mixture begins to thicken, using a wooden spoon. Pour mixture over warm pie. Cool on rack. Makes 6 to 8 servings.

Maple-glazed Apple Pie

Years ago, a Michigan farm woman sent us this recipe
for apple pie flavored with gingersnaps and maple syrup.

Pastry for 2-crust 9″ pie	¼ c. butter or regular
6 c. sliced, pared apples	margarine, melted
½ c. crushed gingersnaps	½ tsp. ground cinnamon
½ c. chopped walnuts	¼ tsp. salt
½ c. sugar	¼ c. maple syrup
¼ c. brown sugar, packed	

Divide pastry almost in half. Roll out larger half on floured surface to 13″ circle. Line 9″ pie plate with pastry. Trim pastry to ½″ beyond rim of pie plate.

Arrange half of the apples in pastry-lined pie plate.

Combine gingersnaps, walnuts, sugar, brown sugar, butter, cinnamon and salt in bowl; mix well. Sprinkle half of the gingersnap mixture over apples. Top with remaining apples and sprinkle with remaining gingersnap mixture.

Roll out remaining pastry to 11″ circle. Cut slits. Place top crust over filling and trim edge to 1″ beyond rim of pie plate. Fold top crust under lower crust and form a ridge. Flute edge.

Bake in 350° oven 35 minutes.

Meanwhile, heat maple syrup in small saucepan over high heat until it boils. Brush hot maple syrup over pie.

Bake 15 minutes more, or until apples are tender. Cool on rack. Makes 6 to 8 servings.

Upside-down Apple Pie

An out-of-the-ordinary apple pie with a crunchy,
candy-like topping glistening with brown sugar and pecans.

¼ c. soft butter or
   regular margarine
½ c. pecan halves
½ c. brown sugar,
   packed
Pastry for 2-crust 9" pie

6 c. sliced, pared apples
½ c. sugar
2 tblsp. flour
½ tsp. ground cinnamon
Dash ground nutmeg

Spread butter over bottom and up sides of 9" pie plate. Press pecan halves, rounded side down, into butter. Sprinkle evenly with brown sugar; pat gently.

Divide pastry almost in half. Roll out larger half on floured surface to 13" circle. Line prepared pie plate with pastry. Trim edge to ½" beyond rim of pie plate.

Combine apples, sugar, flour, cinnamon and nutmeg in bowl; mix well. Spoon apple mixture into prepared pie plate.

Roll out remaining pastry to 11" circle. Cut slits. Place top crust over filling and trim edge to 1" beyond rim of pie plate. Fold top crust under lower crust and form a ridge. Flute edge.

Bake in 400° oven 50 minutes, or until apples are tender. Cool on rack 5 minutes. Place serving plate over pie; invert. Carefully remove pie plate. Cool on rack. Makes 6 to 8 servings.

Lattice Apple Pie

A basic apple pie with a fancy lattice top. To make
the top crust sparkle, brush with milk, sprinkle with sugar, and bake.

Pastry for 2-crust 9" pie
6 c. thinly sliced,
   pared tart apples
1 c. sugar

1 tblsp. cornstarch
½ tsp. ground cinnamon
½ tsp. ground nutmeg

Divide pastry almost in half. Roll out larger half on floured surface to 13" circle. Line 9" pie plate with pastry. Trim edge to 1" beyond rim of pie plate.

Combine apples, sugar, cornstarch, cinnamon and nutmeg in bowl; mix well. Arrange apple mixture in pastry-lined pie plate.

Roll out remaining pastry. Cut into ½"-wide strips. Place half of the strips over filling, about 1" apart. Repeat with remaining strips, placing them in the opposite direction, forming a diamond or square pattern.

Trim strips even with pie edge. Turn bottom crust up over ends of strips. Press firmly to seal edge. Flute edge.

Bake in 400° oven 45 minutes, or until apples are tender. Cool on rack. Makes 6 to 8 servings.

Lattice Apple Pie with Cream

To serve this lattice-topped pie the old-fashioned way,
sprinkle each wedge with brown sugar and add a pour of cream.

Pastry for 2-crust 9" pie
4 large McIntosh apples,
   pared, cored and cut
   into eighths
1 c. sugar
½ tsp. ground cinnamon

½ tsp. ground allspice
3 tblsp. butter or
   regular margarine
Brown sugar
Heavy cream

Divide pastry almost in half. Roll out larger half on floured surface to 13" circle. Line 9" pie plate with pastry. Trim edge to 1" beyond rim of pie plate.

Arrange apples in pastry-lined pie plate. Combine ½ c. of the sugar and cinnamon. Sprinkle sugar-cinnamon mixture over apples.

Combine remaining ½ c. sugar and allspice in bowl. Cut in butter until mixture is crumbly, using a pastry blender. Sprinkle crumb mixture over apple mixture.

Roll out remaining pastry. Cut into ½"-wide strips. Place half of the strips over filling, about 1" apart. Repeat with remaining strips, placing them in the opposite direction, forming a diamond or square pattern. Trim strips even with pie edge. Turn bottom crust up over ends of strips. Press firmly to seal. Flute edge.

Bake in 425° oven 40 minutes, or until apples are tender. Turn off heat and let stand in oven 10 minutes. Remove from oven. Cool on rack.

To serve, sprinkle pie with brown sugar and top with a pour of heavy cream. Makes 6 to 8 servings.

√ *Apple Strip Pie*

Extra-wide strips of pastry on this delectable apple pie
are sprinkled with cinnamon and pecans. Cider flavors the filling.

3 c. grated, pared apples	3 tblsp. flour
½ c. sugar	1 c. apple cider or apple
½ tsp. ground cinnamon	juice
¼ tsp. ground nutmeg	½ c. raisins
⅛ tsp. salt	Pastry for 2-crust 9″ pie
1 tblsp. lemon juice	1 egg white, slightly beaten
2 tsp. grated lemon rind	1 tsp. water
3 tblsp. butter or	Cinnamon Nut Topping
regular margarine	(recipe follows)

Combine apples, sugar, cinnamon, nutmeg, salt, lemon juice and lemon rind in bowl; mix well. Set aside.

Melt butter in 3-qt. saucepan over medium heat. Blend in flour. Gradually stir in apple cider. Cook, stirring constantly, until mixture boils and thickens. Stir in apple mixture and raisins. Cook until mixture returns to a boil. Remove from heat; let stand 20 minutes.

Divide pastry almost in half. Roll out larger half on floured surface to 13″ circle. Line 9″ pie plate with pastry. Trim edge to 1″ beyond rim of pie plate.

Combine egg white and water. Brush some of the egg white mixture over pie shell. Pour apple mixture into pastry-lined pie plate.

Roll out remaining pastry. Cut into three 1½″-wide strips. Arrange strips evenly across top of pie, leaving space between each. Trim strips even with pie edge. Turn bottom crust up over ends of strips. Press firmly to seal. Flute edge. Brush remaining egg white mixture over strips. Prepare Cinnamon Nut Topping and sprinkle between strips.

Bake in 350° oven 1 hour 10 minutes, or until crust is golden brown and filling is bubbly. Cool on rack. Makes 6 to 8 servings.

Cinnamon Nut Topping: Combine ¼ c. chopped pecans, 1 tblsp. sugar and ¼ tsp. ground cinnamon in bowl; mix well.

Apple Crunch Pie

This is a plump, single-crust pie with lots and lots
of apples and a crunchy crumb topping of brown sugar and oats.

9 c. thinly sliced, pared
*   apples*
½ c. sugar
½ tsp. ground cinnamon

⅓ c. orange juice
Unbaked 9" pie shell
Crunchy Oat Topping
*   (recipe follows)*

Combine apples, sugar, cinnamon and orange juice in bowl; mix well.
Arrange apple mixture in unbaked pie shell.

Prepare Crunchy Oat Topping and sprinkle over apple mixture.

Bake in 425° oven 10 minutes. Reduce temperature to 350° and
bake 55 minutes more, or until apples are tender. Cool on rack. Makes 6
to 8 servings.

Crunchy Oat Topping: Combine ½ c. quick-cooking oats, ½ c. flour,
⅓ c. brown sugar (packed), ½ tsp. ground cinnamon and 3 tblsp. melted
butter or regular margarine in bowl; mix until crumbly.

Heritage Dutch Apple Pie

This traditional single-crust apple pie
has a simple crumb topping made with flour, sugar and butter.

6 c. sliced, pared tart
*   apples (6 medium)*
½ c. sugar
1 tsp. ground cinnamon

Unbaked 9" pie shell
*   with fluted edge*
Crumb Topping
*   (recipe follows)*

Combine apples, sugar and cinnamon in bowl; mix well. Arrange apple
mixture in unbaked pie shell.

Prepare Crumb Topping and sprinkle over apple mixture.

Bake in 400° oven 50 minutes, or until apples are tender. Cool on
rack. Makes 6 to 8 servings.

Crumb Topping: Combine 1 c. sifted flour and ¾ c. sugar in bowl. Cut
in ½ c. butter or regular margarine until mixture is crumbly, using a pastry
blender.

Peanut Crunch Apple Pie

If there are peanut butter fans at your house,
try this pie with a crunchy peanut butter-cornflake topping.

5½ c. thinly sliced,
   pared tart apples
¾ c. sugar
2 tblsp. flour
¼ tsp. salt
2 tsp. lemon juice

½ tsp. vanilla
Unbaked 9″ pie shell
3 tblsp. butter or
   regular margarine, melted
Peanut Crunch Topping
(recipe follows)

Combine apples, sugar, flour, salt, lemon juice and vanilla in bowl; mix well. Arrange mixture in unbaked pie shell and drizzle with melted butter.

Prepare Peanut Crunch Topping and sprinkle over apple mixture.

Bake in 350° oven 50 to 60 minutes, or until apples are tender. Cool on rack. Makes 6 to 8 servings.

Peanut Crunch Topping: Combine ½ c. coarsely crushed cornflakes, ¼ c. sugar and ⅛ tsp. salt in bowl. Add 3 tblsp. crunchy peanut butter and mix until blended, using a pastry blender.

Crumb-top Dried Apple Pie

"I dry my own apples, and my family says this pie
is better than plain apple," wrote a Missouri farmer's wife.

1½ c. dried apple
   slices or rings
2 c. water
⅓ c. sugar
2 tblsp. quick-cooking tapioca

1 tsp. ground cinnamon
Unbaked 9″ pie shell
Crumb Topping
(recipe follows)

Combine dried apples and water in 3-qt. saucepan. Cook over high heat until mixture comes to a boil. Reduce heat to low. Cover and simmer 10 minutes, or until apples are tender.

Combine sugar, tapioca and cinnamon in small bowl. Stir into simmering apple mixture. Increase heat to medium. Cook, stirring constantly, until it boils and thickens. Remove from heat. Pour into unbaked pie shell. Prepare Crumb Topping and sprinkle over apple mixture. Bake in 425° oven 15 minutes. Reduce temperature to 375° and bake 20 minutes more, or until golden brown. Cool on rack. Makes 6 to 8 servings.

Crumb Topping: Combine ½ c. brown sugar (packed), ½ c. flour and ½ c. butter or regular margarine (melted) in bowl; mix until crumbly.

Whole-wheat Apple Pie

Both the pie shell and the topping are made
with whole-wheat flour, and you don't have to roll out the crust.

Whole-wheat Pie Shell
  (recipe follows)
6 c. sliced, pared apples
2/3 c. sugar
2 tblsp. whole-wheat flour

1 tsp. ground cinnamon
1/2 c. dairy sour cream
1 tsp. vanilla
Whole-wheat Topping
  (recipe follows)

Prepare Whole-wheat Pie Shell and set aside.

Combine apples, sugar, whole-wheat flour, cinnamon, sour cream and vanilla in bowl; mix well. Arrange mixture in Whole-wheat Pie Shell.

Prepare Whole-wheat Topping and sprinkle over apple mixture.

Bake in 350° oven 1 hour, or until apples are tender. Cool on rack. Makes 6 to 8 servings.

Whole-wheat Pie Shell: Combine 1¼ c. stirred whole-wheat flour, 2 tsp. sugar, 1 tsp. salt, ½ c. cooking oil and 2 tblsp. milk in bowl. Mix well, using a fork. Press mixture evenly into bottom and up sides of 9″ pie plate.

Whole-wheat Topping: Combine 1 c. stirred whole-wheat flour, ½ c. brown sugar (packed) and ½ tsp. ground cinnamon in bowl. Cut in ½ c. butter or regular margarine until crumbly, using a pastry blender.

Easy Apple Puff Pie

This is one of the easiest pies you'll ever make—
just pour sweetened condensed milk over pared apples.

6 medium McIntosh apples,
  pared
Unbaked 9″ pie shell

1 (14-oz.) can sweetened
  condensed milk
Ground cinnamon

Cut apples into halves and remove cores. Prick surface of apples with a fork. Place one apple half, cut side down, in center of unbaked pie shell. Arrange remaining apple halves in ring around center apple, overlapping adjacent apple halves. Pour sweetened condensed milk over apples. Sprinkle with cinnamon.

Bake in 425° oven 20 minutes. Reduce temperature to 300° and bake 50 minutes more, or until apples are tender. Cool on rack. Makes 6 to 8 servings.

Microwaved Apple Pie

If you have a microwave oven, you can use this new recipe
to cook an apple pie from scratch in less than half an hour.

6 c. sliced, pared apples
½ c. sugar
1 tblsp. cornstarch
½ tsp. ground cinnamon

Microwaved Pie Shell
(see Index)
Ginger Crumb Topping
(recipe follows)

Combine apples, sugar, cornstarch and cinnamon in bowl; mix well.
Arrange apple mixture in Microwaved Pie Shell.

Prepare Ginger Crumb Topping and sprinkle over apples. Place a
sheet of waxed paper in bottom of microwave oven.

Microwave (high setting) 8 minutes. Rotate plate one half turn. Microwave 6 to 10 minutes more, or until apples are tender. Cool on rack.
Makes 6 to 8 servings.

Ginger Crumb Topping: Combine 1 c. unsifted flour, ½ c. brown sugar (packed) and ½ tsp. ground ginger in bowl. Cut in ½ c. butter or regular margarine until mixture is crumbly, using a pastry blender. Stir in 1 c.
chopped walnuts.

Sheet Apple Pie

When just one pie isn't enough, bake this easy-to-serve
sheet pie with a golden crumb topping; it makes enough for 16.

Pastry for 2-crust 9" pie
3 lb. apples
¾ c. sugar
1 tblsp. lemon juice

1 tblsp. ground cinnamon
Walnut Crumb Topping
(recipe follows)

Roll out pastry on floured surface to 18x13" rectangle. Fit into
15½x10½x1" jelly roll pan. Trim edge to 1" beyond sides of pan. Fold
under edge of crust and form a ridge. Flute edge.

Quarter apples, but do not pare. Remove cores. Shred apples on medium grater, making 9 to 10 cups shredded apples. Combine shredded apples, sugar, lemon juice and cinnamon in bowl; mix well. Arrange apple
mixture in pastry-lined jelly roll pan.

Prepare Walnut Crumb Topping and sprinkle over apple mixture.

Bake in 400° oven 45 minutes, or until apples are tender. Cool on
rack. Makes 16 servings.

Walnut Crumb Topping: Combine 2 c. sifted flour and 1 c. brown sugar (packed) in bowl. Cut in 1 c. butter or regular margarine until mixture is
crumbly, using a pastry blender. Stir in ½ c. chopped walnuts.

Sour Cream Apple Pie

This pie calls for an egg and a whole cupful
of sour cream. To keep it fresh, be sure to cover and refrigerate.

2 tblsp. flour
¼ tsp. salt
¾ c. sugar
¼ tsp. ground nutmeg
1 egg, beaten
1 c. dairy sour cream

1 tsp. vanilla
3 c. diced, pared apples
Unbaked 9″ pie shell
Cinnamon Topping
(recipe follows)

Stir together flour, salt, sugar and nutmeg in bowl. Combine egg, sour cream and vanilla in another bowl; mix well. Add egg mixture to dry ingredients; mix well. Stir in apples and spoon mixture into unbaked pie shell.

Bake in 400° oven 15 minutes. Reduce temperature to 350° and bake 30 minutes more. Remove pie from oven. Increase temperature to 400°.

Prepare Cinnamon Topping and sprinkle over pie. Return to oven and bake 10 minutes more. Cool on rack. Makes 6 to 8 servings.

Cinnamon Topping: Combine ⅓ c. sugar, ⅓ c. flour and 1 tsp. ground cinnamon in bowl. Cut in 2 tblsp. butter or regular margarine until crumbly, using a pastry blender.

Open-face Apple Pie

Great to satisfy a sweet tooth! This one-crust pie
has thick slices of apples laced with light cream and cinnamon.

6 medium apples
Unbaked 9″ pie shell
1⅓ c. sugar
3 tblsp. flour

¾ tsp. salt
⅓ c. light cream
¼ tsp. ground cinnamon

Pare, core and thinly slice 1 of the apples. Arrange slices in bottom of unbaked pie shell. Pare and core remaining 5 apples. Cut into ¾″ thick slices. Arrange slices in rings in pie shell, with rounded side up.

Combine sugar, flour and salt in bowl. Blend in cream; mix well. Pour cream mixture over apples. Sprinkle with cinnamon.

Bake in 375° oven 1 hour. Cover with foil. Bake 1 hour more, or until apples are tender. Cool on rack. Makes 6 to 8 servings.

Schloss Herblingen Pie

The bread crumbs, almonds, egg and heavy cream in this pie
are the same ingredients found in a classic European tart.

1 tblsp. dry bread
  crumbs
1 tblsp. finely chopped
  toasted almonds
Unbaked 9" pie shell
4 c. thinly sliced,
  pared tart apples
1 egg
1 egg yolk

1 c. heavy cream
1/2 c. sugar
1/8 tsp. salt
1/4 tsp. ground cinnamon
1/4 tsp. ground nutmeg
1 1/2 tblsp. butter or
  regular margarine, melted
3 tblsp. sugar

Sprinkle bread crumbs and almonds in bottom of unbaked pie shell.
Arrange apples in even layer on top.

Bake in 350° oven 5 minutes.

Meanwhile, combine egg and egg yolk in small bowl. Beat slightly, using a fork. Blend in heavy cream, 1/2 c. sugar, salt, cinnamon and nutmeg,
stirring until sugar dissolves. Pour half of the egg mixture over apples.

Bake 30 minutes, or until custard is firm. Pour remaining egg mixture
evenly over partially baked filling.

Bake 30 minutes more, or until a knife inserted near edge comes out
clean. Pour melted butter over pie and sprinkle with 3 tblsp. sugar.

Bake 8 minutes more, or until top looks glazed. Cool slightly on rack.
Serve warm. Makes 6 to 8 servings.

Cheese-topped Apple Pie

If you have prepared apple filling on hand, you have
the makings for this pie. The topping is almost like cheesecake.

1 (24-oz.) jar apple
  pie filling
Unbaked 9" pie shell
  with fluted edge
1 egg, separated
1 tblsp. cold water
1 (3-oz.) pkg. cream
  cheese, softened

1/3 c. graham cracker
  crumbs
2 tblsp. sugar
1/4 tsp. baking powder
1/2 tsp. vanilla
1/4 c. dark corn syrup
1/4 c. chopped walnuts

Spoon apple pie filling into unbaked pie shell.

Beat together egg yolk and water in bowl until foamy, using an electric
mixer at medium speed. Add cream cheese; beat until smooth. Stir in

graham cracker crumbs, sugar, baking powder and vanilla, blending well.

Beat egg white in small bowl until soft peaks form, using an electric mixer at high speed. Gradually add corn syrup, beating until stiff peaks form. Fold cream cheese mixture and walnuts into egg white mixture. Lightly spread over apple filling. Cover completely, sealing to edge.

Bake in 375° oven 30 minutes, or until a knife inserted in center comes out clean. Cool on rack. If you wish, serve with sweetened whipped cream. Makes 6 to 8 servings.

Colonial Apple Pie

The pie shell and the filling are cooked separately;
then they're topped off with a cloud of whipped cream.

¼ c. sugar	¾ c. water
2 tblsp. cornstarch	3½ c. sliced, pared
1 tsp. ground cinnamon	cooking apples
¼ tsp. ground cloves	1 tblsp. lemon juice
¼ tsp. salt	Baked 9″ pie shell
2 tblsp. butter or	½ c. heavy cream,
regular margarine	whipped

Combine sugar, cornstarch, cinnamon, cloves, salt, butter and water in 2-qt. saucepan. Cook over medium heat, stirring constantly, until mixture boils. Cook 1 minute. Add apples; cover and cook 5 minutes, or until apples are tender. Remove from heat. Stir in lemon juice. Cool to room temperature.

Pour cooled apple mixture into baked pie shell. Chill in refrigerator at least 2 hours.

To serve, top with puffs of whipped cream. Makes 6 to 8 servings.

No-Crust Apple Pie

Although this no-crust pie isn't low in calories,
it's a great choice when you need a last-minute dessert.

6 medium apples, pared
  and cut into eighths
½ c. sugar
1 tsp. ground cinnamon

½ c. water
Brown Sugar Topping
  (recipe follows)
Sweetened whipped cream

Combine apples, sugar, cinnamon and water in 2-qt. saucepan. Cook over medium heat 10 minutes, or until apples are partially cooked. Pour apple mixture into 9" pie plate.

Prepare Brown Sugar Topping and sprinkle over apple mixture.

Bake in 350° oven 45 minutes, or until topping is browned and apples are tender. Cool on rack.

To serve, top with sweetened whipped cream. Makes 6 to 8 servings.

Brown Sugar Topping: Stir together ½ c. flour, ¼ c. brown sugar (packed), ½ tsp. baking powder and ½ tsp. salt in bowl. Cut in 3 tblsp. butter or regular margarine until crumbly, using a pastry blender.

Old-time Upside-down Apple Pie

A Pennsylvania farm woman told us that her grandmother
used to make the pastry for this single-crust pie with leftover pie crust.

Easy Margarine Pastry
  (recipe follows)
5 c. sliced, pared apples
1 tblsp. butter or
  regular margarine

⅓ c. sugar
1/16 tsp. ground nutmeg
Heavy cream

Prepare Easy Margarine Pastry and roll out pastry on floured surface to 11" circle. Cut slits.

Place sliced apples in greased 9" pie plate. Top with pastry. Trim edge 1" beyond rim of pie plate. Turn under edge to form a ridge. Flute edge.

Bake in 400° oven 30 minutes, or until apples are tender. Loosen crust around edge of pie plate. Invert onto serving plate. Carefully remove all the apples from the crust and place back into pie plate. Add butter, sugar and nutmeg to apples. Stir lightly with a fork. Arrange apple mixture back on crust. Serve warm with heavy cream. Makes 6 servings.

Easy Margarine Pastry: Combine 1 c. sifted flour and ¼ tsp. salt in bowl. Cut in ⅓ c. regular margarine until coarse crumbs form, using a pastry blender. Sprinkle with 3 tblsp. iced water, tossing with a fork until dough forms. Press dough firmly into a ball.

Fried Apple Pies

Individual-sized fried pies just like the ones Grandmother used to make! They're best served warm with a drizzle of thin icing.

Flaky Pastry	*¼ c. brown sugar,*
(recipe follows)	*packed*
2 c. coarsely chopped,	*¼ tsp. ground cinnamon*
pared apples	*Cooking oil*
¼ c. raisins	*Confectioners' Sugar*
⅓ c. water	*Icing (recipe follows)*

Prepare Flaky Pastry and divide pastry in half. Roll out each half on floured surface to ⅛" thickness. Cut 20 rounds with floured 4" round cookie cutter, rerolling dough as needed.

Combine apples, raisins and water in 2-qt. saucepan. Cook over high heat until mixture comes to a boil. Reduce heat to low and simmer 5 minutes, or until apples are tender. Stir in brown sugar and cinnamon. Increase heat to medium and cook 1 to 2 minutes more, or until most of the liquid is gone. Remove from heat.

Place a rounded teaspoonful of apple mixture on each round of pastry. Moisten edges with water. Fold in half over filling, pressing with a fork to seal.

Pour cooking oil into 4-qt. Dutch oven or electric frypan to a depth of ½". Heat over medium heat until oil reaches a temperature of 375°. Fry pies, five at a time, in hot oil 2 to 3 minutes, or until golden brown, turning once. Drain on paper towels.

Prepare Confectioners' Sugar Icing and drizzle over warm pies. Best if served warm. Makes 20 little pies.

Note: 1 c. prepared cherry pie filling may be substituted for apple filling.

Flaky Pastry: Combine 3 c. sifted flour and 1½ tsp. salt in bowl. Cut in 1 c. shortening until coarse crumbs form, using a pastry blender. Sprinkle ½ c. iced water over crumb mixture, a little at a time, tossing with a fork until dough forms. Press dough firmly into a ball.

Confectioners' Sugar Icing: Combine 1 c. sifted confectioners' sugar, 4 to 5 tsp. milk and ¼ tsp. vanilla in bowl. Stir until smooth.

Swiss Apple-Cherry Pie

Cherries and apples form a colorful twosome. For extra flavor, sprinkle the top crust with sugar and cinnamon before baking.

Pastry for 2-crust 9″ pie
3½ c. thinly sliced,
   pared tart apples
1 (16-oz.) can tart red
   cherries in water,
   drained

1 c. sugar
¼ c. flour
1 tsp. ground cinnamon
⅛ tsp. ground nutmeg
2 tblsp. butter or
   regular margarine

Divide pastry almost in half. Roll out larger half on floured surface to 13″ circle. Line 9″ pie plate with pastry. Trim edge to ½″ beyond rim of pie plate.

Combine apples, cherries, sugar, flour, cinnamon and nutmeg in bowl; mix well. Arrange cherry mixture in pastry-lined pie plate. Dot with butter.

Roll out remaining pastry to 11″ circle. Cut slits. Place top crust over filling and trim edge to 1″ beyond rim of pie plate. Fold top crust under lower crust and form a ridge. Flute edge.

Bake in 400° oven 50 minutes, or until apples are tender. Cool on rack. Makes 6 to 8 servings.

Basic Cherry Pie

Instead of just cutting vents in the top crust, try creating a design with a cookie cutter—adds a decorative touch.

Pastry for 2-crust 9″ pie
2 (16-oz.) cans tart red
   cherries in water
¾ c. sugar
3 tblsp. cornstarch

½ tsp. salt
¼ tsp. almond extract
1 tblsp. butter or
   regular margarine
Sugar

Divide pastry almost in half. Roll out larger half on floured surface to 13″ circle. Line 9″ pie plate with pastry. Trim edge to ½″ beyond rim of pie plate.

Drain cherries, reserving ⅓ c. liquid.

Combine ¾ c. sugar, cornstarch and salt in bowl. Stir in cherries, ⅓ c. reserved liquid and almond extract; mix well. Pour into pastry-lined pie plate. Dot with butter.

Roll out remaining pastry to 11″ circle. Cut slits. Place top crust over filling and trim edge to 1″ beyond rim of pie plate. Fold top crust under lower crust and form a ridge. Flute edge. Sprinkle crust with sugar.

Bake in 425° oven 15 minutes. Reduce temperature to 350° and bake 40 minutes more, or until crust is golden brown. Cool on rack. Makes 6 to 8 servings.

Blue Ribbon Cherry Pie

A great choice for when you're short of time or when
cherry season is over—just make the pastry and add the filling.

Pastry for 2-crust 8" pie
1 (24-oz.) jar cherry pie
  filling
¼ c. sugar

1 tblsp. lemon juice
½ tsp. grated lemon rind
Butter or regular
  margarine

Divide pastry almost in half. Roll out larger half on floured surface to
12" circle. Line 8" pie plate with pastry. Trim pastry to ½" beyond rim of
pie plate.

Combine cherry pie filling, sugar, lemon juice and lemon rind in bowl;
mix well. Pour cherry mixture into pastry-lined pie plate. Dot with butter.

Roll out remaining pastry to 10" circle. Cut slits. Place top crust over
filling and trim edge to 1" beyond rim of pie plate. Fold top crust under
lower crust and form a ridge. Flute edge.

Bake in 425° oven 10 minutes. Reduce temperature to 350° and
bake 30 minutes more, or until crust is golden brown. Cool on rack.
Makes 6 servings.

Fresh Cherry Pie

One of our very favorite cherry pies—a double-crust pie
made with ripe red cherries and flavored with a dash of almond.

Pastry for 2-crust 9" pie
4 c. pitted, tart fresh
  cherries
1⅓ c. sugar
⅓ c. flour

⅛ tsp. salt
3 drops almond extract
2 tblsp. butter or
  regular margarine

Divide pastry almost in half. Roll out larger half on floured surface to
13" circle. Line 9" pie plate with pastry. Trim edge to 1" beyond rim of
pie plate.

Combine cherries, sugar, flour, salt and almond extract in bowl; mix
well. Arrange cherry mixture in pastry-lined pie plate. Dot with butter.

Roll out remaining pastry. Cut into ½"-wide strips. Place half of the
strips over filling, about 1" apart. Repeat with remaining strips, placing
them in the opposite direction, forming a diamond or square pattern.
Trim strips even with pie edge. Turn bottom crust up over ends of strips.
Press firmly to seal edge. Flute edge.

Bake in 425° oven 40 minutes, or until crust is golden brown and filling is bubbly. Cool on rack. Makes 6 to 8 servings.

Luscious Cherry Pie

A down-to-earth, classic cherry pie! In season,
you can substitute a quart of pitted ripe cherries for the canned.

Pastry for 2-crust 9" pie
2 (16-oz.) cans tart red
   cherries in water,
   drained

1¼ c. sugar
2½ tblsp. flour
¼ tsp. salt

Divide pastry almost in half. Roll out larger half on floured surface to 13" circle. Line 9" pie plate with pastry. Trim edge to 1" beyond rim of pie plate.

Combine cherries, sugar, flour and salt in bowl; mix well. Spoon cherry mixture into pastry-lined pie plate.

Roll out remaining pastry. Cut into ½"-wide strips. Place half of the strips over filling, about 1" apart. Repeat with remaining strips, placing them in the opposite direction, forming a diamond or square pattern. Trim strips even with pie edge. Turn bottom crust up over ends of strips. Press firmly to seal edge. Flute edge.

Bake in 450° oven 10 minutes. Reduce temperature to 350° and bake 30 minutes more, or until crust is golden brown and filling is bubbly. Cool on rack. Makes 6 to 8 servings.

Crisscross Cherry Pie

A Farm Journal five-star recipe, with melt-in-your-mouth
pastry forming a lattice top. This pie is picture-perfect, too!

2 (16-oz.) cans tart red
   cherries in water
1¼ c. sugar
2½ tblsp. quick-
   cooking tapioca
1 tsp. lemon juice
¼ tsp. salt

¼ tsp. almond extract
8 drops red food coloring
Rich Pastry (see
   Index)
1 tblsp. butter or
   regular margarine

Drain cherries, reserving ⅓ c. juice. Combine 1 c. of the sugar, tapioca, lemon juice, salt, almond extract, food coloring, cherries and reserved ⅓ c. juice in bowl; mix well. Let stand while preparing pastry.

Prepare Rich Pastry and divide pastry almost in half. Roll out larger half on floured surface to 13" circle. Line 9" pie plate with pastry. Trim edge to 1" beyond rim of pie plate.

Pour cherry mixture into pastry-lined pie plate. Dot with butter. Sprinkle with remaining ¼ c. sugar.

Roll out remaining pastry. Cut into ⅝"-wide strips. Place half of the strips over filling, about 1" apart. Repeat with remaining strips, placing them in the opposite direction, forming a diamond or square pattern. Trim strips even with pie edge. Turn bottom crust up over ends of strips. Press firmly to seal edge. Flute edge. Cover loosely with foil.

Bake in 400° oven 50 minutes, or until filling is bubbly. Cool on rack. Makes 6 to 8 servings.

Regal Cherry Pie

Pretty enough for royalty with its fluffy meringue topping
—and it's rich enough, too, with its cookie-like butter crust.

2 (16-oz.) cans tart red cherries in water	4 egg whites
1 c. sugar	¼ tsp. cream of tartar
¼ c. cornstarch	¼ tsp. salt
½ tsp. almond extract	½ tsp. vanilla
Few drops red food coloring	½ c. sugar
	Butter Crust Pie Shell (see Index)

Drain cherries, reserving ½ c. juice. Combine 1 c. sugar and cornstarch in 2-qt. saucepan. Stir in cherries and reserved juice. Cook over medium heat, stirring constantly, until mixture boils and thickens. Remove from heat. Stir in almond extract and food coloring. Let mixture cool while preparing meringue.

To make meringue, beat egg whites, cream of tartar, salt and vanilla in bowl until foamy, using an electric mixer at high speed. Gradually add ½ c. sugar, 1 tblsp. at a time, beating well after each addition. Continue beating until stiff, glossy peaks form when beaters are slowly lifted.

Pour cherry mixture into Butter Crust Pie Shell. Spoon some of the meringue around edge of crust. Spread meringue so it touches inner edge of crust all around, using back of a spoon. Heap remaining meringue in center. Push out gently to meet meringue border.

Bake in 350° oven 12 to 15 minutes, or until meringue is lightly browned. Cool on rack. Makes 8 servings.

Old-fashioned Peach Pie

What could be better than a fresh peach pie still warm
from the oven, fragrant with cinnamon and just a hint of almond?

Pastry for 2-crust 9" pie
5 c. sliced, pared
  peaches
¾ c. sugar
3 tblsp. flour
1 tsp. lemon juice

¼ tsp. ground cinnamon
⅛ tsp. salt
⅛ tsp. almond extract
2 tblsp. butter or
  regular margarine

Divide pastry almost in half. Roll out larger half on floured surface to
13" circle. Line 9" pie plate with pastry. Trim edge to ½" beyond rim of
pie plate.

Combine peaches, sugar, flour, lemon juice, cinnamon, salt and almond extract in bowl; mix well. Arrange peach mixture in pastry-lined pie
plate. Dot with butter.

Roll out remaining pastry to 11" circle. Cut slits. Place top crust over
filling and trim edge to 1" beyond rim of pie plate. Fold top crust under
lower crust and form a ridge. Flute edge.

Bake in 400° oven 40 to 45 minutes, or until peaches are tender. Cool
on rack. Makes 6 to 8 servings.

Blushing Peach Pie

Tiny cinnamon candies give this peach pie
its delicate pink-red color—and a zingy cinnamon flavor, too.

Pastry for 2-crust 9" pie
1 (29-oz.) can sliced
  peaches in syrup
½ c. sugar
2 tblsp. cornstarch

3 tblsp. red cinnamon
  candies
1 tblsp. butter or
  regular margarine
Sugar

Divide pastry almost in half. Roll out larger half on floured surface to
13" circle. Line 9" pie plate with pastry. Trim edge to ½" beyond rim of
pie plate.

Drain peaches, reserving ¼ c. syrup.

Combine ½ c. sugar and cornstarch in 1-qt. saucepan. Stir in reserved
¼ c. syrup. Cook over medium heat, stirring constantly, until mixture
comes to a boil. Remove from heat.

Combine peaches, cooked syrup and cinnamon candies in bowl; mix
lightly. Pour into pastry-lined pie plate. Dot with butter.

Roll out remaining pastry to 11" circle. Cut slits. Place top crust over

filling and trim edge to 1″ beyond rim of pie plate. Fold top crust under lower crust and form a ridge. Flute edge. Sprinkle crust with sugar.

Bake in 400° oven 25 to 30 minutes, or until crust is golden brown. Cool on rack. Makes 6 to 8 servings.

Glazed Peach Pie

A beautiful open-faced pie featuring fresh slices
of peaches in a shiny glaze flavored with cinnamon and orange.

6 c. sliced, pared peaches	¼ tsp. ground cinnamon
1 c. sugar	½ c. orange juice
3 tblsp. cornstarch	Baked 9″ pie shell
	Sweetened whipped cream

Mash enough sliced peaches to make 1 c., using a fork, reserving remaining peaches.

Combine sugar, cornstarch and cinnamon in 2-qt. saucepan. Gradually stir in orange juice and mashed peaches. Cook over medium heat, stirring constantly, until mixture boils. Cook 1 minute more. Spread half the glaze over bottom of baked pie shell. Arrange reserved peach slices over glaze. Spoon remaining glaze over peach slices, covering completely.

Chill in refrigerator at least 3 hours. To serve, top with sweetened whipped cream. Makes 6 to 8 servings.

Georgia Peach Pie

A Southern tradition—brown sugar and chopped pecans
make this open-face peach pie extra-rich and extra-good.

4 c. sliced, pared peaches	¼ c. flour
¾ c. sugar	3 tblsp. butter or
3 tblsp. flour	regular margarine
1½ tsp. lemon juice	½ c. chopped pecans
⅓ c. brown sugar, packed	Unbaked 9″ pie shell

Combine peaches, sugar, 3 tblsp. flour and lemon juice in bowl; mix well.

Combine brown sugar and ¼ c. flour in another bowl. Cut in butter until mixture is crumbly, using a pastry blender. Add pecans; toss to mix. Sprinkle one half of the pecan mixture in unbaked pie shell. Arrange peach mixture over pecan mixture. Top with remaining pecan mixture.

Bake in 400° oven 40 minutes, or until peaches are tender. Cool on rack. Makes 6 to 8 servings.

Summer Pear Pie

What a scrumptious combination—delicately flavored pears enveloped in a flaky pastry made with sharp Cheddar cheese!

Cheddar Cheese Pastry (see Index)
4 c. sliced, pared Bartlett pears
2 tblsp. lemon juice
⅓ c. sugar

⅓ c. brown sugar, packed
2 tblsp. cornstarch
¼ tsp. salt
¼ tsp. ground mace
2 tblsp. butter or regular margarine

Prepare Cheddar Cheese Pastry and divide pastry almost in half. Roll out larger half on floured surface to 13″ circle. Line 9″ pie plate with pastry. Trim edge to ½″ beyond rim of pie plate.

Combine pears, lemon juice, sugar, brown sugar, cornstarch, salt and mace in bowl; mix well.

Arrange pear mixture in pastry-lined pie plate. Dot with butter.

Roll out remaining pastry to 11″ circle. Cut slits. Place top crust over filling and trim edge to 1″ beyond rim of pie plate. Fold top crust under lower crust and form a ridge. Flute edge.

Bake in 400° oven 35 to 40 minutes, or until pears are tender. Cool on rack. Makes 6 to 8 servings.

Pear-Pineapple Pie

Crushed pineapple adds both contrasting flavor and bright color to this simply flavored, double-crust pie.

Pastry for 2-crust 10″ pie
7 c. thinly sliced, pared Anjou pears
½ c. drained crushed pineapple
3 tblsp. lemon juice

2 tblsp. raisins
½ c. sugar
3 tblsp. flour
¾ tsp. salt
¾ tsp. ground nutmeg

Divide pastry almost in half. Roll out larger half on floured surface to 14″ circle. Line 10″ pie plate with pastry. Trim edge to ½″ beyond rim of pie plate.

Combine pears, pineapple, lemon juice, raisins, sugar, flour, salt and nutmeg in bowl; mix well. Arrange pear mixture in pastry-lined pie plate.

Roll out remaining pastry to 12″ circle. Cut slits. Place top crust over filling and trim edge to 1″ beyond rim of pie plate. Fold top crust under lower crust and form a ridge. Flute edge.

Bake in 375° oven 50 to 60 minutes, or until pears are tender. Cool on rack. Makes 8 servings.

Fresh Pear Pie

The luscious taste of pears straight from the orchard
comes through in this open-face pie with a cap of whipped cream.

3 c. thinly sliced, pared
   pears
½ c. light corn syrup
¾ c. sugar
2 tblsp. butter or
   regular margarine

3 eggs, beaten
2 tsp. vanilla
Unbaked 9″ pie shell
Sweetened whipped cream
Ground nutmeg

Combine pears, corn syrup and sugar in 3-qt. saucepan. Cook over medium heat until mixture comes to a boil. Reduce heat to low and simmer 5 minutes. Add butter; stir until melted. Stir a little of hot pear mixture into eggs; mix well. Then stir egg mixture back into remaining hot pear mixture, blending well. Stir in vanilla. Remove from heat and pour into unbaked pie shell.

Bake in 350° oven 25 minutes, or until a knife inserted halfway between the center and edge comes out clean. Cool on rack.

To serve, spread top of pie with sweetened whipped cream and sprinkle with nutmeg. To store, refrigerate. Makes 6 to 8 servings.

Streusel Pear Pie

Perfect for a company dessert, and simple to prepare.
The easy streusel topping bakes to a beautiful golden brown.

6 c. sliced, pared pears
½ c. sugar
1½ tblsp. quick-
   cooking tapioca
½ tsp. ground cinnamon

⅛ tsp. ground mace
2 tblsp. lemon juice
Unbaked 9″ pie shell
Streusel Topping
   (recipe follows)

Combine pears, sugar, tapioca, cinnamon, mace and lemon juice in bowl; mix well. Let stand 15 minutes.

Arrange pear mixture in unbaked pie shell.

Prepare Streusel Topping and sprinkle over pear mixture.

Bake in 375° oven 45 to 50 minutes, or until topping is golden brown and pears are tender. Cool on rack. Makes 6 to 8 servings.

Streusel Topping: Combine 1 c. sifted flour and 1 c. brown sugar (packed) in bowl. Cut in ½ c. butter or regular margarine until crumbly, using a pastry blender.

French Pear Pie

Orange and lemon accent the light flavor of this
open-face pear pie, and the crumb topping is spiced with ginger.

6 c. thinly sliced,
  pared Bartlett pears
3 tblsp. frozen orange
  juice concentrate

½ tsp. grated lemon rind
Unbaked 9" pie shell
Spicy Crumb Topping
  (recipe follows)

Combine pears, orange juice concentrate and lemon rind in bowl; toss
lightly. Arrange pear mixture in unbaked pie shell.

Prepare Spicy Crumb Topping and sprinkle over pear mixture.

Bake in 400° oven 40 minutes, or until pears are tender. Cover loosely with aluminum foil after 30 minutes, if top becomes too brown. Cool
on rack. Makes 6 to 8 servings.

Spicy Crumb Topping: Combine ¾ c. flour, ½ c. sugar, 1 tsp. ground
cinnamon, ½ tsp. ground ginger and ⅛ tsp. salt in bowl. Cut in ⅓ c. butter or regular margarine until mixture is crumbly, using a pastry blender.

Almond-topped Pear Pie

Spiced with ginger and topped with chopped almonds,
this luscious pie can be made with either summer or winter pears.

3 tblsp. cornstarch
¼ tsp. ground ginger
⅛ tsp. salt
½ c. dark corn syrup
2 tblsp. butter or regular
  margarine, melted
1 tsp. lemon juice

½ tsp. grated lemon rind
4 medium pears, cored,
  pared and thinly
  sliced (4½ c.)
Unbaked 9" pie shell
Almond Topping
  (recipe follows)

Combine cornstarch, ginger and salt in large bowl. Add corn syrup,
butter, lemon juice and lemon rind, stirring until smooth. Add pears and
toss until well coated with corn syrup mixture. Arrange mixture in unbaked pie shell.

Prepare Almond Topping and sprinkle over pears.

Bake in 400° oven 15 minutes. Reduce temperature to 350° and
bake 30 minutes more, or until topping and crust are golden brown. Cool
on rack. Makes 6 to 8 servings.

Almond Topping: Combine 1 c. flour, ½ c. brown sugar (packed) and
¼ tsp. ginger in bowl. Cut in ½ c. butter or regular margarine until crumbly, using a pastry blender. Stir in ½ c. chopped almonds.

Deep-dish Autumn Fruit Pie

Three favorite fall fruits—crimson cranberries, tart apples and succulent pears—are combined in this microwaved dessert.

Pastry for Microwaved
  Pie Shell (see Index)
2½ c. sliced, pared
  pears
2 c. sliced, pared apples
1½ c. fresh or frozen
  cranberries

⅔ c. sugar
3 tblsp. flour
½ tsp. ground cinnamon
⅛ tsp. ground nutmeg
Brown Sugar-Oat Topping
  (recipe follows)

Prepare pastry and roll out on floured surface to 15" circle. Fit loosely into 1½-qt. glass casserole. Trim edge to 1" beyond rim of casserole. Fold under edge of crust and form a ridge. Flute edge. Prick entire surface of pie shell with a fork.

Microwave (high setting) 3 minutes. Rotate casserole one-half turn. Microwave 3 to 4 minutes more, or until pastry is dry and opaque. Cover any brown spots that appear with small pieces of aluminum foil. Cool on rack.

Combine pears, apples, cranberries, sugar, flour, cinnamon and nutmeg in bowl; mix well. Arrange mixture in baked pie shell.

Prepare Brown Sugar-Oat Topping and sprinkle over fruit mixture. Place a sheet of waxed paper in bottom of microwave oven.

Microwave (high setting) 6 minutes. Rotate casserole one-quarter turn. Microwave 4 to 5 minutes more, or until filling is bubbly and fruit is tender, rotating casserole one-quarter turn after 3 minutes. Cool on rack. Makes 8 servings.

Brown Sugar-Oat Topping: Combine ½ c. brown sugar (packed), ½ c. quick-cooking oats, ¼ c. flour and ¼ tsp. ground cinnamon in bowl. Cut in 3 tblsp. butter or regular margarine until mixture is crumbly, using a pastry blender.

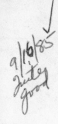
9/16/85
just
good

Pear-Apple Pie

The finest fruits of autumn—slices of apples and pears
mingling under a crumb topping of finely chopped pecans.

3 c. thinly sliced, pared
   Anjou pears
3 c. thinly sliced, pared
   apples
⅓ c. sugar
3 tblsp. flour

½ tsp. ground cinnamon
¼ tsp. salt
Unbaked 9" pie shell
Pecan Crumb Topping
   (recipe follows)

Combine pears, apples, sugar, flour, cinnamon and salt in bowl; mix
well. Arrange pear-apple mixture in unbaked pie shell.

Prepare Pecan Crumb Topping and sprinkle over fruit. Cover pie
loosely with aluminum foil.

Bake in 400° oven 40 minutes. Remove foil and bake 20 minutes
more, or until fruit is tender. Cool on rack. Makes 6 to 8 servings.

Pecan Crumb Topping: Combine ¾ c. flour and ⅓ c. brown sugar
(packed) in bowl. Cut in ⅓ c. butter or regular margarine until mixture is
crumbly, using a pastry blender. Add ½ c. finely chopped pecans, tossing
with a fork to mix.

Basic Rhubarb Pie

An honest-to-goodness, old-fashioned pie just brimming
with flavor. It's slightly tart, with a sugar-sparkled top crust.

Pastry for 2-crust 9" pie
1¼ c. sugar
¼ c. cornstarch
2 tsp. grated orange rind
¼ tsp. salt

5 c. cut-up fresh rhubarb
   (1" lengths)
1 tblsp. butter or regular
   margarine
Sugar

Divide pastry almost in half. Roll out larger half on floured surface to
13" circle. Line 9" pie plate with pastry. Trim edge to ½" beyond rim of
pie plate.

Combine 1¼ c. sugar, cornstarch, orange rind, salt and rhubarb in
bowl; mix well. Arrange rhubarb mixture in pastry-lined pie plate. Dot
with butter.

Roll out remaining pastry to 11" circle. Cut slits. Place top crust over
filling and trim edge to 1" beyond rim of pie plate. Fold top crust under
lower crust and form a ridge. Flute edge. Sprinkle crust with sugar.

Bake in 425° oven 45 minutes, or until rhubarb is tender and crust is
golden brown. Cool on rack. Makes 6 to 8 servings.

Add a professional-looking touch
to your homemade pies with one
of these eye-catching Decorative
Pie Edges (p. 9), or show off
a berry pie with a pretty Wedge
Lattice (p. 10)—so easy to serve.

Luscious Lemon Velvet Pie (p. 176) combines two favorites: lemon chiffon and lemon meringue. The airy chiffon filling is topped with a thin lemony layer and wreathed with puffs of whipped cream.

Celebrate the arrival of spring
with one of these picture-perfect
chiffon pies. From front:
Peppermint Chiffon Pie (p. 190),
Heavenly Lime Pie (p. 178) and
Orange Cloud Pie (p. 180).

Fruit and Cream Tart (p. 92) is
sure to be a show-stopper whenever
you serve it. The cream cheese
filling is topped with colorful
circles of fruit glistening under a
light glaze. Absolutely heavenly!

Rosy Rhubarb Pie

"This is my family's favorite pie," a Kansas farm woman recently told us. She adds an egg to the filling—makes it creamier.

Pastry for 2-crust 8" pie
3 c. cut-up fresh rhubarb
  (½" lengths)
1 c. sugar

3 tblsp. flour
1 egg
3 tblsp. water
Sugar

Divide pastry almost in half. Roll out larger half on floured surface to 12" circle. Line 8" pie plate with pastry. Trim edge to ½" beyond rim of pie plate. Combine rhubarb, 1 c. sugar and flour in bowl; mix well. Arrange rhubarb mixture in pastry-lined pie plate.

Beat together egg and water in another bowl until blended, using a rotary beater. Pour egg mixture over rhubarb mixture.

Roll out remaining pastry to 10" circle. Cut slits. Place top crust over filling and trim edge to 1" beyond rim of pie plate. Fold top crust under lower crust and form a ridge. Flute edge. Sprinkle crust with sugar.

Bake in 400° oven 40 to 45 minutes, or until crust is golden brown and filling is bubbly. Cool on rack. Makes 6 servings.

Honeyed Rhubarb Pie

Welcome spring with this delicately sweetened pie, a Farm Journal recipe that's been popular for more than 20 years.

Pastry for 2-crust 9" pie
4 c. cut-up fresh rhubarb
  (½" lengths)
1¼ c. sugar
⅓ c. honey
6 tblsp. flour

1 tsp. grated lemon rind
¼ tsp. salt
2 tblsp. butter or
  regular margarine
Milk
Sugar

Divide pastry almost in half. Roll out larger half on floured surface to 13" circle. Line 9" pie plate with pastry. Trim edge to ½" beyond rim of pie plate. Combine rhubarb, 1¼ c. sugar, honey, flour, lemon rind and salt in bowl; mix well. Let stand 5 minutes. Arrange rhubarb mixture in pastry-lined pie plate. Dot with butter.

Roll out remaining pastry to 11" circle. Cut slits. Place top crust over filling and trim edge to 1" beyond rim of pie plate. Fold top crust under lower crust and form a ridge. Flute edge. Brush crust with milk and sprinkle with sugar.

Bake in 400° oven 40 minutes, or until rhubarb is tender. Cool on rack. Makes 6 to 8 servings.

Orange-Rhubarb Pie

You can enjoy the special taste of rhubarb all year long
with this recipe; it's just as good made with frozen rhubarb.

Pastry for 2-crust 9" pie
5 c. cut-up fresh rhubarb
   (1" lengths) or
   2 (20-oz.) pkg. frozen
   rhubarb, thawed and
   drained
1¼ c. sugar

¼ c. cornstarch
2 tsp. grated orange
   rind
¼ tsp. salt
1 tblsp. butter or
   regular margarine

Divide pastry almost in half. Roll out larger half on floured surface to
13" circle. Line 9" pie plate with pastry. Trim edge to ½" beyond rim of
pie plate.

Combine rhubarb, sugar, cornstarch, orange rind and salt in bowl; mix
well. Arrange rhubarb mixture in pastry-lined pie plate. Dot with butter.

Roll out remaining pastry to 11" circle. Cut slits. Place top crust over
filling and trim edge to 1" beyond rim of pie plate. Fold top crust under
lower crust and form a ridge. Flute edge.

Bake in 425° oven 45 minutes, or until crust is golden brown and filling is bubbly. Cool on rack. Makes 6 to 8 servings.

Grandmother's Superb Rhubarb Pie

We think this is the best rhubarb pie ever! It has a
bright pink rhubarb-custard filling and a meringue-like topping.

2 eggs
Unbaked 9" pie shell with
   fluted edge *Do not use—10 in*
4 c. diced fresh rhubarb

¾ c. sugar
3 tblsp. flour
1 tsp. ground cinnamon

Break one of the eggs into unbaked pie shell. Roll egg around shell to
seal crust. Remove egg; pour into bowl. Add other egg to bowl.

Arrange rhubarb in prepared pie shell.

Add sugar, flour and cinnamon to eggs. Beat until thick and light-col-
ored, using an electric mixer at high speed. Pour over rhubarb.

Bake in 400° oven 35 minutes, or until rhubarb is tender and top is
golden brown. Cool on rack. Makes 6 to 8 servings.

Microwaved Orange-Rhubarb Pie

This is a double-crust pie made the new-fashioned way—
the top crust is cooked separately to keep it crisp and flaky.

Orange Pastry
  (recipe follows)
Sugar
5 c. cut-up fresh rhubarb
  (¾" lengths)

1¼ c. sugar
¼ c. flour
2 tsp. grated orange rind

Prepare Orange Pastry. Remove one-third of the pastry and set aside. Roll out remaining pastry on floured surface to 13" circle. Fit loosely into 9" pie plate. Trim edge to 1" beyond rim of pie plate. Fold under edge of crust to form a ridge. Flute edge. Prick entire surface of pie shell with a fork.

Microwave (high setting) 3 minutes. Rotate plate one-half turn. Microwave 3 to 4 minutes more, or until pastry is dry and opaque. Cover any brown spots that appear with small pieces of aluminum foil. Cool on rack.

Roll out remaining one-third pastry to 8" circle. Cut into 8 wedges. Sprinkle each with sugar. Place wedges on waxed paper.

Microwave (high setting) 2 to 4 minutes, or until dry and opaque, rotating one-quarter turn after every minute. Cool on rack.

Combine rhubarb, 1¼ c. sugar, flour and orange rind in bowl; mix well. Arrange rhubarb mixture in pie shell. Place a sheet of waxed paper in bottom of microwave oven.

Microwave (high setting) 6 minutes. Rotate plate one-quarter turn. Microwave 3 minutes more. Rotate plate one-quarter turn. Microwave 3 minutes more, or until filling is bubbly. Cool on rack.

To serve, arrange pastry wedges on top of pie. Makes 6 to 8 servings.

Orange Pastry: Combine 1¾ c. sifted flour, ¾ tsp. salt and ½ tsp. grated orange rind in bowl. Cut in ⅔ c. regular margarine until coarse crumbs form, using a pastry blender. Sprinkle 3 to 4 tblsp. cold orange juice over crumb mixture, a little at a time, tossing with a fork until dough forms. Press dough firmly into a ball.

Rhubarb-Rum Pie

This unusually light-textured rhubarb pie is made
with whipped egg whites and flavored with rum, cinnamon and nutmeg.

Unbaked 9" pie shell
2 tblsp. butter or
   regular margarine
1 c. sugar
¼ c. flour
2 eggs, separated
2 c. diced fresh rhubarb

1 c. milk
2 tblsp. dark rum
¼ tsp. salt
¼ tsp. ground cinnamon
¼ tsp. ground nutmeg
Sweetened whipped cream

Bake pie shell in 350° oven 5 minutes. Place on rack.

Meanwhile, cream together butter and sugar in bowl until light and fluffy, using an electric mixer at medium speed. Beat in flour and egg yolks. Stir in rhubarb, milk, rum, salt, cinnamon and nutmeg.

Beat egg whites in another bowl until soft peaks form, using an electric mixer at high speed. Fold egg whites into rhubarb mixture. Turn into partially baked pie shell.

Bake in 350° oven 45 to 50 minutes, or until rhubarb is tender. Cool on rack.

To serve, top with sweetened whipped cream. Makes 6 to 8 servings.

Rhubarb Surprise Pie

Two springtime fruit flavors combine in this
easy-to-make pie—the surprise is the taste of strawberries.

3 c. diced fresh rhubarb
Unbaked Golden Egg
   Pie Shell (see Index)
1 (3-oz.) pkg. strawberry-
   flavored gelatin

½ c. unsifted flour
1 c. sugar
½ tsp. ground cinnamon
¼ c. butter or regular
   margarine, melted

Arrange rhubarb in Golden Egg Pie Shell. Sprinkle with strawberry-flavored gelatin.

Combine flour, sugar, cinnamon and melted butter in bowl; mix until crumbly. Sprinkle crumb mixture over top of pie.

Bake in 350° oven 50 minutes, or until rhubarb is tender and topping is golden brown. Cool on rack. Makes 6 to 8 servings.

Nectarine Pie

Nectarines retain both their color and texture
in this pie—luscious! This recipe is one of our favorites.

Pastry for 2-crust 9" pie
5 c. sliced, pared
  nectarines
1 c. sugar
⅓ c. flour
1 tsp. lemon juice

¼ tsp. grated lemon
  rind
¼ tsp. ground mace
⅛ tsp. salt
2 tblsp. butter or
  regular margarine

Divide pastry almost in half. Roll out larger half on floured surface to 13" circle. Line 9" pie plate with pastry. Trim edge to ½" beyond rim of pie plate.

Combine nectarines, sugar, flour, lemon juice, rind, mace and salt in bowl; mix well. Arrange mixture in pastry-lined pie plate; dot with butter.

Roll out remaining pastry to 11" circle. Cut slits. Place top crust over filling and trim edge to 1" beyond rim of pie plate. Fold top crust under lower crust and form a ridge. Flute edge.

Bake in 400° oven 45 minutes, or until nectarines are tender. Cool on rack. Makes 6 to 8 servings.

Green Grape-Apple Pie

A simply delicious combination: honey-sweet green grapes
and tart apples are combined in this juicy, double-crust pie.

Pastry for 2-crust 9" pie
3 c. sliced, pared apples
¾ lb. seedless green
  grapes (2 c.)
2 tblsp. quick-cooking
  tapioca

1 c. sugar
¼ tsp. ground cardamon
¼ tsp. ground cinnamon
¼ tsp. salt
2 tblsp. butter or
  regular margarine

Divide pastry almost in half. Roll out larger half on floured surface to 13" circle. Line 9" pie plate with pastry. Trim edge to ½" beyond rim of pie plate.

Combine apples, grapes, tapioca, sugar, cardamon, cinnamon and salt in bowl; mix well. Let stand 15 minutes. Arrange apple mixture in pastry-lined pie plate. Dot with butter.

Roll out remaining pastry to 11" circle. Cut slits. Place top crust over filling and trim edge to 1" beyond rim of pie plate. Fold top crust under lower crust and form a ridge. Flute edge.

Bake in 400° oven 50 to 60 minutes, or until apples are tender. Cool on rack. Makes 6 to 8 servings.

Streusel Concord Grape Pie

The filling tastes just like tart grape jam;
the streusel topping adds just the right amount of sweetness.

2 lb. Concord grapes
  (about 4½ c.)
1 c. sugar
¼ c. flour
2 tsp. lemon juice

⅛ tsp. salt
Unbaked 9" pie shell
Oat Streusel
  (recipe follows)

Wash and pick over grapes. Slip skins from grapes by pinching end opposite stem end. Reserve skins.

Place pulp in 2-qt. saucepan. Cook over high heat until it comes to a boil. Reduce heat to low and simmer 5 minutes, or until pulp is soft. Put hot pulp through strainer or food mill to remove seeds.

Combine strained pulp, reserved skins, sugar, flour, lemon juice and salt in bowl; mix well. Pour grape mixture into unbaked pie shell.

Prepare Oat Streusel and sprinkle over grape mixture.

Bake in 425° oven 35 minutes, or until filling is bubbly. Cover loosely with foil after 20 minutes if top becomes too brown. Cool on rack. Makes 6 to 8 servings.

Oat Streusel: Combine ½ c. quick-cooking oats, ½ c. brown sugar (packed) and ⅓ c. flour in bowl. Cut in ¼ c. butter or regular margarine until crumbly, using a pastry blender.

Deep-dish Plum Pie

A dessert that's elegant enough for dinner guests.
Serve it warm from the oven with a scoop of ice cream.

2½ lb. prune plums, halved and pitted	2 tblsp. butter or regular margarine
1 c. sugar	Pastry for 1-crust 9" pie
¼ c. flour	Milk
¼ tsp. ground cinnamon	1 tsp. sugar

Combine plums, 1 c. sugar, flour and cinnamon in bowl; mix well. Arrange plum mixture in 8" square baking pan. Dot with butter.

Roll out pastry on floured surface to 10" square. Cut slits. Place crust over filling and trim edge to 1" beyond sides of pan. Fold edge under and form a ridge. Flute edge. Brush with milk.

Bake in 425° oven 45 to 50 minutes, or until crust is golden brown. Sprinkle top with 1 tsp. sugar. Cool on rack. Makes 6 servings.

Purple Plum Pie

This country favorite is baked an old-fashioned way—
in a brown paper bag. The crumb topping bakes to a golden brown.

4 c. sliced, pitted purple plums (1½ lb.)	¼ tsp. salt
	Unbaked 9" pie shell
½ c. sugar	1 tblsp. lemon juice
2 tblsp. cornstarch	Spicy Topping
¼ tsp. ground cinnamon	(recipe follows)

Combine plums, sugar, cornstarch, cinnamon and salt in bowl; mix well. Arrange plum mixture in unbaked pie shell. Sprinkle with lemon juice.

Prepare Spicy Topping and sprinkle over plum mixture. Place pie in brown paper bag. Fold over open end twice to close and fasten with paper clips. Carefully place on baking sheet.

Bake in 425° oven 45 minutes, or until plums are tender. Cool on rack. Makes 6 to 8 servings.

Spicy Topping: Combine ½ c. flour, ½ c. sugar, ¼ tsp. ground cinnamon and ¼ tsp. ground nutmeg in bowl. Cut in ¼ c. butter or regular margarine until mixture is crumbly, using a pastry blender.

Fresh Plum Pie

The rich sweet taste of small prune plums in an open-face pie
liberally dusted with confectioners' sugar—a real delicacy!

1½ lb. prune plums,
    quartered and pitted
Unbaked Golden Egg Pie Shell
    (see Index)
2 tblsp. sugar
1 tsp. grated orange rind

½ tsp. ground cinnamon
1 tblsp. butter or
    regular margarine
3 tblsp. confectioners'
    sugar

Arrange plums in rings in Golden Egg Pie Shell. Sprinkle with sugar,
orange rind and cinnamon. Dot with butter.

Bake in 400° oven 15 minutes. Reduce temperature to 350° and
bake 45 minutes more, or until plums are tender. Cool slightly on rack.
Sprinkle confectioners' sugar over warm pie. Makes 6 to 8 servings.

Fresh Pineapple Pie

A double-crust pie made with a whole fresh pineapple.
The filling is rich in eggs and has a slightly tart flavor.

Pastry for 2-crust 9" pie
1 medium pineapple (about
    3 lb.)
2 eggs
1½ c. sugar

2 tblsp. flour
1 tblsp. lemon juice
2 tsp. grated lemon rind
⅛ tsp. salt

Divide pastry almost in half. Roll out larger half on floured surface to
13" circle. Line 9" pie plate with pastry. Trim edge to ½" beyond rim of
pie plate.

Cut slices from stem and crown ends of pineapple; discard. Cut remaining pineapple into ¾" thick slices. Remove rind and core from slices
and discard. Cut pineapple into ¾" pieces. (You should have about 3 c.)

Beat eggs slightly in bowl, using a rotary beater. Beat in sugar, flour,
lemon juice, lemon rind and salt. Stir in pineapple. Turn pineapple mixture into pastry-lined pie plate.

Roll out remaining pastry to 11" circle. Cut slits. Place top crust over
filling and trim edge to 1" beyond rim of pie plate. Fold top crust under
lower crust and form a ridge. Flute edge.

Bake in 425° oven 40 minutes, or until crust is lightly browned. Cool
on rack. Makes 6 to 8 servings.

Strawberry-Pineapple Pie

A tropical treat of fresh strawberries and pineapple,
with a dash of rum in the filling and a topping of flaked coconut.

3 c. sliced fresh
  strawberries
2 c. cubed fresh
  pineapple
1 c. sugar
	1/4 c. cornstarch
	2 tblsp. rum
	Unbaked 9" pie shell
	Coconut Crumb Topping
	  (recipe follows)

Combine strawberries, pineapple, sugar, cornstarch and rum in bowl; mix well. Arrange strawberry-pineapple mixture in unbaked pie shell.

Prepare Coconut Crumb Topping and sprinkle over fruit mixture.

Bake in 425° oven 15 minutes. Reduce temperature to 350° and bake 30 minutes more, or until fruit is tender. Cool on rack. Makes 6 to 8 servings.

Coconut Crumb Topping: Combine 1/2 c. flour, 1/3 c. sugar and 1/4 c. flaked coconut in bowl. Cut in 1/3 c. butter or regular margarine until crumbly, using a pastry blender.

Pineapple-Apricot Pie

Looks bright and colorful, tastes juicy—and it's
made with ingredients you can keep on hand all year 'round.

1 (20-oz.) can crushed
  pineapple in juice
1 (11-oz.) pkg. dried
  apricots, cut up
3 c. water
1/4 c. sugar
	2 tblsp. cornstarch
	1/8 tsp. salt
	Unbaked 9" pie shell
	  with fluted edge
	Golden Crumb Topping
	  (recipe follows)

Combine pineapple, apricots and water in 2-qt. saucepan. Cook over high heat until mixture comes to a boil. Reduce heat to low. Cover and simmer 25 minutes, or until apricots are tender.

Combine sugar, cornstarch and salt in small bowl. Stir into apricot mixture. Cook over medium heat, stirring constantly, until mixture boils and thickens. Turn into unbaked pie shell.

Prepare Golden Crumb Topping and sprinkle over fruit mixture.

Bake in 400° oven 30 minutes, or until golden brown. Cool on rack. Makes 6 to 8 servings.

Golden Crumb Topping: Combine 1/2 c. flour, 1/4 c. sugar and 1/8 tsp. ground ginger in bowl. Cut in 3 tblsp. butter or regular margarine until crumbly, using a pastry blender.

Coconut-topped Pineapple-Cherry Pie

A colorful microwave version with maraschino cherries
in the filling and brown sugar flavoring the coconut topping.

2 (20-oz.) cans sliced
   pineapple
3 tblsp. brown sugar,
   packed
2 tblsp. cornstarch
1 tblsp. lemon juice

12 red maraschino
   cherries, halved
Microwaved Pie Shell
   (see Index)
Coconut Topping
   (recipe follows)

Drain pineapple, reserving 1 c. juice. Cut pineapple slices in half and set aside.

Combine brown sugar and cornstarch in glass bowl. Stir in lemon juice and reserved 1 c. pineapple juice. Microwave (high setting) 2 minutes. Stir mixture and microwave 1 minute more, or until thickened. Stir in cherries and pineapple. Turn mixture into Microwaved Pie Shell.

Prepare Coconut Topping and sprinkle over pineapple mixture. Place a sheet of waxed paper in bottom of microwave oven.

Microwave (medium setting) 15 minutes, or until filling is bubbly, rotating pie one-quarter turn every 3 minutes. Cool on rack. Makes 6 to 8 servings.

Coconut Topping: Combine ½ c. brown sugar (packed) and ¾ c. flour in bowl. Cut in ½ c. butter or regular margarine until crumbly, using a pastry blender. Stir in ⅔ c. flaked coconut.

Walnut-Mince Pie

"This recipe was given to me by my first-grade teacher,
who taught me 54 years ago!" a Kansas farm woman told us.

Pastry for 2-crust 9" pie
1 c. raisins
1 c. walnuts
2 c. chopped, pared
   apples
1½ c. sugar
1 tsp. ground cinnamon

¼ tsp. ground cloves
¼ tsp. salt
¼ c. vinegar
⅔ c. water
Milk
Sugar

Divide pastry almost in half. Roll out larger half on floured surface to 13" circle. Line 9" pie plate with pastry. Trim edge to ½" beyond rim of pie plate.

Grind raisins and walnuts in a food grinder, using fine blade. Combine raisin mixture, apples, 1½ c. sugar, cinnamon, cloves, salt, vinegar and water in bowl; mix well. Arrange mixture in pastry-lined pie plate.

Roll out remaining pastry to 11" circle. Cut slits. Place top crust over filling and trim edge to 1" beyond rim of pie plate. Fold top crust under lower crust and form a ridge. Flute edge. Brush top crust with milk and sprinkle with sugar.

Bake in 400° oven 40 minutes, or until golden brown. Cool on rack. Makes 6 to 8 servings.

Green Tomato Mincemeat

Every autumn after the first frost, a New York woman
picks her green tomatoes for this delicious homemade mincemeat.

3 lb. green tomatoes,
    quartered and cored
3½ lb. apples, pared
    and quartered
1 lb. currants
1 lb. raisins
1 c. ground beef suet
2 lb. brown sugar
1 c. vinegar

3 tblsp. lemon juice
2½ tblsp. ground
    cinnamon
1 tblsp. ground nutmeg
1 tblsp. ground cloves
1 tblsp. salt
1 tblsp. grated lemon
    rind

Grind tomatoes in a food grinder, using medium blade. (You should have 2 qt.) Drain well.

Grind apples in a food grinder, using medium blade.

Combine currants, raisins, suet, brown sugar, vinegar, lemon juice, cinnamon, nutmeg, cloves, salt, lemon rind and ground tomatoes and apples in 8-qt. kettle. Cook over medium heat until mixture comes to a boil. Reduce heat to low and simmer 35 minutes, stirring occasionally.

Immediately pack into 8 hot pint jars, leaving 1" head space. Wipe rims of jars and adjust lids. Process in pressure canner at 10 pounds pressure 25 minutes.

Cool canner before opening vent. Wait 2 minutes and then remove lid. Remove jars from canners. Cool. Test for seals and store in cool, dark place. Makes 8 pt. or enough filling for 4 (9") pies.

Mincemeat Pie Filling

Use part of this filling right now, and store the rest.
Makes enough for four 9" pies, or about five dozen tarts.

4 lb. pears	5 c. sugar
3 lb. apples	1 tblsp. salt
3 thin-skinned oranges	4 tsp. ground cinnamon
2 (15-oz.) pkg. raisins	1 tsp. ground cloves

Cut pears, apples and oranges into quarters. Remove cores from pears and apples and seeds from oranges. Grind pears, apples and oranges in a food grinder, using medium blade.

Combine raisins, sugar, salt, cinnamon, cloves and ground fruit in 8-qt. kettle. Cook over medium heat until mixture comes to a boil. Reduce heat to low and simmer 1 hour, or until thickened, stirring often.

Immediately, pack into 8 hot pint jars, leaving ½" head space. Wipe rims of jars and adjust lids. Process in boiling water bath 25 minutes. Remove jars from canner. Cool. Test for seals and store in cool, dark place. Makes 8 pt. or enough filling for 4 (9") pies.

Easy Mincemeat Pie

Add apples, raisins and lemon juice to a commercial filling, and no one will know it isn't homemade mincemeat. Delicious!

Pastry for 2-crust 10" pie	1 c. water
1 (28-oz.) jar prepared	1 tblsp. lemon juice
mincemeat	½ c. sugar
1 c. raisins	2 tblsp. flour
2 c. cubed, pared apples	

Divide pastry almost in half. Roll out larger half on floured surface to 14" circle. Line 10" pie plate with pastry. Trim edge to 1" beyond rim of pie plate.

Combine mincemeat, raisins, apples, water and lemon juice in 3-qt. saucepan. Cook over medium heat, stirring constantly, until mixture comes to a boil. Combine sugar and flour in another bowl; mix well and stir into mincemeat mixture. Pour mixture into pastry-lined pie plate.

Roll out remaining pastry. Cut into ½"-wide strips. Place half of the strips over filling, about 1" apart. Repeat with remaining strips, placing them in the opposite direction, forming a diamond or square pattern. Trim strips even with edge. Turn bottom crust up over ends of strips. Press firmly to seal edge. Flute edge.

Bake in 350° oven 55 minutes, or until crust is golden brown. Cool on rack. Makes 8 servings.

Microwaved *apple* Mince Pie

A filling that's lighter than most, with the fresh taste
of apples blended with prepared mincemeat under a buttery topping.

1 (28-oz.) jar prepared
  mincemeat
2 c. chopped, pared
  apples
2 tblsp. sugar

Microwaved Pie Shell
  (see Index)
Butter Crumb Topping
  (recipe follows)

Combine mincemeat, apples and sugar in bowl; mix well. Turn into Microwaved Pie Shell.

Prepare Butter Crumb Topping and sprinkle over filling. Place a sheet of waxed paper in bottom of microwave oven.

Microwave (high setting) 6 minutes. Rotate plate one-quarter turn. Microwave 8 minutes more, or until filling is very bubbly around edges, rotating plate one-quarter turn every 3 minutes. Cool on rack. Makes 6 to 8 servings.

Butter Crumb Topping: Combine 1 c. flour and ¼ tsp. salt in bowl. Cut in 6 tblsp. butter or regular margarine until crumbly, using a pastry blender.

Sliced Green Tomato Pie

A great way to use up a bumper crop of green tomatoes!
The filling is on the sweet side, with undertones of lemon and spice.

Pastry for 2-crust 9" pie
2 lb. green tomatoes,
  thinly sliced (4 c.)
1¼ c. sugar
5 tblsp. flour

2 tblsp. lemon juice
½ tsp. ground cinnamon
½ tsp. ground nutmeg
¼ tsp. salt

Divide pastry almost in half. Roll out larger half on floured surface to 13" circle. Line 9" pie plate with pastry. Trim pastry to ½" beyond rim of pie plate.

Combine tomatoes, sugar, flour, lemon juice, cinnamon, nutmeg and salt in bowl; mix well. Arrange tomato mixture in pastry-lined pie plate.

Roll out remaining pastry to 11" circle. Cut slits. Place top crust over filling and trim edge to 1" beyond rim of pie plate. Fold top crust under lower crust and form a ridge. Flute edge.

Bake in 400° oven 50 to 60 minutes, or until tomatoes are tender. Cool on rack. Makes 6 to 8 servings.

Green Tomato Pie

Slice green tomatoes, add a little ingenuity and turn those
garden leftovers into a cinnamon-flavored treat. Good warm or cold.

4 c. sliced green tomatoes	2 tblsp. butter or
1 lemon, thinly sliced	regular margarine
2 tblsp. cornstarch	½ tsp. ground cinnamon
2 tblsp. cold water	¼ tsp. salt
1 c. sugar	Pastry for 2-crust 9″ pie

Place tomatoes and lemon in 2-qt. saucepan. Cook over high heat un-til mixture comes to a boil. Reduce heat to low. Cover and simmer 12 to 15 minutes, or until tomatoes are transparent. Combine cornstarch and water in bowl; stir to blend. Add sugar, butter, cinnamon and salt. Stir cornstarch mixture into tomato mixture. Cook over medium heat, stirring constantly, until mixture comes to a boil. Cook 1 minute more. Remove from heat.

Divide pastry almost in half. Roll out larger half on floured surface to 13″ circle. Line 9″ pie plate with pastry. Trim edge to ½″ beyond rim of pie plate.

Turn tomato mixture into pastry-lined pie plate.

Roll out remaining pastry to 11″ circle. Cut slits. Place top crust over filling and trim edge to 1″ beyond rim of pie plate. Fold top crust under lower crust and form a ridge. Flute edge.

Bake in 425° oven 35 minutes, or until tomatoes are tender and crust is golden brown. Cool on rack. Makes 6 to 8 servings.

Fresh Blueberry Pie

You don't need to wait for the short blueberry season
to make this pie; frozen unsweetened berries will taste just as good.

Pastry for 2-crust 9″ pie	1 tblsp. butter or
1 c. sugar	regular margarine
2½ tblsp. cornstarch	Sugar
2 pt. fresh blueberries	

Divide pastry almost in half. Roll out larger half on floured surface to 13″ circle. Line 9″ pie plate with pastry. Trim edge to ½″ beyond rim of pie plate.

Combine 1 c. sugar and cornstarch in bowl. Add blueberries; toss to coat. Arrange blueberry mixture in pastry-lined pie plate. Dot with butter.

Roll out remaining pastry to 11″ circle. Cut slits. Place top crust over filling and trim edge to 1″ beyond rim of pie plate. Fold top crust under lower crust and form a ridge. Flute edge. Sprinkle crust with sugar.

Bake in 425° oven 40 minutes, or until crust is golden brown. Cool on rack. Makes 6 to 8 servings.

Lattice-topped Blueberry Pie

Imagine microwaving a blueberry pie in just 20 minutes!
To keep the bottom crust extra-flaky, it's microwaved before filling.

Margarine Pastry for
  2-crust 9" Pie (see
  Index)
Sugar
Ground cinnamon
4 c. fresh or frozen
  blueberries

⅔ c. sugar
2 tblsp. cornstarch
½ tsp. ground cinnamon
1 tblsp. lemon juice

Prepare Margarine Pastry for 2-crust 9" Pie. Remove one-third of the pastry and set aside. Roll out remaining pastry to 13" circle. Fit loosely into 9" pie plate. Trim edge to 1" beyond rim of pie plate. Fold under edge of crust to form a ridge. Flute edge. Prick entire surface of pie shell with a fork.

Microwave (high setting) 3 minutes. Rotate plate one-half turn. Microwave 3 to 4 minutes more, or until pastry is dry and opaque. Cover any brown spots that appear with small pieces of aluminum foil. Cool on rack.

Roll out remaining one-third pastry on floured surface to ⅛" thickness. Cut into 8 (1") strips. Arrange 4 strips, 1" apart, on a sheet of waxed paper. Weave 4 strips, crosswise, over and under strips on waxed paper. Sprinkle with sugar and cinnamon.

Microwave (high setting) 3 to 5 minutes, or until dry and opaque, rotating one-quarter turn after every minute. Cool on rack.

Combine blueberries, ⅔ c. sugar, cornstarch, ½ tsp. cinnamon and lemon juice in bowl; mix well. Turn into microwaved pie shell. Place a sheet of waxed paper in bottom of microwave oven.

Microwave (high setting) 6 minutes. Rotate plate one-quarter turn. Microwave 3 minutes more, or until filling is bubbly around the edge. Cool on rack.

Before serving, top with lattice pastry. Makes 6 to 8 servings.

Double-good Blueberry Pie

Sometimes the simplest recipes are the best, and we think
this one is an example. If you love blueberries, this is for you!

¾ c. sugar	1 tblsp. butter or
3 tblsp. cornstarch	regular margarine
⅛ tsp. salt	Baked 9" pie shell
2 pt. fresh or frozen	1 c. heavy cream
blueberries	1 tblsp. sugar
¼ c. water	½ tsp. vanilla
1 tblsp. lemon juice	

Combine ¾ c. sugar, cornstarch and salt in 2-qt. saucepan. Stir in 2 c.
of the blueberries and water. Cook over medium heat, stirring constantly,
until mixture comes to a boil. Cook 1 minute more. Remove from heat.
(Mixture will be thick.) Stir in lemon juice and butter. Cool to room temperature.

Arrange remaining 2 c. blueberries in baked pie shell. Spoon blueberry
mixture over blueberries in pie shell. Chill in refrigerator at least 1 hour.

Combine heavy cream, 1 tblsp. sugar and vanilla in chilled bowl. Beat
until soft peaks form, using an electric mixer at high speed. Spread over
chilled pie. Makes 6 to 8 servings.

Blueberry-Apple Pie

An uncommonly good late summer's treat—the first
apples of the season mingled with a sprinkling of blueberries.

Pastry for 2-crust 9" pie	1 tblsp. lemon juice
5 c. sliced, pared apples	½ tsp. salt
1 c. fresh blueberries	2 tblsp. butter or
¾ c. sugar	regular margarine
3 tblsp. cornstarch	

Divide pastry almost in half. Roll out larger half on floured surface to
13" circle. Line 9" pie plate with pastry. Trim edge to ½" beyond rim of
pie plate.

Combine apples, blueberries, sugar, cornstarch, lemon juice and salt in
bowl; mix well. Arrange apple-blueberry mixture in pastry-lined pie plate.
Dot with butter.

Roll out remaining pastry to 11" circle. Cut slits. Place top crust over
filling and trim edge to 1" beyond rim of pie plate. Fold top crust under
lower crust and form a ridge. Flute edge.

Bake in 425° oven 15 minutes. Reduce temperature to 350° and bake 35 minutes more, or until crust is golden brown and apples are tender. Cool on rack. Makes 6 to 8 servings.

Blueberry-Lemon Sponge Pie

A two-layer delight that features a classic filling
and a light, airy layer of tangy lemon sponge. Luscious!

1 pt. fresh or frozen blueberries	1/4 c. sugar
3/4 c. sugar	2 tblsp. flour
2 tblsp. flour	1/8 tsp. salt
1/8 tsp. salt	1/2 c. water
3 eggs, separated	1 tblsp. lemon juice
1/4 c. orange juice	1 tsp. grated lemon rind
Baked 9" pie shell	1/4 c. sugar

Heat blueberries in 3-qt. saucepan over low heat. Combine 3/4 c. sugar, 2 tblsp. flour and 1/8 tsp. salt in small bowl. Add 2 of the egg yolks and orange juice, mixing until smooth. Stir egg yolk mixture into blueberries. Cook over low heat, stirring constantly, until mixture thickens slightly. Pour mixture into baked pie shell.

Combine 1/4 c. sugar, 2 tblsp. flour and 1/8 tsp. salt in 2-qt. saucepan. Stir in water and 1 beaten egg yolk. Cook over low heat, stirring constantly, until mixture thickens. Remove from heat. Stir in lemon juice and lemon rind.

Beat egg whites in another bowl until foamy, using an electric mixer at high speed. Gradually add 1/4 c. sugar, 1 tblsp. at a time, beating well after each addition. Continue beating until stiff peaks form. Fold lemon mixture into egg white mixture. Spoon mixture over blueberry layer, spreading so it touches inner edge of crust all around.

Bake in 325° oven 30 minutes, or until lightly browned. Cool on rack. Makes 6 to 8 servings.

Blueberry-Peach Pie

Just bursting with flavor! Golden peaches and blueberries
sprinkled with cinnamon in an extra-juicy, double-crust pie.

Pastry for 2-crust 9" pie
4 medium fresh
  peaches, pared and
  sliced (3 c.)
2 c. fresh blueberries
1 c. sugar

3 tblsp. cornstarch
1 tblsp. lemon juice
½ tsp. ground cinnamon
1 tblsp. butter or
  regular margarine

Divide pastry almost in half. Roll out larger half on floured surface to
13" circle. Line 9" pie plate with pastry. Trim edge to ½" beyond rim of
pie plate.

Combine peaches, blueberries, sugar, cornstarch, lemon juice and cinnamon in bowl; mix well. Arrange peach-blueberry mixture in pastry-lined
pie plate. Dot with butter.

Roll out remaining pastry to 11" circle. Cut slits. Place top crust over
filling and trim edge to 1" beyond rim of pie plate. Fold top crust under
lower crust and form a ridge. Flute edge.

Bake in 425° oven 15 minutes. Reduce temperature to 350° and
bake 40 minutes more, or until filling is bubbly. Cool on rack. Makes 6 to
8 servings.

Orange-flavored Cranberry Pie

"Even people who say they don't like cranberries
enjoy this heirloom recipe," says the Wisconsin woman who sent it.

Orange Pastry
  (recipe follows)
1 c. sugar
1 tblsp. flour
1 c. fresh or frozen
  cranberries

½ c. water
1 c. heavy cream
2 tblsp. sugar
1 tsp. vanilla
½ tsp. grated orange rind

Prepare Orange Pastry and divide pastry almost in half. Roll out larger
half on floured surface to 13" circle. Line 9" pie plate with pastry. Trim
edge to 1" beyond rim of pie plate.

Combine 1 c. sugar and flour in bowl.

Cut cranberries in half. Add to sugar-flour mixture, tossing with a fork
to coat. Stir in water. Arrange cranberry mixture in pastry-lined pie plate.

Roll out remaining pastry. Cut into ½"-wide strips. Place half of the
strips over filling, about 1" apart. Repeat with remaining strips, placing
them in the opposite direction, forming a diamond or square pattern.

Trim strips even with pie edge. Turn bottom crust up over ends of strips. Press edge firmly to seal, using a floured fork.

Bake in 400° oven 15 minutes. Reduce temperature to 350° and bake 30 minutes more, or until cranberries are tender and crust is golden brown. Cool on rack.

Whip heavy cream, 2 tblsp. sugar and vanilla in bowl until soft peaks form, using an electric mixer at high speed. To serve, top pie with puffs of whipped cream and sprinkle with orange rind. Makes 6 to 8 servings.

Orange Pastry: Combine 2 c. sifted flour, ½ tsp. salt and ½ tsp. grated orange rind in bowl. Cut in ⅔ c. regular margarine until coarse crumbs form, using a pastry blender. Sprinkle 6 tblsp. iced water, a little at a time, tossing with a fork until dough forms. Press dough firmly into a ball.

Cranberry-Raspberry Pie

A festive-looking, luscious pie combining tart cranberries
with sweet raspberries. A perfect choice for Christmas entertaining.

2 c. fresh or frozen cranberries, chopped	¼ tsp. salt
	¼ tsp. almond extract
1 (10-oz.) pkg. frozen raspberries, thawed	Almond Pastry (recipe follows)
1½ c. sugar	1 tblsp. butter or
2 tblsp. quick-cooking tapioca	regular margarine

Combine cranberries, raspberries, sugar, tapioca, salt and almond extract in bowl; mix well. Let stand while preparing Almond Pastry.

Prepare Almond Pastry and divide almost in half. Roll out larger half on floured surface to 13" circle. Line 9" pie plate with pastry. Trim edge to 1" beyond rim of pie plate.

Pour cranberry mixture into pastry-lined pie plate. Dot with butter.

Roll out remaining pastry. Cut into ½"-wide strips. Place half of the strips over filling about 1" apart. Repeat with remaining strips, placing them in the opposite direction, forming a diamond or square pattern. Trim strips even with pie edge. Turn bottom crust up over ends of strips. Press firmly to seal edge. Flute edge.

Bake in 425° oven 10 minutes. Reduce temperature to 350° and bake 40 minutes more, or until crust is golden brown and filling is bubbly. Makes 6 to 8 servings.

Almond Pastry: Combine 2¼ c. sifted flour, 1 tsp. salt and 1 tblsp. sugar in bowl. Cut in ¾ c. shortening until mixture forms fine crumbs, using a pastry blender. Beat together 1 egg yolk, 2 tsp. almond extract and ¼ c. iced water in bowl. Sprinkle egg mixture over crumb mixture. Toss with a fork until soft dough forms. Press dough firmly into a ball.

Cranberry-Apple Pie

One of those pies you'll want to bake all winter long.
Delicious whether you serve it plain or with a scoop of ice cream.

Pastry for 2-crust 9" pie
3½ c. sliced, pared
  apples
2 c. finely chopped fresh
  or frozen cranberries
½ c. sugar

2 tblsp. cornstarch
1 tblsp. grated orange
  rind
2 tblsp. butter or
  regular margarine

Divide pastry almost in half. Roll out larger half on floured surface to 13" circle. Line 9" pie plate with pastry. Trim edge to 1" beyond rim of pie plate.

Combine apples, cranberries, sugar, cornstarch and orange rind in bowl; mix well. Arrange apple-cranberry mixture in pastry-lined pie plate. Dot with butter.

Roll out remaining pastry. Cut into ¾"-wide strips. Place half of the strips over filling, about 1" apart. Repeat with remaining strips, placing them in the opposite direction, forming a diamond or square pattern. Trim strips even with pie edge. Turn bottom crust up over ends of strips. Press firmly to seal edge. Flute edge.

Bake in 400° oven 15 minutes. Reduce temperature to 350° and bake 30 minutes more, or until apples are tender and crust is golden brown. Cool on rack. Makes 6 to 8 servings.

Cranberry-Blueberry Pie

Tart cranberries and sweet plump blueberries in a flaky crust
—a double treat that's especially good with a pour of heavy cream.

Pastry for 2-crust 9" pie
2 c. fresh or frozen
  cranberries
1 pt. fresh or frozen
  blueberries

1½ c. sugar
3 tblsp. cornstarch
⅛ tsp. salt
2 tblsp. butter or
  regular margarine

Divide pastry almost in half. Roll out larger half on floured surface to 13" circle. Line 9" pie plate with pastry. Trim edge to 1" beyond rim of pie plate.

Combine cranberries, blueberries, sugar, cornstarch and salt in bowl; mix well. Turn mixture into pastry-lined pie plate. Dot with butter.

Roll out remaining pastry. Cut into ½"-wide strips. Place half of the strips over filling, about 1" apart. Repeat with remaining strips, placing them in the opposite directions, forming a diamond or square pattern. Trim strips even with pie edge. Turn bottom crust up over ends of strips. Press firmly to seal edge. Flute edge.

Bake in 425° oven 45 to 50 minutes, or until crust is golden brown and filling is bubbly. Cool on rack. Makes 6 to 8 servings.

Cranberry-Pear Sheet Pie

Baked in a jelly roll pan, this big-batch pie provides a dozen servings, each one juicy with slices of fresh Bosc pears.

Sheet Pie Pastry (recipe follows)	3 c. fresh or frozen cranberries
9 c. sliced, pared Bosc pears	2½ c. sugar
	¾ c. flour

Prepare Sheet Pie Pastry and divide pastry almost in half. Roll out larger half on floured surface to 18x13" rectangle. Line 15½x 10½x1" jelly roll pan with pastry. Trim edges to 1" beyond sides of pan.

Combine pears, cranberries, sugar and flour in bowl; mix well. Arrange pear-cranberry mixture in pastry-lined pan.

Roll out remaining pastry. Cut into ½"-wide strips. Place half of the strips over filling, about 1" apart. Repeat with remaining strips, placing them in the opposite direction, forming a diamond or square pattern. Trim strips even with edge. Turn bottom crust up over ends of strips. Press firmly to seal edges. Flute edges.

Bake in 400° oven 45 minutes, or until pears are tender. Cool on rack. Makes 12 servings.

Sheet Pie Pastry: Combine 3 c. sifted flour and 1½ tsp. salt in bowl. Cut in 1 c. shortening until coarse crumbs form, using a pastry blender. Sprinkle ½ c. iced water over crumb mixture, tossing with a fork until dough forms. Press dough firmly into a ball.

Basic Raspberry Pie

You can enjoy this pie year 'round because it calls for
frozen raspberries. Utterly delightful with its crown of whipped cream.

2 (10-oz.) pkg. frozen
  raspberries, thawed
2½ tblsp. quick-cooking
  tapioca

¼ c. sugar
Unbaked 9" pie shell
Sweetened Cream
  (recipe follows)

Combine undrained raspberries, tapioca and sugar in bowl; mix well.
Let stand 15 minutes.

Meanwhile, bake pie shell in 425° oven 5 minutes.

Pour raspberry mixture into partially baked pie shell. Reduce temperature to 375°. Bake 35 minutes more, or until crust is golden brown. Cool
on rack.

To serve, prepare Sweetened Cream and spread over top of pie.
Makes 6 to 8 servings.

Sweetened Cream: Combine ½ c. heavy cream, ½ tsp. vanilla and
1 tblsp. sugar in chilled bowl. Beat until soft peaks form, using an electric
mixer at high speed.

Raspberry Glacé Pie

An absolutely heavenly three-layer pie: cream cheese
topped with glazed fresh raspberries and puffs of whipped cream.

2 pt. fresh red
  raspberries
⅔ c. water
1 c. sugar
3 tblsp. cornstarch
⅓ c. water
2 tsp. lemon juice

4 drops red food coloring
1 (3-oz.) pkg. cream
  cheese, softened
1 tblsp. milk
Baked 9" pie shell
Sweetened whipped cream

Combine 1 c. of the raspberries and ⅔ c. water in 2-qt. saucepan.
Cook over high heat until mixture comes to a boil. Reduce heat to low
and simmer 3 minutes. Force mixture through sieve to remove seeds.

Combine sugar and cornstarch in 2-qt. saucepan. Blend in ⅓ c. water.
Stir in sieved raspberries. Cook over medium heat, stirring constantly, until mixture boils and thickens. Remove from heat; stir in lemon juice and
food coloring. Cool to room temperature.

Beat cream cheese in bowl until smooth, using an electric mixer at high
speed. Blend in milk. Spread cream cheese mixture in bottom of baked

pie shell. Arrange remaining raspberries on cheese filling, reserving some for garnish. Spoon cooled glaze over raspberries.

Chill in refrigerator at least 2 hours. To serve, decorate wedges with puffs of sweetened whipped cream. Top each puff with a reserved raspberry. Makes 8 servings.

Raspberry Pie in Meringue Crust

A Missouri homemaker says that her minister's wife gave her the recipe for this pie. It's a favorite at their church suppers.

Meringue Crust
  (recipe follows)
1 (10-oz.) pkg. frozen
  raspberries, thawed
1 tblsp. cornstarch

1 c. heavy cream
2 tblsp. sugar
¼ tsp. vanilla
⅓ c. flaked coconut

Prepare Meringue Crust and let cool while preparing filling.

Drain raspberries, reserving syrup. Combine cornstarch and reserved syrup in 2-qt. saucepan. Cook over medium heat, stirring constantly, until mixture comes to a boil. Cook 1 minute more. Remove from heat and cool slightly.

Stir raspberries into slightly cooled syrup. Pour mixture into Meringue Crust. Chill in refrigerator at least 3 hours.

To serve, combine heavy cream, sugar and vanilla in chilled bowl. Beat until soft peaks form, using an electric mixer at high speed. Spread whipped cream over raspberry filling. Sprinkle with coconut. Makes 6 to 8 servings.

Meringue Crust: Beat 3 egg whites, ¼ tsp. baking powder, ¼ tsp. cream of tartar, ¼ tsp. salt and ½ tsp. vanilla in bowl until foamy, using an electric mixer at high speed. Gradually add 1 c. sugar, 1 tblsp. at a time, beating well after each addition. Continue beating until stiff, glossy peaks form. Fold in ¾ c. quick-cooking oats and ½ c. chopped walnuts. Spread meringue on bottom and up sides of well-greased 9" pie plate. Bake in 325° oven 25 minutes, or until lightly browned. Cool on rack.

Fresh Strawberry Pie

It just isn't spring at some farm houses until the first
strawberry pie of the season is set out on the dinner table.

Pastry for 2-crust 9" pie
1 c. sugar
¼ c. cornstarch
2 pt. fresh strawberries,
   hulled

1 tblsp. butter or
   regular margarine
Sugar

Divide pastry almost in half. Roll out larger half on floured surface to
13" circle. Line 9" pie plate with pastry. Trim edge to ½" beyond rim of
pie plate.

Combine 1 c. sugar and cornstarch in bowl.

Cut strawberries in half. Add to sugar-cornstarch mixture, tossing with
a fork to coat. Arrange strawberry mixture in pastry-lined pie plate. Dot
with butter.

Roll out remaining pastry to 11" circle. Cut slits. Place top crust over
filling and trim edge to 1" beyond rim of pie plate. Fold top crust under
lower crust and form a ridge. Flute edge. Sprinkle crust with sugar.

Bake in 425° oven 40 minutes, or until crust is golden brown. Cool on
rack. Makes 6 to 8 servings.

Strawberry-Rhubarb Pie

Two spring favorites combined in one dessert—
strawberries and rhubarb. Try it topped with a dollop of sour cream.

Pastry for 2-crust 9" pie
1¼ c. sugar
⅓ c. flour
⅛ tsp. salt
1 pt. fresh strawberries,
   hulled

2 c. cut-up fresh rhubarb
   (1" lengths)
2 tblsp. butter or
   regular margarine
Water
1 tblsp. sugar

Divide pastry almost in half. Roll out larger half on floured surface to
13" circle. Line 9" pie plate with pastry. Trim edge to ½" beyond rim of
pie plate.

Mix together 1¼ c. sugar, flour and salt in bowl.

Combine strawberries and rhubarb in another bowl; mix well. Arrange
half of the fruit mixture in bottom of pastry-lined pie plate. Sprinkle with
half of the sugar mixture. Repeat with remaining fruit and sugar mixture.
Dot with butter.

Roll out remaining pastry to 11" circle. Cut slits. Place top crust over

filling and trim edge to 1″ beyond rim of pie plate. Fold top crust under lower crust and form a ridge. Flute edge. Brush crust with water. Sprinkle with 1 tblsp. sugar.

Bake in 425° oven 40 to 50 minutes, or until rhubarb is tender. Cool on rack. Makes 6 to 8 servings.

Glazed Fresh Strawberry Pie

Simple and elegant: glazed whole strawberries
arranged in a baked pie shell and topped with whipped cream.

3 pt. fresh strawberries, hulled	Few drops red food coloring
1 c. sugar	Baked 9″ pie shell
3½ tblsp. cornstarch	Sweetened whipped cream
½ c. water	

Mash 1 pt. of the strawberries, using a fork. Set aside.

Combine sugar and cornstarch in 3-qt. saucepan. Stir in water and mashed berries. Cook over medium heat, stirring constantly, until mixture comes to a boil. Cook 2 minutes more. Remove from heat. Stir in food coloring. Cool to room temperature.

Fold remaining 2 pt. strawberries into cooled mixture. Turn into baked pie shell. Chill in refrigerator at least 2 hours.

To serve, top with puffs of sweetened whipped cream. Makes 6 to 8 servings.

✓ Strawberry Festival Pie

If you're not lucky enough to live in an area where
there's an annual strawberry festival, create your own celebration.

Toasted Oat Topping (recipe follows)	2 pt. fresh strawberries, hulled
3 tblsp. cornstarch	2 drops red food coloring
¾ c. sugar	Baked 9″ pie shell
¼ c. water	Sweetened whipped cream

Prepare Toasted Oat Topping and set aside.

Combine cornstarch and sugar in 2-quart saucepan. Blend in water. Add 2 c. of the strawberries. Cook over medium heat, stirring constantly, until mixture boils and thickens. (Mixture will be very thick.) Remove from heat.

Stir remaining 2 c. strawberries and food coloring into cornstarch mixture. Cool to room temperature.

Pour strawberry mixture into baked pie shell. Sprinkle with Toasted Oat Topping. Chill in refrigerator at least 2 hours. To serve, top with puffs of sweetened whipped cream. Makes 6 to 8 servings.

Toasted Oat Topping: Combine 1 c. quick-cooking oats, ¼ c. brown sugar (packed) and ¼ c. butter or regular margarine (melted) in bowl; mix well. Spread mixture in 9″ square baking pan. Bake in 350° oven 10 minutes, or until golden brown. Toss lightly with a fork.

✓ Microwaved Strawberry Pie

Extra-large whole berries can turn this simple dessert
into an extravaganza. Super served with a dollop of heavy cream.

⅓ c. sugar
4½ tsp. cornstarch
1 (10-oz.) pkg. frozen
   strawberries, thawed
1 tblsp. lemon juice

2 pt. fresh strawberries,
   hulled
Microwaved 9″ Pie Shell
   (see Index)
Sweetened whipped cream

Combine sugar and cornstarch in small glass bowl. Stir in thawed strawberries.

Microwave (high setting) 2 minutes. Stir mixture. Microwave 2 to 3 minutes more, or until mixture thickens, stirring after every minute. Stir in lemon juice. Cool slightly.

Arrange strawberries, stem end down, in Microwaved Pie Shell. Spoon sauce evenly over strawberries.

Chill in refrigerator at least 2 hours. To serve, top with puffs of sweetened whipped cream. Makes 8 servings.

Fresh Gooseberry Pie

An old-time favorite recipe—gooseberries picked
fresh from the bush and baked in an almond-flavored pastry.

Almond Pastry
   (recipe follows)
3 c. fresh gooseberries
1½ c. sugar
3 tblsp. quick-cooking
   tapioca

⅛ tsp. salt
2 tblsp. butter or
   regular margarine
Milk

Prepare Almond Pastry and divide pastry almost in half. Roll out larger half on floured surface to 13″ circle. Line 9″ pie plate with pastry. Trim edge to ½″ beyond rim of pie plate.

Crush ¾ c. of the gooseberries.

Combine sugar, tapioca, salt and crushed berries in 3-qt. saucepan. Stir in remaining 2¼ c. gooseberries. Cook over medium heat, stirring constantly, until mixture boils and thickens. Remove from heat.

Pour mixture into pastry-lined pie plate. Dot with butter.

Roll out remaining pastry to 11″ circle. Cut slits. Place top crust over filling and trim edge to 1″ beyond rim of pie plate. Fold top crust under lower crust and form a ridge. Flute edge. Brush crust with milk.

Bake in 425° oven 35 to 45 minutes, or until crust is golden brown and filling is bubbly. Cool on rack. Makes 6 to 8 servings.

Almond Pastry: Combine 2 c. sifted flour and 1 tsp. salt in bowl. Cut in ¾ c. shortening until coarse crumbs form, using a pastry blender. Sprinkle 1 tsp. almond extract and 4 to 5 tblsp. iced water over crumb mixture, a little at a time, tossing with a fork until dough forms. Press dough firmly into a ball.

Pioneer Elderberry Pie

To serve this pie the traditional way, slice it
while it's still warm and top it with a scoop of ice cream.

Pastry for 2-crust 9″ pie	⅓ c. flour
3½ c. fresh elderberries	¼ tsp. salt
1 tblsp. vinegar or lemon	1 tblsp. butter or
juice	regular margarine
1 c. sugar	

Divide pastry almost in half. Roll out larger half on floured surface to 13″ circle. Line 9″ pie plate with pastry. Trim edge to ½″ beyond rim of pie plate.

Wash elderberries and remove stems. Arrange berries in pastry-lined pie plate. Sprinkle with vinegar. Combine sugar, flour and salt and sprinkle over berries. Dot with butter.

Roll out remaining pastry to 11″ circle. Cut slits. Place top crust over filling and trim edge to 1″ beyond rim of pie plate. Fold top crust under lower crust and form a ridge. Flute edge.

Bake in 400° oven 35 to 45 minutes, or until crust is golden brown and filling is bubbly. Cool on rack. Makes 6 to 8 servings.

Elderberry-Apple Pie

This combination was popular among farm folks
a generation ago, and it's every bit as popular today.

Pastry for 2-crust 9" pie
2 c. fresh elderberries
1½ c. chopped, pared
  tart apples
1 c. sugar

3 tblsp. quick-cooking
  tapioca
⅛ tsp. salt
2 tblsp. butter or
  regular margarine

Divide pastry almost in half. Roll out larger half on floured surface to 13" circle. Line 9" pie plate with pastry. Trim edge to 1" beyond rim of pie plate.

Wash elderberries and remove stems. Combine elderberries, apples, sugar, tapioca and salt in bowl; mix well. Arrange elderberry-apple mixture in pastry-lined pie plate. Dot with butter.

Roll out remaining pastry. Cut into ½"-wide strips. Place half of the strips over filling, about 1" apart. Repeat with remaining strips, placing them in the opposite direction, forming a diamond or square pattern. Trim strips even with pie edge. Turn bottom crust up over ends of strips. Press firmly to seal edge. Flute edge.

Bake in 400° oven 35 to 40 minutes, or until crust is golden brown and apples are tender. Cool on rack. Makes 6 to 8 servings.

Mulberry-Rhubarb Pie

If you freeze fresh mulberries and fresh rhubarb,
you can enjoy this wonderful summertime pie any month of the year.

Pastry for 2-crust 9" pie
2 c. fresh mulberries
1 c. thinly sliced fresh
  rhubarb

1 c. sugar
¼ c. flour
2 tblsp. butter or
  regular margarine

Divide pastry almost in half. Roll out larger half on floured surface to 13" circle. Line 9" pie plate with pastry. Trim edge to ½" beyond rim of pie plate.

Combine mulberries and rhubarb in bowl; mix well.

Mix together sugar and flour. Sprinkle one-third of the sugar-flour mixture over bottom of pastry-lined pie plate. Turn mulberry-rhubarb mixture into pie plate. Sprinkle with remaining sugar-flour mixture. Dot with butter.

Roll out remaining pastry to 11" circle. Cut slits. Place top crust over filling and trim edge to 1" beyond rim of pie plate. Fold top crust under lower crust and form a ridge. Flute edge.

Bake in 425° oven 40 to 50 minutes, or until crust is golden brown and filling is bubbly. Cool on rack. Makes 6 to 8 servings.

Blackberry-Apple Pie

For a really superior summertime pie,
combine lustrous blackberries with tart, juicy apples.

Pastry for 2-crust 9" pie
3 c. fresh blackberries
1 c. thinly sliced, pared
   green apples
1 c. sugar

2½ to 3 tblsp. quick-
   cooking tapioca
½ tsp. ground cinnamon
2 tblsp. butter or
   regular margarine

Divide pastry almost in half. Roll out larger half on floured surface to 13" circle. Line 9" pie plate with pastry. Trim edge to ½" beyond rim of pie plate.

Combine blackberries, apples, sugar, tapioca and cinnamon in bowl; mix well. Arrange blackberry-apple mixture in pastry-lined pie plate. Dot with butter.

Roll out remaining pastry to 11" circle. Cut slits. Place top crust over filling and trim edge to 1" beyond rim of pie plate. Fold top crust under lower crust and form a ridge. Flute edge.

Bake in 425° oven 40 to 50 minutes, or until crust is golden brown and filling is bubbly. Cool on rack. Makes 6 to 8 servings.

Apricot Lattice Pie

A state champion pie-baker divulged the recipe
for this unusually good pie made with dried apricots.

2 (8-oz.) pkg. dried
   apricots
Water
1¼ c. sugar
¼ tsp. salt
¼ tsp. ground nutmeg
¼ tsp. ground cinnamon
2½ tblsp. quick-cooking
   tapioca

2 tblsp. soft butter or
   regular margarine
1 tblsp. lemon juice
Pastry for 2-crust 9" pie
Milk
Sugar

Place apricots in 3-qt. saucepan. Add enough water to cover. Cook over high heat until mixture comes to a boil. Reduce heat to low and simmer 25 minutes, or until apricots are tender. Drain apricots, reserving

1¼ c. liquid. Cool to room temperature.

Combine 1¼ c. sugar, salt, nutmeg, cinnamon, tapioca, butter and lemon juice in bowl. Add apricots and reserved liquid to sugar mixture; mix well. Let stand 20 minutes.

Divide pastry almost in half. Roll out larger half on floured surface to 13" circle. Line 9" pie plate with pastry. Trim edge to 1" beyond rim of pie plate.

Spoon apricot mixture into pastry-lined pie plate.

Roll out remaining pastry. Cut into ½"-wide strips. Place half of the strips over filling, about 1" apart. Repeat with remaining strips, placing them in the opposite direction, forming a diamond or square pattern. Trim strips even with pie edge. Turn bottom crust up over ends of strips. Press firmly to seal edge. Flute edge. Brush strips with milk and sprinkle with sugar.

Bake in 350° oven 1 hour, or until crust is golden brown and filling is bubbly. Cool on rack. Makes 6 to 8 servings.

Raisin-Apricot Pie

"This is one of my experimental pies that turned out pretty well," a Pennsylvania woman modestly told us. We agree!

Pastry for 2-crust 9" pie	1 tsp. grated lemon rind
1½ c. raisins	1 (16-oz.) can apricot
1½ c. water	halves, drained
¼ c. sugar	2 tblsp. butter or
2 tblsp. flour	regular margarine
2 tsp. lemon juice	

Divide pastry almost in half. Roll out larger half on floured surface to 13" circle. Line 9" pie plate with pastry. Trim edge to ½" beyond rim of pie plate.

Combine raisins and water in 2-qt. saucepan. Cook over medium heat until mixture comes to a boil. Reduce heat to low. Cover and simmer 5 minutes.

Combine sugar and flour, mixing well. Stir into simmering raisin mixture. Increase heat to medium. Cook, stirring constantly, until mixture comes to a boil. Cook 1 minute more. Remove from heat. Stir in lemon juice, lemon rind and apricots. Arrange mixture in pastry-lined pie plate. Dot with butter.

Roll out remaining pastry to 11" circle. Cut slits. Place top crust over filling and trim edge to 1" beyond rim of pie plate. Fold top crust under lower crust and form a ridge. Flute edge.

Bake in 400° oven 35 to 45 minutes, or until crust is golden brown and filling is bubbly. Cool on rack. Makes 6 to 8 servings.

Old-fashioned Raisin Pie

"A highlight of attending neighborhood auctions as a child was to buy a piece of raisin pie," a Minnesota farm woman recalls.

Pastry for 2-crust 9" pie	1¼ c. water
1 (15-oz.) pkg. raisins (3 c.)	2 tblsp. lemon juice
¾ c. brown sugar, packed	1 c. chopped walnuts
2 tblsp. cornstarch	2 tblsp. butter or
2 tblsp. orange-flavored	regular margarine
instant breakfast drink mix	

Divide pastry almost in half. Roll out larger half on floured surface to 13" circle. Line 9" pie plate with pastry. Trim edge to ½" beyond rim of pie plate. Combine raisins, brown sugar, cornstarch and drink mix in 3-qt. saucepan. Stir in water and lemon juice. Cook over medium heat, stirring constantly, until mixture boils and thickens. Remove from heat; stir in walnuts. Turn mixture into pastry-lined pie plate. Dot with butter.

Roll out remaining pastry to 11" circle. Cut slits. Place top crust over filling and trim edge to 1" beyond rim of pie plate. Fold top crust under lower crust and form a ridge. Flute edge.

Bake in 400° oven 30 minutes, or until crust is golden brown and filling is bubbly. Cool on rack. Makes 6 to 8 servings.

Country-style Raisin Pie

An Iowa corn grower's wife makes this pie often for her husband, especially during the busy harvest season.

Pastry for 2-crust 9" pie	3 tblsp. lemon juice
1 (15-oz.) pkg. raisins (3 c.)	1½ tsp. grated lemon rind
2¼ c. hot water	½ tsp. salt
¾ c. sugar	2 tblsp. butter or
3 tblsp. cornstarch	regular margarine

Divide pastry almost in half. Roll out larger half on floured surface to 13" circle. Line 9" pie plate with pastry. Trim edge to ½" beyond rim of pie plate. Combine raisins and hot water in 3-qt. saucepan. Let stand 5 minutes. Mix together sugar and cornstarch; stir into raisin mixture. Cook over low heat, stirring constantly, until it boils and thickens. Remove from heat. Stir in lemon juice, lemon rind, salt and butter. Pour mixture into pastry-lined pie plate.

Roll out remaining pastry to 11" circle. Cut slits. Place top crust over filling and trim edge to 1" beyond rim of pie plate. Fold top crust under lower crust and form a ridge. Flute edge.

Bake in 425° oven 20 to 25 minutes, or until crust is golden brown. Cool on rack. Makes 6 to 8 servings.

Raisin-Nut Pie

"Friends who don't normally like raisin pie love this one,"
a Kansas woman told us. (She says her husband loves it, too.)

1½ c. raisins
1 c. water
Pastry for 2-crust 9" pie
2 eggs
1 c. sugar

1 tblsp. butter or
  regular margarine
½ c. light cream
½ c. coarsely chopped
  walnuts

Combine raisins and water in 2-qt. saucepan. Cook over high heat until mixture comes to a boil. Reduce heat to low. Cover and simmer 5 minutes. Drain well.

Divide pastry almost in half. Roll out larger half on floured surface to 13" circle. Line 9" pie plate with pastry. Trim edge to ½" beyond rim of pie plate.

Beat together eggs, sugar and butter in bowl until light and fluffy, using an electric mixer at high speed. Stir in light cream, walnuts and raisins. Pour mixture into pastry-lined pie plate.

Roll out remaining pastry to 11" circle. Cut slits. Place top crust over filling and trim edge to 1" beyond rim of pie plate. Fold top crust under lower crust and form a ridge. Flute edge.

Bake in 375° oven 50 minutes, or until golden brown. Cool on rack. Makes 6 to 8 servings.

Harvest Festival Raisin Pie

Stiffly beaten egg whites give a light touch
to the filling, which rises to form its own puffy topping.

2 c. raisins
1 c. water
2 eggs, separated
¾ c. sugar
1 tblsp. flour

½ c. butter or
  regular margarine
¾ c. coarsely chopped
  walnuts
Unbaked 9" pie shell

Combine raisins and water in 3-qt. saucepan. Cook over high heat until mixture comes to a boil. Reduce heat to low. Cover and simmer 10 minutes. Remove from heat.

Beat egg yolks slightly, using a fork. Add sugar, flour, butter and beaten egg yolks to raisin mixture. Cook over medium heat, stirring constantly, until mixture is slightly thickened. Remove from heat.

Beat egg whites in bowl until stiff peaks form, using an electric mixer at high speed. Fold egg whites and walnuts into raisin mixture. Pour into un-baked pie shell.

Bake in 325° oven 50 to 55 minutes, or until top is golden brown. Cool on rack. Makes 6 to 8 servings.

Sour Cream-Raisin Pie

No collection of country pies would be complete without a sour cream-raisin pie. This one's topped with meringue.

1 c. sugar	1½ c. raisins
1½ tblsp. cornstarch	1½ tblsp. lemon juice
½ tsp. ground cinnamon	¼ tsp. cream of tartar
¼ tsp. ground nutmeg	6 tblsp. sugar
¼ tsp. salt	½ tsp. vanilla
1½ c. dairy sour cream	Baked 9" pie shell
3 eggs, separated	

Combine 1 c. sugar, cornstarch, cinnamon, nutmeg and salt in 3-qt. saucepan. Blend in sour cream.

Beat egg yolks slightly, using a fork. Stir beaten egg yolks, raisins and lemon juice into saucepan. Cook over medium heat, stirring constantly, until mixture comes to a boil. Cook 1 minute more. Remove from heat. Let mixture cool while preparing meringue.

To make meringue, beat egg whites and cream of tartar in bowl until foamy, using an electric mixer at high speed. Gradually add 6 tblsp. sugar, 1 tblsp. at a time, beating well after each addition. Continue beating until stiff, glossy peaks form when beaters are slowly lifted. Beat in vanilla.

Pour slightly cooled raisin mixture into baked pie shell. Spoon some of the meringue around edge of filling. Spread meringue so it touches inner edge of crust all around, using back of a spoon. Heap remaining meringue in center. Push out gently to meet meringue border.

Bake in 400° oven 10 minutes, or until meringue is lightly browned. Cool on rack. Makes 6 to 8 servings.

Custard Apple Tarts

This European-type apple tart is spiced with cinnamon,
laced with a rich egg custard and glazed with apple jelly.

Flaky Tart Shells
  (recipe follows)
2/3 c. dry bread crumbs
1/2 tsp. sugar
2 tsp. ground cinnamon
1/2 tsp. salt
6 c. sliced, pared apples

1/4 c. butter or
  regular margarine
4 eggs
1 1/2 c. heavy cream
1/2 c. sugar
1/2 tsp. ground nutmeg
2/3 c. apple jelly

Prepare Flaky Tart Shells and set aside.

Combine bread crumbs, 1/2 tsp. sugar, cinnamon and salt in bowl. Sprinkle half of bread crumb mixture in bottom of each pastry-lined tart pan. Arrange apple slices in a swirl pattern over crumbs, overlapping slices. Dot with butter.

Bake in 425° oven 15 minutes.

Beat eggs until well blended, using a rotary beater. Stir in heavy cream, 1/2 c. sugar and nutmeg. Pour over apples in each pan. Reduce temperature to 375°; bake 25 minutes more, or until custard is set and apples are tender.

Heat apple jelly in saucepan over low heat; stir until smooth. Spoon over hot tarts. Cool in pans on racks. Makes 2 (10") tarts.

Flaky Tart Shells: Combine 2 c. sifted flour and 1/2 tsp. salt in bowl. Cut in 2/3 c. shortening until coarse crumbs form, using a pastry blender. Sprinkle 6 tblsp. iced water over crumb mixture, tossing with a fork until dough forms. Press dough firmly into a ball. Divide dough in half. Roll out one half on floured surface to 12" circle. Line 10" tart or quiche pan with dough. Trim edge even with rim of pan. Repeat with remaining dough.

√ Apple Pizza Pie

Dramatic, but a snap to make. This fruit "pizza"
features spiced apples on a rich Cheddar cheese pastry. So good!

Golden Cheese Pastry
  (recipe follows)
1/2 c. powdered non-dairy
  coffee creamer
1/2 c. brown sugar, packed
1/2 c. sugar
1/3 c. flour
1/4 tsp. salt

1 tsp. ground cinnamon
1/2 tsp. ground nutmeg
1/4 c. butter or regular
  margarine
6 c. sliced, pared apples
  (1/2" thick)
2 tblsp. lemon juice

Prepare Golden Cheese Pastry and roll out pastry on floured surface to 15" circle. Place in 14" pizza pan or on baking sheet. Form ½" ridge around edge. Flute edge. Set aside.

Combine non-dairy coffee creamer, brown sugar, sugar, flour, salt, cinnamon and nutmeg in bowl; mix well. Sprinkle half of the sugar mixture over pastry. Cut butter into remaining sugar mixture until crumbly, using a pastry blender. Set aside.

Starting from the center, arrange apples in rings, overlapping slices slightly. Sprinkle with lemon juice. Top with crumb mixture.

Bake in 450° oven 30 minutes, or until apples are tender. Serve warm. Makes 12 servings.

Golden Cheese Pastry: Combine 1¼ c. sifted flour and 1 tsp. salt in bowl. Cut in ½ c. shortening until coarse crumbs form, using a pastry blender. Stir in 1 c. shredded Cheddar cheese. Sprinkle ¼ c. iced water over crumb mixture, a little at a time, tossing with a fork until dough forms. Press dough firmly into a ball.

Apricot-Raspberry Pastry Bars

This impressive-looking dessert is just right for a crowd.
Easy to make, too—preserves are spread on a cookie-like crust.

Golden Cookie Pastry   ¾ c. apricot preserves
(recipe follows)   ¾ c. raspberry preserves

Prepare Golden Cookie Pastry. Roll out three-fourths of the dough on floured surface to 16x12" rectangle. Place dough on baking sheet. Form ½" rim around edges of dough.

Spread apricot preserves on one-half of the dough and raspberry preserves on the other half.

Roll out remaining pastry to 13x9" rectangle. Cut into 18 (13") strips. Place 9 strips at an angle across filling on narrow side. Then place 9 remaining strips in the opposite direction, forming a diamond pattern. Trim strips even with pie edges. Press firmly to rim to seal. Flute edges.

Bake in 325° oven 30 minutes, or until crust is golden brown. Cool on baking sheet on rack. Makes 32 servings.

Golden Cookie Pastry: Sift together 3 c. sifted flour, 1 c. sugar, 1 tsp. baking powder and ½ tsp. salt into bowl. Cut in 1 c. butter or regular margarine until fine crumbs form, using a pastry blender. Add 2 eggs (beaten) and 2 tsp. vanilla, tossing with a fork until dough forms. Press dough firmly into a ball.

Danish Apple Bars

Extra-flaky glazed pastry bars with lots of apples
and cinnamon—one of our favorite recipes from 'way back.

Egg Yolk Pastry	1 c. sugar
(recipe follows)	1 tsp. ground cinnamon
1 c. crushed cornflakes	1 egg white
8 large apples, pared	Confectioners' Sugar
and sliced (8 c.)	Glaze (recipe follows)

Prepare Egg Yolk Pastry and divide pastry almost in half. Roll out larg-er half on floured surface to 18x13" rectangle. Line 15½x 10½x1" jelly roll pan with pastry. Trim edges to ½" beyond sides of pan.

Sprinkle cornflakes in bottom of pastry-lined pan. Arrange apple slices over cornflakes. Combine sugar and cinnamon and sprinkle over apples.

Roll out remaining pastry to 17x12" rectangle. Cut slits. Place top crust over filling and trim edges to 1" beyond sides of pan. Fold top crust under lower crust. Press to pan to seal.

Beat egg white in small bowl until stiff, using an electric mixer at high speed. Spread egg white over crust.

Bake in 375° oven 1 hour, or until crust is golden brown and apples are tender. Prepare Confectioners' Sugar Glaze and spread on bars while warm. Cool on rack. Makes 12 servings.

Egg Yolk Pastry: Combine 3 c. sifted flour and 1 tsp. salt in bowl. Cut in 1 c. shortening until coarse crumbs form, using a pastry blender. Add enough milk to 1 egg yolk (beaten) to make ½ c. Add to crumb mixture, tossing with a fork until dough forms. Press dough firmly into a ball.

Confectioners' Sugar Glaze: Combine 1 c. sifted confectioners' sugar, 3 tblsp. water and 1 tsp. vanilla in bowl. Stir until smooth.

Cherry-Blueberry Tart

This is a big-batch tart—one generous rectangle
that serves 12-16. Make it when you're pressed for time.

Sweet Pastry	1 (24-oz.) jar
(recipe follows)	blueberry pie filling
1 (24-oz.) jar cherry	
pie filling	

Prepare Sweet Pastry. Remove one-third of the pastry and set aside. Press remaining pastry into bottom and up sides of 15½x10½x1" jelly roll pan.

Spread half of the cherry pie filling in a strip over one-fourth of the pastry. Spread half of the blueberry pie filling over next fourth. Repeat strips with remaining cherry and blueberry pie filling.

Divide remaining pastry into 20 pieces. Shape each piece into a rope, by rolling back and forth with hands on floured surface. Place half of the ropes diagonally over filling. Repeat with remaining ropes, placing them in the opposite direction, forming a diamond pattern. Trim ropes even with edge of pan.

Bake in 350° oven 35 minutes, or until pastry is golden brown. Cool on rack. Makes 12 to 16 servings.

Sweet Pastry: Sift together 3 c. sifted flour, 2 tsp. baking powder, ½ tsp. baking soda and ½ tsp. salt; set aside. Cream together 1 c. shortening and 1 c. sugar in bowl until light and fluffy, using an electric mixer at medium speed. Beat in 1 egg, ½ c. milk and 1 tsp. vanilla. Stir in dry ingredients, blending well. Press dough firmly into a ball.

Ambrosia Tarts

Petite tarts in a shortbread pastry filled with lots of fruit, coconut, walnuts and whipped cream. Perfect for a special party.

1 (8¼-oz.) can crushed
  pineapple
1 c. miniature
  marshmallows
1 tblsp. sugar
1 (11-oz.) can mandarin
  orange segments,
  drained

1 c. green grapes, halved
½ c. flaked coconut
½ c. coarsely chopped
  walnuts
1 c. heavy cream, whipped
Golden Tart Shells
  (see Index)
Flaked coconut

Combine undrained pineapple, marshmallows and sugar in bowl; mix well. Cover and chill in refrigerator 2 hours, or until pineapple juice is absorbed.

Reserve 12 orange segments and 12 grape halves. Stir remaining orange segments, remaining grape halves, ½ c. coconut and walnuts into pineapple mixture. Fold in whipped cream.

Divide filling evenly in Golden Tart Shells and sprinkle with coconut. Decorate each tart with an orange segment or grape half.

Chill in refrigerator until serving time. Makes 24 tarts.

Fruit and Cream Tart

Absolutely elegant! The flaky pie crust base is spread
with cream cheese filling and topped with circles of glazed fruit.

Pastry for 2-crust 9" pie
1 (3-oz.) pkg. cream
  cheese, softened
¾ c. sugar
1 tblsp. milk
1 tblsp. grated orange rind
⅔ c. heavy cream
2 tblsp. cornstarch

¼ c. water
½ c. orange juice
¼ c. lemon juice
1 pt. fresh strawberries
2 medium bananas, sliced
1 (11-oz.) can mandarin
  orange segments,
  drained

Roll out pastry on floured surface to 15" circle. Line 14" pizza pan or baking sheet with pastry and form ½" rim. Flute edge. Prick entire surface of tart shell with a fork.

Bake in 425° oven 12 to 15 minutes, or until golden brown. Cool on rack.

Combine cream cheese, ¼ c. of the sugar, milk and orange rind in bowl. Beat with an electric mixer at medium speed until smooth. Gradually add heavy cream, beating until thick and creamy. Spread mixture over cooled crust and chill in refrigerator.

Combine remaining ½ c. sugar and cornstarch in 2-qt. saucepan. Stir in water, orange juice and lemon juice. Cook over medium heat, stirring constantly, until mixture boils. Cook 1 minute more. Remove from heat. Let mixture cool while preparing fruit.

Reserve 3 large strawberries with leaves; set aside. Hull remaining strawberries and cut into slices. Arrange sliced strawberries around inner edge of crust. Then form a ring of sliced bananas. Continue making concentric circles with mandarin oranges and remaining bananas. Place any remaining sliced strawberries in last ring with whole strawberries in center. Spoon cooled sauce evenly over fruit.

Chill in refrigerator at least 2 hours. Makes 12 to 16 servings.

Apple Meringue Tarts

These small apple tarts are flavored and colored
with red cinnamon candies and swirled with puffs of meringue.

4 c. chopped, pared apples
3 tblsp. sugar
3 tblsp. red cinnamon candies
¾ c. water
1 tsp. cornstarch
¼ c. water

3 egg whites
¼ tsp. cream of tartar
½ tsp. vanilla
6 tblsp. sugar
Baked Tart Shells
  (see Index)

Combine apples, 3 tblsp. sugar, cinnamon candies and ¾ c. water in 3-qt. saucepan. Cook over medium heat until mixture comes to a boil. Continue cooking, stirring occasionally, until most of the liquid evaporates, about 7 minutes.

Blend together cornstarch and ¼ c. water in bowl; stir until blended. Stir cornstarch mixture into apple mixture. Cook, stirring constantly, until mixture boils and thickens. Remove from heat. Spoon hot filling into Baked Tart Shells.

To make meringue, beat egg whites, cream of tartar and vanilla in bowl until foamy, using an electric mixer at high speed. Gradually add 6 tblsp. sugar, 1 tblsp. at a time, beating well after each addition. Continue beating until stiff, glossy peaks form when beaters are slowly lifted.

Spoon meringue onto filling and spread so it touches inner edge of crust all around, using back of a spoon.

Bake in 400° oven 5 minutes, or until meringue is lightly browned. Cool on rack. Makes 8 tarts.

Peach Melba Tarts

An interesting way to serve a classic combination.
Each tart contains cream cheese, peaches and raspberry sauce.

2 (3-oz.) pkg. cream
   cheese, softened
¼ c. sugar
½ tsp. vanilla
⅓ c. heavy cream
Graham Cracker Tart
   Shells (see Index)

1 (16-oz.) can sliced
   peaches, drained
1 (10-oz.) pkg. frozen
   raspberries, thawed
Water
2 tblsp. sugar
1 tblsp. cornstarch

Combine cream cheese, ¼ c. sugar and vanilla in bowl. Beat until smooth, using an electric mixer at medium speed. Add heavy cream and beat at high speed until creamy. Spoon mixture into Graham Cracker Tart Shells. Cut peach slices in half and arrange on top of cream cheese filling. Cover and chill in refrigerator until serving time.

Drain raspberries, reserving juice. Add enough water to juice to make ¾ c. Combine 2 tblsp. sugar and cornstarch in small saucepan. Stir ¾ c. juice into saucepan. Cook over medium heat, stirring constantly, until mixture boils and thickens. Remove from heat; cool to room temperature. Stir in raspberries.

To serve, spoon raspberry sauce over each tart. Makes 18 tarts.

Strawberry-glazed Pear Tart

Dazzle your company with this breathtaking dessert
any time of year—it features canned pears and frozen strawberries.

Sweet Tart Shell
  (recipe follows)
⅓ c. butter or
  regular margarine
1 c. sifted
  confectioners' sugar
1 egg
½ tsp. vanilla

2 (16-oz.) cans pear
  halves, drained
1 (10-oz.) pkg. frozen
  strawberries, thawed
4 tsp. cornstarch
3 tblsp. currant jelly
6 drops red food coloring

Prepare Sweet Tart Shell and set aside.

Cream together butter and confectioners' sugar in bowl until light and fluffy, using an electric mixer at medium speed. Add egg and vanilla; beat well. Spread mixture in bottom of Sweet Tart Shell.

Arrange pear halves, cut side down, in shell. Chill in refrigerator while preparing glaze.

Drain strawberries, reserving juice. Stir together cornstarch and reserved juice in small saucepan. Cook over medium heat, stirring constantly, until mixture boils and thickens. Add currant jelly and food coloring, stirring until jelly melts. Remove from heat; cool slightly. Stir in strawberries. Spoon mixture evenly over pears.

Chill in refrigerator at least 3 hours. Makes 8 servings.

Sweet Tart Shell: Cream together ½ c. butter or regular margarine and ¼ c. sugar in bowl until light and fluffy, using an electric mixer at medium speed. Gradually stir in 1 c. sifted flour, mixing until dough forms. Press dough firmly into a ball. Roll out dough on floured surface to 13″ circle. Line 10″ quiche or tart pan with pastry. Trim edge even with rim of pan. Prick entire surface with a fork. Bake in 325° oven 15 to 20 minutes, or until golden brown. Cool on rack.

Microwaved Cherry Tarts

These pretty cherry tarts can be microwaved in 15 minutes
or less, and they're every bit as good as oven-baked pastries!

Microwaved Tart Pastry
  (recipe follows)
Sugar
1 (16-oz.) can tart red
  cherries in water

6 tblsp. sugar
1½ tblsp. cornstarch
⅛ tsp. salt
⅛ tsp. almond extract
10 drops red food coloring

Prepare Microwaved Tart Pastry and roll out pastry on floured surface to $1/8''$ thickness. Cut 6 rounds, using a floured 5″ round cookie cutter. Cut remaining pastry into 6 decorative shapes, using cookie cutters. Fit rounds over inverted 6-oz. glass custard cups. Prick entire surface of shells with a fork. Arrange custard cups in ring in microwave oven.

Microwave (high setting) 3 minutes. Rearrange custard cups. Microwave 2 to 3 minutes more, or until pastry is dry and opaque. Cover any brown spots that appear with small pieces of aluminum foil. Cool on rack.

Carefully loosen pastry with spatula and remove from custard cups.

Sprinkle pastry cut-outs with sugar and place on waxed paper. Microwave (high setting) 2 to 3 minutes, rotating one-quarter turn after every minute. Cool on rack.

Drain cherries, reserving $1/2$ c. liquid. Combine 6 tblsp. sugar, cornstarch and salt in glass bowl. Stir in almond extract, food coloring, cherries and reserved liquid.

Microwave (high setting) 3 minutes. Stir mixture. Microwave 3 minutes more, or until mixture boils and thickens, stirring after every minute. Spoon cherry mixture into tart shells. Cool on rack. Top each tart with pastry cut-out. Makes 6 tarts.

Microwaved Tart Pastry: Combine $1\frac{1}{4}$ c. sifted flour and $1/2$ tsp. salt in bowl. Cut in $1/2$ c. regular margarine until coarse crumbs form, using a pastry blender. Sprinkle 2 to 3 tblsp. iced water over crumb mixture, a little at a time, tossing with a fork until dough forms. Press dough firmly into a ball.

Peachy Turnovers

You can make these excellent turnovers in almost no time
if you use frozen puff pastry: the taste of homemade without the fuss.

3 tblsp. sugar	1 tsp. lemon juice
2 tsp. cornstarch	1 (17¼-oz.) pkg.
½ tsp. ground cinnamon	frozen puff pastry
1 (16-oz.) can sliced	Confectioners' sugar
peaches, drained	

Combine sugar, cornstarch and cinnamon in 2-qt. saucepan. Drain peaches, reserving $1/4$ c. juice. Add peaches, reserved juice and lemon juice to saucepan. Cook over medium heat, stirring constantly, until mixture boils and thickens. Remove from heat and cool completely.

Thaw puff pastry, according to package directions. Gently unfold thawed pastry. Cut each pastry sheet into 4 squares. Spoon 2 tblsp. filling onto each square. Moisten edges with water. Fold pastry diagonally in half over filling, forming a triangle. Press edges with a fork to seal. Place about 2″ apart, on ungreased baking sheets.

Bake in 350° oven 35 minutes, or until golden brown. Sprinkle with confectioners' sugar. Serve warm. Makes 8 turnovers.

Golden Sunburst Tart

A Kansas homemaker sent us this picture-perfect tart
with a crunchy cookie crust topped by colorful rings of fruit.

*Cookie Crust
  (recipe follows)
1 (8-oz.) pkg. cream
  cheese, softened
½ c. sugar
2 tsp. pineapple juice
¼ c. sugar
4 tsp. cornstarch
1 c. pineapple juice*

*1 (17-oz.) can apricot
  halves, drained
10 red maraschino
  cherries, halved
1 medium banana, sliced
1 (8¾-oz.) can sliced
  peaches, drained
1 (8-oz.) can pineapple
  chunks, drained*

Prepare Cookie Crust and set aside.

Combine cream cheese, ½ c. sugar and 2 tsp. pineapple juice in bowl.
Beat until smooth and creamy, using an electric mixer at medium speed.
Spread mixture over cooled Cookie Crust.

Combine ¼ c. sugar and cornstarch in small saucepan. Gradually stir
in 1 c. pineapple juice. Cook over medium heat, stirring constantly, until
mixture boils and thickens. Remove from heat. Let mixture cool while
preparing fruit.

Arrange apricots, cut side down, around inner edge of crust. Place a
cherry half between each apricot half. Then form a ring of banana slices,
and then one of peach slices. Arrange pineapple chunks in center. Spoon
cooled sauce evenly over all fruit.

Chill in refrigerator at least 2 hours. Makes 12 to 16 servings.

Cookie Crust: Sift together 1½ c. sifted flour, 1 tsp. cream of tartar,
½ tsp. baking soda and ¼ tsp. salt into bowl; set aside. Cream together
½ c. butter or regular margarine and ¾ c. sugar in bowl until light and
fluffy, using an electric mixer at medium speed. Beat in 1 egg and ½ tsp.
vanilla. Stir dry ingredients into creamed mixture, mixing until crumbs
form. Press mixture into 12″ pizza pan. Bake in 350° oven 20 minutes,
or until golden brown. Cool on rack.

4 Extra-Rich Cream Pies

Whether they're topped with billows of whipped cream or crowned by a cloud of golden-tinged meringue, cream pies deserve their reputation as the beauty queens of the pie world. The tantalizing pies in this chapter feature velvety-smooth fillings rich with eggs—and each one tastes as good as it looks.

Country women make the best cream pies you'll find anywhere; they almost always have the ingredients on hand, and they get lots of practice because their families ask for cream pies year 'round. It's not unusual in many farm homes for lemon meringue or banana cream pie to be requested instead of a birthday cake.

Unlike the fillings for fruit pies, which are usually baked in the crust, cream pie fillings are cooked separately and poured, semi-set, into a baked pie shell or crumb crust. We've streamlined the cooking method for most of the fillings by using direct heat, but if you prefer the double-boiler method, we've included several recipes made that way, too. Making a cream filling that sets just right can be tricky unless you know how, so this chapter opens with step-by-step directions for turning out a perfect cream pie.

There's a wealth of flavors to choose from, including new recipes for Chocolate-Coconut Meringue Pie, Strawberry Cream Pie, Butterscotch Meringue Pie and a no-bake pumpkin pie with a surprise praline layer lining the pie shell. Anyone who loves peanut butter will think other desserts are ordinary once they've tasted our new recipe for Banana Cream Tarts. Each tart has a graham cracker crust flavored with peanut butter and filled with a home-made vanilla pudding layered with sliced bananas—simply heavenly.

For traditionalists, you'll find recipes for meringue-topped and whipped cream-decorated versions of coconut, chocolate and banana cream pies. And for those who prefer plain vanilla over any other flavor, there's a versatile recipe for Vanilla Cream Pie that also can be used to make three other flavors of meringue pie.

When you think of meringue pie, you probably think of lemon, so we've begun this chapter with five outstanding variations of this handsome dessert, including a new, quick-cooking recipe for Lemony Meringue Pie. Other citrus flavors are represented by Orange Meringue Pie and a cool-looking Lime Meringue Pie that's mildly tart.

Meringue-topped cream pies are at their best the same day they're made, and if you've ever tried to freeze any kind of cream pie, you were probably disappointed when the filling thawed. We've included a recipe for Frozen Cream Pie Fillings that won't disappoint you; it can be frozen up to four weeks and used to make strawberry, peach, banana or coconut cream pie.

Because women who live on farms and ranches know what it's like to be busy, they're experts at finding ways to make a satisfying dessert in a hurry. Our new recipe for Banana-Coconut Cream Pie was created by an Iowa farm woman with the help of a pudding mix, and an Idaho homemaker combined two pudding mixes to make Rancher's Delight, an "instant" pie with a chocolate-pistachio filling in a nutlike oatmeal crust.

On special occasions, a Minnesota farm woman makes Grasshopper Pie spread with minty whipped cream and garnished with chocolate curls. She says "it's rich, pretty and just plain yummy—my husband's favorite pie."

Any one of these refreshing cream pies will answer the question of what to serve for dessert, and can turn an everyday meal into a party.

How to Make Perfect Cream Pies

Here is the basic method for making a cream pie:

1. Blend the dry ingredients thoroughly, using a wooden spoon. It's important to mix the dry ingredients well so that the liquid will blend in easily.

2. To cook the filling, use a heavy-gauge saucepan; there's less chance of scorching. Be sure to stir slowly and constantly to prevent burning; we suggest stirring in the shape of a figure 8. Don't stir too quickly or the mixture will break down and won't thicken.

3. To combine the hot mixture with the egg yolks, begin by carefully stirring some of the hot mixture into the beaten egg yolks. (If the egg yolks are added directly to the hot mixture, they'll probably curdle.) Blend thoroughly. Then immediately stir the egg yolk mixture into the remaining mixture in the saucepan and cook as recipe directs.

4. If butter or margarine is added to the filling, stir it in very gently, or the mixture will break down and become thin.

5. Pour the filling into a baked pie shell as recipe directs. Cover with plastic wrap or waxed paper and chill several hours, or until set.

How to Make Perfect Meringue

Here is the basic method for making meringue:

1. Separate the eggs for the meringue as soon as you take them out of the refrigerator because they separate more easily when they're cold. Be sure to separate eggs carefully; even a trace of egg yolk can prevent the whites from whipping properly.

2. Place the egg whites in a medium-sized glass or metal bowl; don't use plastic bowls because the oils in it can prevent the egg whites from whipping properly. If you let the egg whites stand at room temperature for about an hour, they'll beat to a much higher volume.

3. Beat the egg whites until they're foamy before you begin to add the sugar. If you beat them until stiff peaks form, you may overbeat the whites before all the sugar is added and lose volume in the finished meringue.

4. Add the sugar very gradually, about a tablespoon at a time, so that it will dissolve completely and prevent the baked meringue from "beading"—forming small golden beads on top.

5. Beat the meringue until it forms stiff, glossy peaks. Then rub some meringue between your fingers to see whether all the sugar is dissolved. If it feels grainy, continue beating until it feels smooth.

6. Spread the meringue over the still-warm filling so that the heat of the filling will help cook the underside of the meringue and keep it from "weeping"—forming liquid between the meringue and the filling. Each of our meringue pie recipes suggests pouring the hot filling into the baked pie shell before starting to beat the meringue so that the filling will be slightly cooled, but still warm, when the meringue is ready.

7. Spread the meringue over the filling, starting all around the edge of the crust, using a tablespoon. Shape the meringue into peaks and swirls, but don't make the peaks too high or the tips will burn during baking. Be sure to seal the meringue all around the edge to prevent it from pulling away from the crust as it bakes.

8. Bake as recipe directs until the meringue is lightly browned and cool the pie on a rack, away from drafts, about 3 hours before cutting. If the pie is cooled in a drafty area, the meringue may pull away from the crust.

To serve, dip the knife into water before cutting pie to keep meringue from sticking to the knife. If you plan to transport the pie to another location, insert several toothpicks halfway into the meringue and cover loosely.

Basic Lemon Meringue Pie

If you've ever had trouble making a perfect lemon meringue pie, try this one. Cornstarch keeps the meringue high and dry.

1 1/4 c. sugar
1/3 c. cornstarch
1/4 tsp. salt
2 c. boiling water
3 eggs, separated
2 tblsp. butter or
   regular margarine
1/3 c. lemon juice

1 tsp. grated lemon rind
Baked 9" pie shell
2 tblsp. sugar
1 tblsp. cornstarch
1/8 tsp. salt
1/2 c. cold water
4 tblsp. sugar

Combine 1 1/4 c. sugar, 1/3 c. cornstarch and 1/4 tsp. salt in 2-qt. saucepan; mix well. Gradually stir in 2 c. boiling water. Cook over medium heat, stirring constantly, until mixture comes to a boil, about 5 to 7 minutes. Cook 1 minute more. Remove from heat.

Beat egg yolks slightly, using a fork. Stir a small amount of hot mixture into egg yolks, blending well. Immediately pour egg yolk mixture back into remaining hot mixture, blending well. Cook over low heat 2 minutes more, stirring constantly. Gently stir in butter, lemon juice and lemon rind. Pour into baked pie shell.

Combine 2 tblsp. sugar, 1 tblsp. cornstarch, 1/8 tsp. salt and 1/2 c. cold water in small saucepan. Cook over medium heat, stirring constantly, until mixture is thick and clear. Remove from heat; cool well.

To make meringue, beat egg whites in bowl until foamy, using an electric mixer at high speed. Gradually add 4 tblsp. sugar, 1 tblsp. at a time, beating well after each addition. Slowly add cooled cornstarch mixture, beating until stiff, glossy peaks form when beaters are slowly lifted.

Spoon some of the meringue around edge of filling. Spread mixture so it touches inner edge of crust all around, using back of a spoon. Heap remaining meringue in center. Push out gently to meet meringue border.

Bake in 350° oven 12 to 15 minutes, or until meringue is lightly browned. Cool on rack. Makes 6 to 8 servings.

Lemony Meringue Pie

A classic American dessert with its meringue crown.
The filling is stirred up in a saucepan over direct heat.

1 c. sugar
3 tblsp. cornstarch
1½ c. cold water
3 eggs, separated
¼ c. lemon juice

1 tblsp. grated lemon rind
1 tblsp. butter or
   regular margarine
Baked 9" pie shell
⅓ c. sugar

Combine 1 c. sugar and cornstarch in 2-qt. saucepan; mix well. Gradually add cold water, stirring well. Beat egg yolks slightly, using a fork. Stir into sugar mixture. Cook over medium heat, stirring constantly, until mixture comes to a boil. Cook 1 minute more. Remove from heat. Gently stir in lemon juice, lemon rind and butter. Pour into baked pie shell.

To make meringue, beat egg whites in bowl until foamy, using an electric mixer at high speed. Gradually add ⅓ c. sugar, 1 tblsp. at a time, beating well after each addition. Continue beating until stiff, glossy peaks form when beaters are slowly lifted.

Spoon some of the meringue around edge of filling. Spread meringue so it touches inner edge of crust all around, using back of a spoon. Heap remaining meringue in center. Push out gently to meet meringue border.

Bake in 350° oven 15 to 20 minutes, or until meringue is lightly browned. Cool on rack. Makes 6 to 8 servings.

Sunny Lemon Pie

A lemony filling as light as a cloud—half the meringue
is folded into the filling, and the rest is mounded in a circle on top.

4 eggs, separated
¼ c. lemon juice
1 tsp. grated lemon rind

3 tblsp. water
1 c. sugar
Baked 9" pie shell

Beat egg yolks until thick in top of double boiler, using an electric mixer at high speed. Gradually stir in lemon juice, lemon rind, water and ½ c. of the sugar. Cook over simmering water, stirring constantly, until thick. Remove from heat.

To make meringue, beat egg whites in bowl until foamy, using an electric mixer at high speed. Gradually add remaining ½ c. sugar, 1 tblsp. at a time, beating well after each addition. Continue beating until stiff, glossy peaks form when beaters are slowly lifted.

Fold half of the egg white mixture into warm egg yolk mixture, folding until no egg whites show. Pour into baked pie shell.

Spoon remaining egg white mixture around edge of pie. Spread mixture so it touches inner edge of crust all around, using back of a spoon.

Bake in 350° oven 15 minutes, or until meringue is lightly browned. Cool on rack. Makes 6 to 8 servings.

All-American Lemon Meringue Pie

This tart and tangy lemony treat whirled with meringue wins a blue ribbon every time. It's everybody's favorite.

½ c. sugar
5 tblsp. cornstarch
¼ tsp. salt
1½ c. boiling water
3 eggs, separated
½ c. sugar
1 tblsp. butter or
   regular margarine

⅓ c. lemon juice
1½ tblsp. grated
   lemon rind
Baked 9" pie shell
6 tblsp. sugar

Combine ½ c. sugar, cornstarch and salt in top of double boiler; mix well. Gradually stir in boiling water. Cook over boiling water, stirring constantly, until mixture is thick enough to mound when dropped from a spoon. Cover and cook 10 minutes, stirring occasionally.

Combine egg yolks and ½ c. sugar in small bowl; mix well. Stir a small amount of hot mixture into egg yolk mixture, blending well. Immediately pour egg yolk mixture back into remaining hot mixture, blending well. Cook 2 minutes more, stirring constantly. Remove from heat. Gently stir in butter, lemon juice and lemon rind. Pour into baked pie shell.

To make meringue, beat egg whites until foamy, using an electric mixer at high speed. Gradually add 6 tblsp. sugar, 1 tblsp. at a time, beating well after each addition. Continue beating until stiff, glossy peaks form when beaters are slowly lifted.

Spoon some of the meringue around edge of filling. Spread meringue so it touches inner edge of crust all around, using back of a spoon. Heap remaining meringue in center. Push out gently to meet meringue border.

Bake in 425° oven 5 minutes, or until meringue is lightly browned. Cool on rack. Makes 6 to 8 servings.

Lemon-Orange Meringue Pie

This good basic lemon pie with the added flavor
of orange makes a cool and refreshing meringue-topped treat.

½ c. sugar.	2 tblsp. lemon juice
4 tblsp. cornstarch	3 tblsp. orange juice
¼ tsp. salt	1 tsp. grated lemon rind
1½ c. cold water	1½ tsp. grated orange rind
3 eggs, separated	Baked 9" pie shell
½ c. sugar	6 tblsp. sugar
2 tblsp. butter or	
regular margarine	

Combine ½ c. sugar, cornstarch and salt in top of double boiler; mix well. Gradually add cold water, stirring well. Cook over boiling water, stirring constantly, until mixture is thick enough to mound when dropped from a spoon. Cover and cook 10 minutes more, stirring occasionally.

Combine egg yolks and ½ c. sugar; mix well. Stir a small amount of hot mixture into egg yolk mixture, blending well. Immediately pour egg yolk mixture back into remaining hot mixture, blending well. Cook 2 minutes more, stirring constantly. Remove from heat. Add butter, lemon juice, orange juice, lemon rind and orange rind; stir gently to mix. Pour into baked pie shell.

To make meringue, beat egg whites in bowl until foamy, using an electric mixer at high speed. Gradually add 6 tblsp. sugar, 1 tblsp. at a time, beating well after each addition. Continue beating until stiff, glossy peaks form when beaters are slowly lifted.

Spoon some of the meringue around edge of filling. Spread meringue so it touches inner edge of crust all around, using back of a spoon. Heap remaining meringue in center. Push out gently to meet meringue border.

Bake in 325° oven 12 to 15 minutes, or until meringue is lightly browned. Cool on rack. Makes 6 to 8 servings.

Orange Meringue Pie

Cream of tartar is added to the meringue, so it whips
up easily. A pleasant change from the classic lemon meringue pie.

1 c. sugar
3 tblsp. cornstarch
1/8 tsp. salt
3 eggs, separated
1 c. orange juice
1/2 c. water
3 tblsp. butter or
   regular margarine

1 tblsp. lemon juice
1 tblsp. grated orange rind
Baked 9" pie shell
1/4 tsp. cream of tartar
6 tblsp. sugar
1/4 tsp. vanilla

Combine 1 c. sugar, cornstarch and salt in 2-qt. saucepan; mix well.
Beat together egg yolks, orange juice and water in bowl until blended, using a rotary beater. Gradually add egg yolk mixture to cornstarch mixture,
blending well. Cook over medium heat, stirring constantly, until mixture
comes to a boil. Cook 1 minute more. Remove from heat. Gently stir in
butter, lemon juice and orange rind. Pour into baked pie shell.

To make meringue, beat egg whites and cream of tartar in bowl until
foamy, using an electric mixer at high speed. Gradually add 6 tblsp. sugar,
1 tblsp. at a time, beating well after each addition. Add vanilla. Continue
beating until stiff, glossy peaks form when beaters are slowly lifted.

Spoon some of the meringue around edge of filling. Spread meringue
so it touches inner edge of crust all around, using back of a spoon. Heap
remaining meringue in center. Push out gently to meet meringue border.

Bake in 350° oven 12 to 15 minutes, or until meringue is lightly
browned. Cool on rack. Makes 6 to 8 servings.

Lime Meringue Pie

Looks every bit as cool and refreshing as it tastes—
a light, mildly tart pie pretty enough for any occasion.

½ c. sugar
4 tblsp. cornstarch
¼ tsp. salt
1½ c. cold water
3 eggs, separated
½ c. sugar
5 tblsp. lime juice

2 tblsp. butter or
   regular margarine
1 tsp. grated lime rind
2 drops green food
   coloring
Baked 9" pie shell
6 tblsp. sugar

Combine ½ c. sugar, cornstarch and salt in top of double boiler; mix well. Gradually add cold water, stirring well. Cook over boiling water, stirring constantly, until mixture is thick enough to mound when dropped from a spoon. Cover and cook 10 minutes more, stirring occasionally.

Combine egg yolks and ½ c. sugar in small bowl; mix well. Stir a small amount of hot mixture into egg yolk mixture, blending well. Immediately pour egg yolk mixture back into remaining hot mixture, blending well. Cook 2 minutes, stirring constantly. Remove from heat. Add lime juice, butter, lime rind and coloring; stir gently. Pour into baked pie shell.

To make meringue, beat egg whites in bowl until foamy, using an electric mixer at high speed. Gradually add 6 tblsp. sugar, 1 tblsp. at a time, beating well after each addition. Continue beating until stiff, glossy peaks form when beaters are slowly lifted.

Spoon some of the meringue around edge of filling. Spread meringue so it touches inner edge of crust all around, using back of a spoon. Heap remaining meringue in center. Push out gently to meet meringue border.

Bake in 325° oven 12 to 15 minutes, or until meringue is lightly browned. Cool on rack. Makes 6 to 8 servings.

Butterscotch Meringue Pie

A real treat for anyone with a sweet tooth—the creamy filling
is mostly brown sugar and eggs, and it's topped with golden meringue.

1 c. brown sugar, packed
¼ c. cornstarch
½ tsp. salt
1½ c. water
1 c. milk
3 eggs, separated

⅓ c. butter or
   regular margarine
1 tsp. vanilla
Baked 9" pie shell
6 tblsp. sugar

Combine brown sugar, cornstarch and salt in 2-qt. saucepan. Gradually add water and milk, stirring well. Cook over medium heat, stirring constantly, until it comes to a boil. Cook 1 minute more. Remove from heat.

Beat egg yolks slightly, using a fork. Stir a small amount of hot mixture into egg yolks, blending well. Immediately pour egg yolk mixture back into remaining hot mixture, blending well. Cook 2 minutes more over low heat, stirring constantly. Remove from heat. Gently stir in butter and vanilla. Pour into baked pie shell.

To make meringue, beat egg whites in bowl until foamy, using an electric mixer at high speed. Gradually add sugar, 1 tblsp. at a time, beating well after each addition. Continue beating until stiff, glossy peaks form when beaters are slowly lifted.

Spoon some of the meringue around edge of filling. Spread meringue so it touches inner edge of crust all around, using back of a spoon. Heap remaining meringue in center. Push out gently to meet meringue border.

Bake in 350° oven 15 to 20 minutes, or until meringue is lightly browned. Cool on rack. Makes 6 to 8 servings.

Caramel Cream Pie

A slightly richer, slightly smaller pie with a creamy,
caramel-colored butterscotch filling and a meringue topping.

1 c. dark brown sugar, packed	2 tblsp. water
¼ c. cornstarch	1 tblsp. butter or regular margarine
¼ tsp. salt	Baked 8" pie shell
1½ c. milk	2 tblsp. sugar
2 eggs, separated	¼ tsp. vanilla

Combine brown sugar, cornstarch and salt in 2-qt. saucepan. Gradually stir in milk. Cook over medium heat, stirring constantly, until mixture comes to a boil. Cook 1 minute more. Remove from heat.

Beat together egg yolks and water until blended, using a fork. Stir a small amount of hot mixture into egg yolk mixture, blending well. Immediately pour egg yolk mixture back into remaining hot mixture, blending well. Cook 1 minute more over low heat, stirring constantly. Remove from heat. Gently stir in butter. Pour into baked pie shell.

To make meringue, beat egg whites in bowl until foamy, using an electric mixer at high speed. Gradually add sugar, 1 tblsp. at a time, beating well after each addition. Continue beating until stiff, glossy peaks form when beaters are slowly lifted. Beat in vanilla.

Spoon some of the meringue around edge of filling. Spread meringue so it touches inner edge of crust all around, using back of a spoon. Heap remaining meringue in center. Push out gently to meet meringue border.

Bake in 350° oven 5 to 10 minutes, or until meringue is lightly browned. Cool on rack. Makes 6 servings.

Coconut Meringue Pie

A sprinkle of coconut on the meringue is just a hint
of the coconut lavishly blended into the luscious vanilla filling.

⅔ c. sugar
¼ c. cornstarch
½ tsp. salt
3 c. milk
3 eggs, separated

¾ c. flaked coconut
1 tsp. vanilla
Baked 9″ pie shell
6 tblsp. sugar
¼ c. flaked coconut

Combine ⅔ c. sugar, cornstarch and salt in top of double boiler; mix well. Gradually add milk, stirring well. Cook over boiling water, stirring constantly, until mixture is thick enough to mound when dropped from a spoon. Cover and cook 10 minutes more, stirring occasionally.

Beat egg yolks slightly, using a fork. Stir a small amount of hot mixture into egg yolks, blending well. Immediately pour egg yolk mixture back into remaining hot mixture, blending well. Cook 2 minutes more, stirring constantly. Remove from heat. Gently stir in ¾ c. coconut and vanilla. Pour into baked pie shell.

To make meringue, beat egg whites in bowl until foamy, using an electric mixer at high speed. Gradually add 6 tblsp. sugar, 1 tblsp. at a time, beating well after each addition. Continue beating until stiff, glossy peaks form when beaters are slowly lifted.

Spoon some of the meringue around edge of filling. Spread meringue so it touches inner edge of crust all around, using back of a spoon. Heap remaining meringue in center. Push out gently to meet meringue border. Sprinkle with ¼ c. coconut.

Bake in 425° oven 5 minutes, or until meringue is lightly browned. Cool on rack. Makes 6 to 8 servings.

Banana Meringue Pie

A layer of sliced bananas tucked between layers
of creamy vanilla custard and smothered with meringue.

⅔ c. sugar
¼ c. cornstarch
½ tsp. salt
2½ c. milk
3 eggs, separated

1 tsp. vanilla
Baked 9″ pie shell
2 medium bananas, sliced
6 tblsp. sugar

Combine ⅔ c. sugar, cornstarch and salt in top of double boiler; mix well. Gradually stir in milk. Cook over boiling water, stirring constantly, until mixture is thick enough to mound when dropped from a spoon. Cover and cook 10 minutes more, stirring occasionally.

Beat egg yolks slightly, using a fork. Stir a small amount of hot mixture into egg yolks. Immediately pour egg yolk mixture back into remaining hot mixture, blending well. Cook 2 minutes more, stirring constantly. Remove from heat. Gently stir in vanilla. Pour half of filling into baked pie shell. Arrange sliced bananas over filling. Top with remaining filling.

To make meringue, beat egg whites in bowl until foamy, using an electric mixer at high speed. Gradually add 6 tblsp. sugar, 1 tblsp. at a time, beating well after each addition. Continue beating until stiff, glossy peaks form when beaters are slowly lifted.

Spoon some of the meringue around edge of filling. Spread meringue so it touches inner edge of crust all around, using back of a spoon. Heap remaining meringue in center. Push out gently to meet meringue border.

Bake in 325° oven 12 to 15 minutes, or until meringue is lightly browned. Cool on rack. Makes 6 to 8 servings.

Chocolate-Coconut Meringue Pie

Two of the all-time favorite flavors of cream pies
are blended into one smooth filling in this scrumptious pie.

⅔ c. sugar	1 (3½-oz.) can flaked
¼ c. cornstarch	coconut (1⅓ c.)
½ tsp. salt	1 tsp. vanilla
2½ c. milk	Baked 9″ pie shell
3 eggs, separated	⅓ c. sugar
2 (1-oz.) squares	
unsweetened chocolate	

Combine ⅔ c. sugar, cornstarch and salt in 2-qt. saucepan; mix well. Gradually add milk, stirring well. Beat egg yolks slightly, using a fork. Add egg yolks and chocolate to milk mixture. Cook over medium heat, stirring constantly, until mixture comes to a boil. Cook 1 minute more. Remove from heat. Gently stir in 1 c. of the coconut and vanilla. Pour into baked pie shell.

To make meringue, beat egg whites in bowl until foamy, using an electric mixer at high speed. Gradually add ⅓ c. sugar, 1 tblsp. at a time, beating well after each addition. Continue beating until stiff, glossy peaks form when beaters are slowly lifted.

Spoon some of the meringue around edge of filling. Spread meringue so it touches inner edge of crust all around, using back of a spoon. Heap remaining meringue in center. Push out gently to meet meringue border. Sprinkle with remaining coconut.

Bake in 350° oven 15 to 20 minutes, or until meringue is lightly browned. Cool on rack. Makes 6 to 8 servings.

Cottage Cheese Meringue Pie

The lemony, cheesecake-like filling in this pie
is just waiting to be discovered under an airy cloud of meringue.

1 c. small-curd creamed
   cottage cheese
½ c. sugar
¼ c. flour
⅔ c. milk
2 eggs, separated

2 tblsp. butter or
   regular margarine
3 tblsp. lemon juice
1½ tsp. grated lemon rind
Baked 8" pie shell
¼ c. sugar

Place cottage cheese in blender jar. Blend until smooth; set aside.

Combine ½ c. sugar and flour in 2-qt. saucepan; mix well. Gradually stir in milk. Cook over medium heat, stirring constantly, until mixture thickens. Remove from heat.

Beat egg yolks slightly, using a fork. Stir a small amount of hot mixture into egg yolks, blending well. Immediately pour egg yolk mixture back into remaining hot mixture, blending well. Cook 2 minutes more over low heat, stirring constantly. Remove from heat. Gently stir in cottage cheese, butter, lemon juice and lemon rind. Pour into baked pie shell.

To make meringue, beat egg whites in bowl until foamy, using an electric mixer at high speed. Gradually add ¼ c. sugar, 1 tblsp. at a time, beating well after each addition. Continue beating until stiff, glossy peaks form when beaters are slowly lifted.

Spoon some of the meringue around edge of filling. Spread meringue so it touches inner edge of crust all around, using back of a spoon. Heap remaining meringue in center. Push out gently to meet meringue border.

Bake in 325° oven 12 to 15 minutes, or until meringue is lightly browned. Cool on rack. Makes 6 servings.

Peanut Butter Meringue Pie

Change a plain vanilla meringue pie into something special
by using peanut butter to flavor the filling and form a crumb topping.

¾ c. sifted confectioners'
  sugar
⅓ c. creamy peanut
  butter
Baked 9" pie shell
3 tblsp. cornstarch
¾ c. sugar
⅛ tsp. salt
2 c. milk

3 eggs, separated
2 tblsp. butter or
  regular margarine
1 tsp. vanilla
¼ tsp. cream of tartar
1 tsp. cornstarch
2 tblsp. sifted confectioners'
  sugar

Place ¾ c. confectioners' sugar in bowl. Cut in peanut butter, using a pastry blender, until coarse crumbs form. Sprinkle half of crumb mixture in baked pie shell, reserving remaining crumb mixture.

Combine 3 tblsp. cornstarch, sugar and salt in top of double boiler; mix well. Gradually stir in milk. Cook over boiling water, stirring constantly, until mixture thickens. Cover and cook 10 minutes more, stirring occasionally.

Beat egg yolks slightly, using a fork. Stir a small amount of hot mixture into egg yolks, blending well. Immediately pour egg yolk mixture back into remaining hot mixture, blending well. Cook 2 minutes more, stirring constantly. Remove from heat. Gently stir in butter and vanilla. Pour into baked pie shell.

To make meringue, beat egg whites, cream of tartar and 1 tsp. cornstarch in bowl until foamy, using an electric mixer at high speed. Gradually add 2 tblsp. confectioners' sugar, 1 tblsp. at a time, beating well after each addition. Continue beating until stiff, glossy peaks form when beaters are slowly lifted.

Spoon some of the meringue around edge of filling. Spread meringue so it touches inner edge of crust all around, using back of a spoon. Heap remaining meringue in center. Push out gently to meet meringue border. Sprinkle with remaining crumb mixture.

Bake in 350° oven 12 to 15 minutes, or until meringue is lightly browned. Cool on rack. Makes 6 to 8 servings.

Chocolate Macaroon Cream Pie

Half a cup of coconut folded into the meringue
gives this dark chocolate cream pie a macaroon-like topping.

¾ c. sugar
3 tblsp. flour
1 tblsp. cornstarch
¼ tsp. salt
3 eggs, separated
1½ c. milk
1½ (1-oz.) squares
   unsweetened chocolate,
   melted and cooled

1 tblsp. butter or
   regular margarine
1 tsp. vanilla
Baked 9" pie shell
⅓ c. sugar
½ c. flaked coconut

Combine ¾ c. sugar, flour, cornstarch and salt in top of double boiler; mix well. Beat egg yolks slightly, using a fork. Add egg yolks, milk and cooled chocolate to sugar mixture; mix well. Cook over boiling water, stirring constantly, until mixture thickens, about 10 minutes. Remove from heat. Gently stir in butter and vanilla. Pour into baked pie shell.

To make meringue, beat egg whites in bowl until foamy, using an electric mixer at high speed. Gradually add ⅓ c. sugar, 1 tblsp. at a time, beating well after each addition. Beat until stiff, glossy peaks form when beaters are slowly lifted. Fold in coconut. Drop meringue mixture by spoonfuls over top of filling.

Place under broiler, about 10" from source of heat. Broil until delicately browned. Cool on rack. Makes 6 to 8 servings.

Rich Chocolate Pie

The dark, fudgy filling sweetened with brown sugar
makes a striking contrast to the pale swirls of meringue.

2 (1-oz.) squares
   unsweetened chocolate
1½ c. milk
1 c. brown sugar, packed
⅓ c. flour
3 eggs, separated

2 tblsp. butter or
   regular margarine
½ tsp. vanilla
Baked 9" pie shell
   with fluted edge
6 tblsp. sugar

Combine chocolate and 1 c. of the milk in 2-qt. saucepan. Cook over medium heat, stirring often, until chocolate melts. Stir in brown sugar.

Combine remaining ½ c. milk and flour in jar. Cover and shake until blended. Gradually stir flour mixture into chocolate mixture. Cook over medium heat, stirring constantly, until mixture boils and thickens. Remove from heat.

Beat egg yolks slightly, using a fork. Stir a small amount of hot mixture into egg yolks, blending well. Immediately pour egg yolk mixture back into remaining hot mixture, blending well. Cook 2 minutes more over low heat, stirring constantly. Remove from heat. Gently stir in butter and vanilla. Pour into baked pie shell.

To make meringue, beat egg whites in bowl until foamy, using an electric mixer at high speed. Gradually add 6 tblsp. sugar, 1 tblsp. at a time, beating well after each addition. Continue beating until stiff, glossy peaks form when beaters are slowly lifted.

Spoon some of the meringue around edge of filling. Spread meringue so it touches inner edge of crust all around, using back of a spoon. Heap remaining meringue in center. Push out gently to meet meringue border.

Bake in 325° oven 12 to 15 minutes, or until meringue is lightly browned. Cool on rack. Makes 6 to 8 servings.

Frozen Cream Pie Fillings

To make your family's favorite cream pie in a flash,
just keep this ready-to-use filling on hand in your freezer.

2 tsp. unflavored gelatin	6 egg yolks, beaten
6 c. milk	6 tblsp. butter or
2 c. sugar	regular margarine
9 tblsp. cornstarch	3 tsp. vanilla
½ tsp. salt	

Sprinkle gelatin over ¼ c. of the milk to soften.

Scald remaining 5¾ c. milk in saucepan over medium heat.

Combine sugar, cornstarch and salt in 3-qt. saucepan. Gradually stir in scalded milk. Cook over medium heat, stirring constantly, until mixture boils and thickens, about 10 minutes. Remove from heat.

Beat egg yolks slightly, using a fork. Stir a small amount of hot mixture into egg yolks, blending well. Immediately pour egg yolk mixture back into remaining hot mixture, blending well. Cook 5 minutes more, stirring constantly. Remove from heat. Gently stir in softened gelatin, butter and vanilla. Pour mixture evenly into 3 foil-lined 8″ pie plates. Cool to room temperature.

Freeze until firm. Remove filling from pie plates and wrap securely in aluminum foil.

Return to freezer. Use to make Banana Cream Pie, Strawberry Cream Pie, Peach Cream Pie and Coconut Cream Pie (recipes follow).   Makes 6 c. filling or enough for 3 (9″) pies.

Banana Cream Pie

If you have homemade filling and a baked pie shell in your freezer,
you can assemble and bake this popular pie in less than half an hour.

1 Frozen Cream Pie Filling
Baked 9″ pie shell
2 medium bananas, sliced
1 tblsp. confectioners'
   sugar

3 egg whites
¼ tsp. cream of tartar
6 tblsp. sugar

Place unthawed Frozen Cream Pie Filling in baked pie shell. Arrange
bananas over filling. Sprinkle with confectioners' sugar.

To make meringue, beat egg whites and cream of tartar in bowl until
foamy, using an electric mixer at high speed. Gradually add sugar, 1 tblsp.
at a time, beating well after each addition. Continue beating until stiff,
glossy peaks form when beaters are slowly lifted.

Spoon some of the meringue around edge of filling. Spread meringue
so it touches inner edge of crust all around, using back of a spoon. Heap
remaining meringue in center. Push out gently to meet meringue border.

Bake in 375° oven 10 to 12 minutes, or until meringue is lightly
browned. Cool on rack. Makes 6 to 8 servings.

Strawberry Cream Pie

Fresh strawberries in a vanilla-scented custard
topped with meringue—a treat for young and old alike.

1 Frozen Cream Pie Filling
Baked 9″ pie shell
1½ c. sliced fresh
   strawberries
3 tblsp. confectioners'
   sugar

3 egg whites
¼ tsp. cream of tartar
6 tblsp. sugar

Place unthawed Frozen Cream Pie Filling in baked pie shell. Arrange
strawberries over filling. Sprinkle with confectioners' sugar.

To make meringue, beat egg whites and cream of tartar in bowl until
foamy, using an electric mixer at high speed. Gradually add sugar, 1 tblsp.
at a time, beating well after each addition. Continue beating until stiff,
glossy peaks form when beaters are slowly lifted.

Spoon some of the meringue around edge of filling. Spread meringue
so it touches inner edge of crust all around, using back of a spoon. Heap
remaining meringue in center. Push out gently to meet meringue border.

Bake in 375° oven 10 to 12 minutes, or until meringue is lightly
browned. Cool on rack. Makes 6 to 8 servings.

Peach Cream Pie

An old-fashioned combination, peaches and cream,
in a dessert that will bring any meal to happy conclusion.

1 Frozen Cream Pie Filling	3 egg whites
Baked 9" pie shell	1/4 tsp. cream of tartar
1 1/2 c. sliced, pared	6 tblsp. sugar
peaches	
3 tblsp. confectioners'	
sugar	

Place unthawed Frozen Cream Pie Filling in baked pie shell. Arrange peaches over filling. Sprinkle with confectioners' sugar.

To make meringue, beat egg whites and cream of tartar in bowl until foamy, using an electric mixer at high speed. Gradually add sugar, 1 tblsp. at a time, beating well after each addition. Continue beating until stiff, glossy peaks form when beaters are slowly lifted.

Spoon some of the meringue around edge of filling. Spread meringue so it touches inner edge of crust all around, using back of a spoon. Heap remaining meringue in center. Push out gently to meet meringue border.

Bake in 375° oven 10 to 12 minutes, or until meringue is lightly browned. Cool on rack. Makes 6 to 8 servings.

Coconut Cream Pie

When you don't have time to fuss over dessert,
this cream pie generously dressed with coconut is just the thing.

1 Frozen Cream Pie Filling	3 egg whites
Baked 9" pie shell	1/4 tsp. cream of tartar
1 1/2 c. flaked coconut	6 tblsp. sugar

Place unthawed Frozen Cream Pie Filling in baked pie shell. Sprinkle with coconut.

To make meringue, beat egg whites and cream of tartar in bowl until foamy, using an electric mixer at high speed. Gradually add sugar, 1 tblsp. at a time, beating well after each addition. Continue beating until stiff, glossy peaks form when beaters are slowly lifted.

Spoon some of the meringue around edge of filling. Spread meringue so it touches inner edge of crust all around, using back of a spoon. Heap remaining meringue in center. Push out gently to meet meringue border.

Bake in 375° oven 10 to 12 minutes, or until meringue is lightly browned. Cool on rack. Makes 6 to 8 servings.

Vanilla Cream Pie

You can make any of three favorite meringue pies—
banana, coconut or chocolate—from this basic vanilla pie recipe.

⅔ c. sugar
¼ c. cornstarch
½ tsp. salt
2½ c. milk

3 eggs, separated
1 tsp. vanilla
Baked 9" pie shell
6 tblsp. sugar

Combine ⅔ c. sugar, cornstarch and salt in 2-qt. saucepan; mix well. Gradually add milk, stirring well. Beat egg yolks slightly, using a fork. Stir into milk mixture. Cook over medium-low heat, stirring constantly, until mixture comes to a boil. Cook 1 minute more. Remove from heat. Gently stir in vanilla. Pour into baked pie shell.

To make meringue, beat egg whites in bowl until foamy, using an electric mixer at high speed. Gradually add 6 tblsp. sugar, 1 tblsp. at a time, beating well after each addition. Continue beating until stiff, glossy peaks form when beaters are slowly lifted.

Spoon some of the meringue around edge of filling. Spread meringue so it touches inner edge of crust all around, using back of a spoon. Heap remaining meringue in center. Push out gently to meet meringue border.

Bake in 350° oven 15 to 20 minutes, or until meringue is lightly browned. Cool on rack. Makes 6 to 8 servings.

Banana Pie: Follow recipe for Vanilla Cream Pie, but pour half of the filling into baked pie shell. Top with 2 medium bananas (sliced). Pour remaining filling over bananas. Continue as for Vanilla Cream Pie.

Coconut Cream Pie: Follow recipe for Vanilla Cream Pie, but gently stir ¾ c. flaked coconut into hot filling. Continue as for Vanilla Cream Pie. Sprinkle meringue with ¼ c. flaked coconut. Bake in 425° oven 5 minutes, or until meringue is lightly browned and coconut is toasted.

Chocolate Cream Pie: Follow recipe for Vanilla Cream Pie, but add 2 (1-oz.) squares unsweetened chocolate to milk mixture before cooking.

Easy Banana Cream Pie

Let a child help with this one—the easy filling
is made with lots of bananas, and it's poured into a no-roll crust.

2 c. mashed bananas
   (about 5 medium)
½ c. light corn syrup
1 tblsp. butter or
   regular margarine
⅛ tsp. salt

2 tblsp. lime juice
½ tsp. ground nutmeg
Baked No-Roll Margarine Pie
   Shell (see Index)
1 c. heavy cream, whipped

Combine mashed bananas, corn syrup, butter and salt in 2-qt. saucepan. Cook over medium heat, stirring occasionally, until mixture comes to a boil. Remove from heat. Cool 10 minutes.

Stir lime juice and nutmeg into slightly cooled banana mixture. Pour into baked No-Roll Margarine Pie Shell.

Cover and chill in refrigerator until set.

To serve, decorate with puffs of whipped cream. Makes 6 to 8 servings.

Banana-Coconut Cream Pie

A shortcut recipe created for the busy harvest season
by an Iowa farmer's wife who says there's never any left over.

1 (3¾-oz.) pkg. banana
   cream instant pudding
   and pie filling mix
2 c. milk
½ c. flaked coconut

Baked 9" pie shell
2 large bananas, sliced
Whipped Cream Topping
   (recipe follows)
¼ c. flaked coconut

Combine banana cream pudding mix and milk in bowl. Beat until well blended, using an electric mixer at low speed, about 2 minutes. Fold in ½ c. coconut.

Pour half of the pudding mixture into baked pie shell. Arrange bananas on pudding layer. Pour remaining pudding over bananas.

Cover and chill in refrigerator 1 hour, or until set.

To serve, prepare Whipped Cream Topping and spread over pie. Sprinkle with ¼ c. coconut. Makes 6 to 8 servings.

Whipped Cream Topping: Combine 1 c. heavy cream, 1 tblsp. sugar and ½ tsp. vanilla in bowl. Beat until soft peaks form, using an electric mixer at high speed.

Basic Banana Cream Pie

You've never tasted banana cream pie this good
unless you've already tried this all-time favorite recipe.

¾ c. sugar
2 tblsp. flour
2 tblsp. cornstarch
¼ tsp. salt
2 c. milk
3 egg yolks
2 tblsp. butter or
    regular margarine

1 tsp. vanilla
2 large bananas, sliced
Baked 9″ pie shell
1 c. heavy cream
2 tblsp. sugar
½ tsp. vanilla

Combine ¾ c. sugar, flour, cornstarch and salt in 3-qt. saucepan. Gradually stir in milk. Cook over medium heat, stirring constantly, until mixture comes to a boil. Cook 2 minutes more. Remove from heat.

Beat egg yolks slightly, using a fork. Stir a small amount of hot mixture into egg yolks, blending well. Immediately pour egg yolk mixture back into remaining hot mixture, blending well. Cook 2 minutes more over low heat, stirring constantly. Remove from heat.

Gently stir in butter and 1 tsp. vanilla. Cool 5 minutes.

Arrange sliced bananas in bottom of baked pie shell. Pour slightly cooled filling over bananas.

Cover and chill in refrigerator until set, about 3 hours.

To serve, whip heavy cream with 2 tblsp. sugar and ½ tsp. vanilla in bowl until soft peaks form, using an electric mixer at high speed. Spread whipped cream over pie. Makes 6 to 8 servings.

Banana-Yogurt Pie

A new variation of the classic banana cream pie—
extra-nutritious because it's made with plain yogurt and bananas.

¾ c. sugar
⅓ c. cornstarch
¼ tsp. salt
3 c. skim milk
2 tblsp. butter or
    regular margarine

1 tsp. vanilla
1 (8-oz.) container plain
    yogurt
2 medium bananas, sliced
Baked 9″ pie shell

Combine sugar, cornstarch and salt in 2-qt. saucepan. Gradually add skim milk, stirring well. Cook over medium heat, stirring constantly, until mixture comes to a boil. Cook 1 minute more. Gently stir in butter and vanilla. Pour into bowl.

Cover and chill in refrigerator 1 hour, or until mixture is cool and thick.

Add yogurt to cooled custard. Beat until creamy, using an electric mixer at medium speed.

Place sliced bananas in bottom of baked pie shell. Pour yogurt mixture over bananas.

Cover and chill in refrigerator 1 hour, or until set. Makes 6 to 8 servings.

Coconut Cream Pie

This extra-creamy coconut pie is so light that it just
melts in your mouth. The secret ingredient is whipped cream.

⅔ c. sugar
¼ c. cornstarch
¼ tsp. salt
2½ c. milk
3 egg yolks
1 tblsp. butter or
    regular margarine

2 tsp. vanilla
1 c. heavy cream, whipped
1⅓ c. flaked coconut
Baked 9″ pie shell

Combine sugar, cornstarch and salt in 3-qt. saucepan. Gradually stir in milk. Cook over medium heat, stirring constantly, until mixture comes to a boil. Cook 2 minutes more. Remove from heat.

Beat egg yolks slightly, using a fork. Stir a small amount of hot mixture into egg yolks, blending well. Immediately pour egg yolk mixture back into remaining hot mixture, blending well. Cook 2 minutes more over low heat, stirring constantly. Remove from heat.

Gently stir in butter and vanilla. Cool completely.

Fold whipped cream into cooled filling. Then fold in 1 c. of the coconut. Pour into baked pie shell.

Cover and chill in refrigerator until set, about 2 hours. To serve, sprinkle pie with remaining ⅓ c. coconut. Makes 6 to 8 servings.

Cherry Cream Pie

A bright bounty of almond-scented cherries spread
over a layer of vanilla pudding in a flaky pie crust.

1 (3¼-oz.) pkg. vanilla pudding and pie filling mix
2 c. milk
2 egg yolks
1 tblsp. butter or
   regular margarine

¼ tsp. vanilla
Baked 9″ pie shell
1 (24-oz.) jar cherry pie
   filling
¼ tsp. almond extract

Combine pudding mix and milk in 2-qt. saucepan. Cook over medium heat, stirring constantly, until mixture comes to a boil. Cook 1 minute more. Remove from heat.

Beat egg yolks slightly, using a fork. Stir a small amount of hot mixture into egg yolks, blending well. Immediately pour egg yolk mixture back into remaining hot mixture, blending well. Cook 2 minutes more over low heat, stirring constantly. Remove from heat.

Gently stir in butter and vanilla. Cool 5 minutes. Pour slightly cooled filling into baked pie shell.

Cover and chill in refrigerator until set.

To serve, combine cherry pie filling with almond extract; mix well. Spread cherry mixture over filling. Makes 6 to 8 servings.

Old-fashioned Butterscotch Pie

A caramel-colored pie with a whipped cream topping
and a rich taste that will please even the fussiest eaters.

½ c. butter or
   regular margarine
1¼ c. brown sugar,
   packed
1½ c. boiling water
4 tblsp. cornstarch
3 tblsp. flour
¾ tsp. salt

1 c. milk
4 egg yolks
1½ tsp. vanilla
Baked 9″ pie shell
1 c. heavy cream
1 tblsp. sugar
½ tsp. vanilla

Melt butter in 3-qt. saucepan over low heat until butter turns a light golden brown. Stir in brown sugar and boiling water. Cook over medium heat until mixture comes to a boil. Cook 2 minutes more, stirring constantly. Remove from heat.

Combine cornstarch, flour and salt in bowl. Gradually stir in milk. Stir milk mixture into butter mixture. Cook over medium heat, stirring constantly, until mixture comes to a boil, about 5 to 7 minutes. Cook 1 minute more. Remove from heat.

Beat egg yolks slightly, using a fork. Stir a small amount of hot mixture into egg yolks, blending well. Immediately pour egg yolk mixture back into remaining hot mixture, blending well. Cook 2 minutes more over low heat, stirring constantly. Remove from heat.

Gently stir in 1½ tsp. vanilla. Cool 5 minutes. Pour slightly cooled filling into baked pie shell.

Cover and chill in refrigerator until set.

To serve, whip heavy cream, sugar and ½ tsp. vanilla in bowl until soft peaks form, using an electric mixer at high speed. Spread whipped cream over pie. Makes 6 to 8 servings.

Creamy Chocolate Pie

Grated chocolate and a swirl of whipped cream
are the finishing touches to this delicately set chocolate pie.

2 (1-oz.) squares unsweetened chocolate	2 tblsp. butter or regular margarine
3 c. milk	1 tsp. vanilla
1 c. sugar	Baked 9" pie shell
⅓ c. flour	Sweetened whipped cream
¼ tsp. salt	Grated semisweet chocolate
3 egg yolks	

Combine unsweetened chocolate and milk in 2-qt. saucepan. Cook over medium heat until chocolate is melted.

Combine sugar, flour and salt in small bowl. Pour some of the hot mixture into sugar-flour mixture. Beat until smooth, using a rotary beater. Then stir back into remaining hot mixture. Cook over medium heat, stirring constantly, until mixture comes to a boil. Cook 1 minute more. Remove from heat.

Beat egg yolks slightly, using a fork. Pour some of the hot mixture into egg yolks, blending well. Immediately pour egg yolk mixture back into remaining hot mixture, blending well. Cook 2 minutes more over low heat, stirring constantly. Remove from heat.

Gently stir in butter and vanilla. Cool 10 minutes. Pour slightly cooled filling into baked pie shell.

Cover and chill in refrigerator 2 hours, or until set.

To serve, spread sweetened whipped cream over pie. Decorate with grated semisweet chocolate. Makes 6 to 8 servings.

Chocolate Velvet Pie

Irresistible—a silky-smooth, cocoa-flavored cream filling
beneath a whipped cream topping garnished with shaved chocolate.

1¼ c. sugar
½ c. baking cocoa
4 tblsp. cornstarch
¼ tsp. salt
3 c. milk
3 tblsp. butter or
   regular margarine

1½ tsp. vanilla
Baked 9″ pie shell
1 (1-oz.) square
   unsweetened chocolate
1 c. heavy cream
2 tblsp. sugar
1 tsp. vanilla

Sift together 1¼ c. sugar, baking cocoa, cornstarch and salt; set aside.

Scald milk in top of double boiler. Gradually stir in sugar mixture. Cook over boiling water, stirring constantly, until mixture begins to thicken. Cover and cook over simmering water 15 minutes more, stirring occasionally. Remove from heat.

Add butter and 1½ tsp. vanilla. Stir gently until butter melts. Cool 10 minutes. Pour slightly cooled filling into baked pie shell.

Cover and chill in refrigerator at least 2 hours, or until set.

To serve, cut unsweetened chocolate into shavings, using a vegetable peeler. Whip heavy cream in bowl until it begins to thicken, using an electric mixer at high speed. Gradually add 2 tblsp. sugar and 1 tsp. vanilla, beating until soft peaks form. Spread whipped cream over pie and garnish with chocolate shavings. Makes 6 to 8 servings.

German Sweet Chocolate Pie

A blend of chopped pecans and coconut forms the crunchy crust
of this sweet chocolate pudding pie. It's a sure company-pleaser.

⅓ c. butter or
   regular margarine
⅓ c. brown sugar, packed
⅓ c. chopped pecans
⅓ c. flaked coconut
Baked 9″ pie shell
1 (4¾-oz.) pkg. vanilla
   pudding and pie filling mix

1 (4-oz.) bar sweet
   cooking chocolate, cut up
2½ c. milk
Sweetened whipped cream
Flaked coconut

Combine butter, brown sugar, pecans and ⅓ c. coconut in small saucepan. Cook over medium heat, stirring often, until mixture comes to a boil. Remove from heat; cool slightly.

Spread slightly cooled pecan-coconut mixture in bottom of baked pie shell.

Bake in 450° oven 5 minutes to set filling. Cool on rack.

Combine pudding mix, chocolate and milk in 2-qt. saucepan. Cook according to package directions for pie filling. Remove from heat; cool 5 minutes. Pour slightly cooled filling over pecan-coconut layer.

Cover and chill in refrigerator 4 hours, or until set.

To serve, decorate with puffs of sweetened whipped cream and coconut. Makes 6 to 8 servings.

Chocolate Rum Pie

Devilishly delicious—spiked with rum flavoring
and generously studded with toasted slivers of almonds.

1 (5½-oz.) pkg. chocolate pudding and pie filling mix	⅔ c. toasted slivered almonds
2 c. milk	Baked 9″ pie shell
1 c. heavy cream	4 tsp. sugar
	¼ tsp. rum flavoring

Cook pudding mix according to package directions for pie filling, using 2 c. milk. (Filling will be thick.) Remove from heat; pour into bowl. Cover and cool completely.

Whip ⅓ c. of the heavy cream in bowl until soft peaks form, using an electric mixer at high speed. Fold whipped cream into chocolate mixture.

Remove 3 tblsp. almonds; set aside. Arrange remaining almonds in bottom of baked pie shell. Add chocolate filling.

Cover and chill in refrigerator until set.

To serve, whip remaining heavy cream in bowl until it begins to thicken, using an electric mixer at high speed. Gradually add sugar and rum flavoring, beating until soft peaks form. Spread whipped cream over pie. Decorate with remaining 3 tblsp. almonds. Makes 6 to 8 servings.

Milk Chocolate Pie

Cocoa gives this pie its light, gentle flavor.
You can serve the filling alone as chocolate pudding.

¾ c. sugar
6 tblsp. cornstarch
2 tblsp. baking cocoa
4 c. milk

½ tsp. vanilla
Baked 9" pie shell
Sweetened whipped cream
Walnut halves

Combine sugar, cornstarch and baking cocoa in top of double boiler. Gradually stir in milk. Cook over boiling water 15 minutes, stirring constantly, until mixture thickens. Remove from heat.

Gently stir in vanilla. Cool 5 minutes. Pour slightly cooled filling into baked pie shell.

Cover and chill in refrigerator 4 hours, or until set.

To serve, decorate with puffs of sweetened whipped cream and walnut halves. Makes 6 to 8 servings.

No-Bake Pumpkin Pie

Because it's cooked on top of the range, the filling
is extra-creamy. It's topped with whipped cream and almonds.

¾ c. sugar
2 tblsp. cornstarch
1 tsp. ground cinnamon
¼ tsp. ground nutmeg
¼ tsp. ground ginger
¼ tsp. ground cloves
1 (16-oz.) can mashed
    pumpkin (2 c.)

1 c. milk
2 eggs
Baked 9" pie shell
Sweetened whipped cream
Toasted slivered almonds

Combine sugar, cornstarch, cinnamon, nutmeg, ginger and cloves in 3-qt. saucepan. Blend in pumpkin. Gradually add milk, stirring well. Cook over medium heat, stirring constantly, until mixture comes to a boil. Cook 1 minute more. Remove from heat.

Beat eggs slightly, using a fork. Stir a small amount of hot mixture into eggs, blending well. Immediately pour egg mixture back into remaining hot mixture, blending well. Cook 2 minutes more over low heat, stirring constantly. Remove from heat.

Cover and cool at room temperature, about 30 minutes. Pour slightly cooled filling into baked pie shell.

Cover and chill in refrigerator 2 hours, or until set.

To serve, decorate with whipped cream and almonds. Makes 6 to 8 servings.

No-Bake Pumpkin Praline Pie

A farm family in Ohio loves the crunchy pecan-
brown sugar layer that lines the crust of this creamy pumpkin pie.

1/4 c. butter or
   regular margarine
1/2 c. coarsely chopped
   pecans
1/2 c. brown sugar, packed
Baked 9" pie shell
1/2 c. sugar
1/3 c. cornstarch
2 tsp. pumpkin pie spice

1/8 tsp. salt
1 c. milk
2 eggs, beaten
1 (16-oz.) can mashed
   pumpkin (2 c.)
1 tsp. vanilla
1 c. heavy cream, whipped
Pecan halves

Melt butter in small saucepan over medium heat. Add 1/2 c. pecans and brown sugar. Cook, stirring often, until mixture comes to a boil. Spread over bottom of baked pie shell.

Combine sugar, cornstarch, pumpkin pie spice and salt in 2-qt. saucepan. Gradually add milk, stirring well. Blend eggs and pumpkin into milk mixture. Cook over medium heat, stirring constantly, until mixture comes to a boil. Cook 1 minute more. (Mixture will be very thick.) Remove from heat. Gently stir in vanilla. Cool completely.

Fold half of the whipped cream into cooled pumpkin mixture. Turn in-to prepared pie shell.

Cover and chill in refrigerator 2 hours, or until set.

To serve, decorate with remaining whipped cream and pecan halves. Makes 6 to 8 servings.

Grasshopper Pie

This cool and refreshing pie with its minty filling
in a chocolate cookie crust is a Minnesota farmer's favorite pie.

¾ c. sugar
3 tblsp. cornstarch
1/₁₆ tsp. salt
1¾ c. half-and-half
3 egg yolks
¼ c. creme de menthe

Chocolate Cookie Crust
  (see Index)
Minty Whipped Cream
  (recipe follows)
Chocolate curls

Combine sugar, cornstarch and salt in 2-qt. saucepan. Gradually stir in half-and-half. Cook over medium heat, stirring constantly, until mixture boils and thickens. Cook 1 minute more. Remove from heat.

Beat egg yolks slightly, using a fork. Stir a small amount of hot mixture into egg yolks, blending well. Immediately pour egg yolk mixture back into remaining hot mixture, blending well. Cook 1 minute more over low heat, stirring constantly. Remove from heat. Stir in creme de menthe. Cool 5 minutes. Pour slightly cooled filling into Chocolate Cookie Crust.

Cover and chill in refrigerator until set, about 4 hours.

To serve, prepare Minty Whipped Cream and spread over pie. Garnish with chocolate curls. Makes 6 to 8 servings.

Minty Whipped Cream: Combine 1 c. heavy cream, 2 tblsp. creme de menthe and 1 tblsp. sugar in chilled bowl. Beat until soft peaks form, using an electric mixer at high speed.

Black-and-White Date Pie

Velvety custard and a blanket of whipped cream
over a rich, dark layer of chopped dates. Uniquely delicious.

1 c. chopped, pitted
  dates (8 oz.)
½ c. water
1/₈ tsp. salt
½ c. sugar
1 tsp. cornstarch
1 tsp. butter or
  regular margarine
1 tblsp. lemon juice
¾ c. sugar

¼ c. flour
2 tblsp. cornstarch
¼ tsp. salt
2 c. milk, scalded
3 egg yolks, beaten
½ tsp. lemon juice
½ tsp. vanilla
Baked 9" pie shell
¾ c. heavy cream, whipped

Combine dates, water and 1/₈ tsp. salt in 2-qt. saucepan. Cook over medium heat until dates soften. Combine ½ c. sugar and 1 tsp. cornstarch. Add sugar mixture to date mixture, blending well. Cook until mixture thickens, stirring constantly. Remove from heat. Stir in butter and 1 tblsp. lemon juice. Cool.

Combine ¾ c. sugar, flour, 2 tblsp. cornstarch and ¼ tsp. salt in top of double boiler. Gradually stir in milk. Cook over boiling water, stirring constantly, until mixture thickens.

Stir a small amount of hot mixture into egg yolks, blending well. Immediately pour egg yolk mixture back into remaining hot mixture, blending well. Cook 3 minutes more, stirring constantly. Remove from heat. Gently stir in ½ tsp. lemon juice and vanilla. Cool slightly.

Spread cooled date mixture in baked pie shell. Carefully spread slightly cooled filling over date mixture.

Cover and chill in refrigerator until set.

To serve, spread whipped cream over pie. Makes 6 to 8 servings.

Rancher's Delight Pies

Oatmeal gives this pie crust a mild nutty flavor,
and instant pudding mixes make the filling a snap to prepare.

Oatmeal Crust (recipe follows)	3½ c. milk
	1 tsp. vanilla
1 (4½-oz.) pkg. instant chocolate pudding mix	1 (2-oz.) env. whipped topping mix
1 (3¾-oz.) pkg. instant pistachio pudding mix	½ c. milk
	½ tsp. vanilla

Prepare Oatmeal Crust and divide pastry in half. Roll out each half on floured surface to 12″ circle. Line 2 (8″) pie plates with pastry. Trim edge to 1″ beyond rim of each pie plate. Turn under edge to form a ridge. Flute edge. Prick with a fork.

Bake in 375° oven 10 to 15 minutes, or until golden. Cool on racks.

Combine chocolate pudding mix, pistachio pudding mix, 3½ c. milk and 1 tsp. vanilla in bowl. Beat slowly 2 minutes, using a rotary beater. Chill in refrigerator 5 minutes. Spoon filling into pie shells.

Cover and chill in refrigerator until set.

Prepare whipped topping mix with ½ c. milk and ½ tsp. vanilla according to package directions.

To serve, decorate each pie with puffs of whipped topping. Makes 2 (8″) pies, 6 servings each.

Oatmeal Crust: Combine 2 c. sifted flour, ½ c. quick-cooking oats, 1 tblsp. sugar, ½ tsp. salt and ¼ tsp. baking powder in bowl. Cut in 1 c. butter or regular margarine until coarse crumbs form, using a pastry blender. Stir in 1 egg (beaten). Add 1 to 2 tblsp. iced water, tossing with a fork until dough forms. Press dough firmly into a ball.

Cream Tarts

Individual tarts with a choice of three fillings
—a versatile recipe that you can use all year 'round.

2 c. sifted flour	1 (2-oz) env. whipped
1 tsp. salt	topping mix
¾ c. shortening or ⅔ c. lard	½ c. milk
4 to 5 tblsp. iced water	½ tsp. vanilla
1⅓ c. Pumpkin Paste or	Yellow food coloring
½ c. Cocoa Paste or	(optional)
½ c. Lemon Paste	
(recipes follow)	

Combine flour and salt in bowl. Cut in shortening until coarse crumbs form, using a pastry blender. Sprinkle iced water over crumb mixture, a little at a time, tossing with a fork until dough forms.

Divide pastry into 6 parts. Shape each part into a ball. Roll out each on floured surface to 4½" circle. Fit pastry rounds over the backs of 3" muffin-pan cups. Or roll each part to 5" circle; fit over inverted 6-oz. custard cups and place on baking sheet. Make pleats so pastry will fit snugly. Prick entire surface of each with a fork.

Chill in refrigerator 30 minutes.

Bake in 450° oven 10 to 20 minutes, or until golden brown. Cool on racks. Carefully remove shells from muffin-pan cups or custard cups.

Meanwhile, remove paste from refrigerator or thaw frozen paste.

Prepare whipped topping mix with milk and vanilla, according to package directions. Add 1⅓ c. Pumpkin Paste or ½ c. Cocoa Paste or ½ c. Lemon Paste, beating until smooth and creamy. If you wish, add a few drops yellow food coloring to lemon filling. Spoon filling into each tart shell.

Cover and chill in refrigerator before serving. Makes 6 tarts.

Pumpkin Paste: Combine 1 c. sugar, ½ c. brown sugar (packed), ⅓ c. sifted flour, 1½ tsp. ground cinnamon, 1½ tsp. ground nutmeg and ¾ tsp. salt in 2-qt. saucepan. Add 3 c. canned mashed pumpkin and ¾ c. water; blend well. Cook over low heat, stirring occasionally, 15 minutes. Remove from heat; cool. Freeze in 1⅓-c. portions. (May be stored in freezer up to 4 weeks.) Makes 4 c.

Cocoa Paste: Combine 1⅓ c. baking cocoa and 1 c. sugar in 2-qt. saucepan. Gradually add 2 c. boiling water, stirring until smooth. Cook over medium heat until mixture comes to a boil. Reduce heat to low and cook, stirring occasionally, 15 minutes. Remove from heat; cool. Freeze in ½-c. portions or store in refrigerator. (May be stored in refrigerator or freezer up to 4 weeks.) Makes 2 c.

Lemon Paste: Melt ½ c. butter or regular margarine in 2-qt. saucepan over low heat. Blend in ⅓ c. sifted flour and ¼ c. sugar. Gradually add 1 c. boiling water, stirring until smooth. Stir in ¾ c. sugar, ½ c. lemon juice and 1 tblsp. grated lemon rind. Cook over medium heat, stirring constantly, until mixture comes to a boil. Reduce heat to low and cook, stirring occasionally, 15 minutes. Remove from heat; cool. Freeze in ½-c. portions or store in refrigerator. (May be stored in refrigerator or freezer up to 4 weeks.) Makes 2 c.

Strawberry Cream Tarts

One whole, luscious strawberry, surrounded by slices
of strawberries and glazed with jelly, tops a creamy custard filling.

Flaky Tart Shells
  (recipe follows)
¼ c. sugar
4 tsp. cornstarch
1 c. milk

1 egg yolk
1 tsp. vanilla
1 pt. fresh strawberries,
  hulled
½ c. strawberry jelly

Prepare Flaky Tart Shells and set aside.

Combine sugar and cornstarch in small saucepan. Gradually stir in milk. Cook over medium heat, stirring constantly, until mixture boils and thickens. Remove from heat.

Beat egg yolk slightly, using a fork. Stir a small amount of hot mixture into egg yolk, blending well. Immediately pour egg yolk mixture back into remaining hot mixture, blending well. Cook over low heat 1 minute more, stirring constantly. Remove from heat. Gently stir in vanilla. Cool 5 minutes.

Spoon slightly cooled filling into Flaky Tart Shells.

Place one strawberry, stem end down, on each tart. Slice remaining berries and arrange in a ring around edge of each tart.

Heat jelly in small saucepan over low heat until melted. Spoon melted jelly over strawberries.

Cover and chill in refrigerator 1 hour, or until set. Makes 12 tarts.

Flaky Tart Shells: Combine 2 c. sifted flour and 1 tsp. salt in bowl. Cut in ⅔ c. regular margarine until coarse crumbs form, using a pastry blender. Sprinkle 5 tblsp. iced water over crumb mixture, a little at a time, tossing with a fork until dough forms. Press dough firmly into a ball. Roll out pastry on floured surface to ⅛" thickness. Cut 12 rounds, using floured 4½" round cookie cutter. Line 3" muffin-pan cups with pastry rounds. Flute edges. Prick entire surface of each shell with a fork. Bake in 425° oven 12 to 15 minutes, or until golden brown. Cool on racks. Remove from pans.

Banana Cream Tarts

A young New York homemaker's children love these tiny tarts made with graham cracker crusts flavored with peanut butter.

Peanut-Graham Shells
   (recipe follows)
¼ c. sugar
2 tblsp. cornstarch
1½ c. milk
2 egg yolks

1 tblsp. butter or
   regular margarine
1½ tsp. vanilla
2 medium bananas, sliced
Vanilla Whipped Cream
   (recipe follows)

Prepare Peanut-Graham Shells and set aside.

Combine sugar and cornstarch in 2-qt. saucepan. Gradually add milk, stirring well. Cook over medium heat, stirring constantly, until mixture comes to a boil. Cook 1 minute more. Remove from heat.

Beat egg yolks slightly, using a fork. Stir a small amount of hot mixture into egg yolks, blending well. Immediately pour egg yolk mixture back into remaining hot mixture, blending well. Cook 2 minutes more over low heat, stirring constantly. Remove from heat. Gently stir in butter and vanilla. Cool 5 minutes.

Stir in bananas. Spoon banana mixture into Peanut-Graham Shells.

Cover and chill in refrigerator at least 2 hours.

To serve, prepare Vanilla Whipped Cream and spread over each tart. Makes 12 tarts.

Peanut-Graham Shells: Melt ¼ c. peanut butter and ¼ c. butter or regular margarine in small saucepan over low heat; stir until smooth. Combine 1½ c. graham cracker crumbs and 3 tblsp. sugar in bowl. Add peanut butter mixture; mix well. Divide mixture evenly among 12 paper-lined 3″ muffin-pan cups. Press crumb mixture into bottom and up sides. Bake in 350° oven 8 minutes, or until edges are golden. Cool on racks.

Vanilla Whipped Cream: Combine 1 c. heavy cream, 2 tblsp. sugar and ½ tsp. vanilla in bowl. Beat until soft peaks form, using an electric mixer at high speed.

Silky-Smooth
5 Custard Pies

You'll never taste creamier or more velvety custard pies than the ones in this chapter!

Custard pies are honest-to-goodness country pies because they're extra-rich in eggs and milk, and their popularity in farm kitchens is second only to that of fruit pies. Country cooks serve these pies often because they always have the ingredients on hand, and they can stir up a custard pie on short notice.

Some farm families like their custard pies served slightly warm, while others prefer them thoroughly chilled. There are six simply delicious traditional custard pies in this chapter, including Speedy Custard Pie, which bakes in just 15 minutes, and Low-Calorie Custard Pie, with the rich taste of the classic version and only 250 calories a slice.

There are plenty of variations of the classic custard pie, too, some made with milk and eggs and others made with cheese or corn syrup or molasses—each one smooth and delicious. There are golden pumpkin pies; crunchy custard pies generously studded with pecans, walnuts and peanuts; light, lemon-flavored chess pies; an old-fashioned shoofly pie made with lots of butter and brown sugar; dark, creamy chocolate custard pies garnished with coconut and almonds; and cheese pies topped with raspberries, blueberries and cherries shimmering under a transparent glaze.

Thanksgiving wouldn't be the same without pumpkin pie, and there are ten tempting choices in this chapter, every one just a bit different. Pumpkin Meringue Pie, with its lightly spiced filling and crown of meringue, has been the traditional Thanksgiving dessert in one Wisconsin family for several generations. If you like a more richly spiced version, try Creamy Pumpkin Pie, made with a perfect balance of four spices, or Tawny Pumpkin Pie, flavored with ginger and vanilla.

Chess pies, originally brought to the States from England, still are very popular in our southern and New England states. Our selection includes lemon, chocolate and a recipe for Raisin-Pecan Pie sent to us by a Tennessee woman who told us it was handed down to her by her grandmother.

From Pennsylvania Dutch country, we've collected four extra-sweet, densely textured pies: Shoofly, Old-fashioned Vinegar, Heirloom Molasses and Amish Vanilla Pie. These pies have changed little over the generations and are still made from such simple ingredients as the corn syrup, eggs, molasses and brown sugar in the original German recipes.

Pecan pie lovers can choose from nine tantalizing recipes in this chapter. Our Basic Pecan Pie has won a blue ribbon, and once you taste it, you'll know why: each forkful is smooth and sweet and loaded with pecans. The North Carolina farm wife who sent us her own Special Pecan Pie told us proudly that her friends and relatives think her pecan pie is "out of this world." There's even a recipe for a Chocolate Chip-Pecan Pie—a rich, very sweet pie that tastes like a buttery chocolate chip cookie in a crust.

At the end of this chapter we've included our very best baked cheese pies. Most are topped with glazed fruit—blueberries, strawberries, peaches or cherries—and are pretty enough for any occasion. A much-asked-for recipe, Chocolate Cheese Swirl Pie, can be either baked or microwaved, and both methods turn out a creamy-smooth cheese filling swirled with chocolate that just melts on your tongue.

Next time you need a last-minute dessert for a club meeting or family reunion, turn to this chapter and stir up one of these custard pies—they're the simplest of all pies to make, and just as easy to tote!

How to Make Perfect Custard Pies

Here is the basic method for making a custard pie:

1. Use a pie shell with a high, fluted edge; this is helpful when the pie has a lot of filling. (For step-by-step directions on how to make a fluted edge, see page 9.)

2. Be sure to mix the ingredients for the filling thoroughly so that the filling will thicken evenly.

3. Place the pie shell on the oven rack before you pour in the filling to avoid the risk of spilling the filling when carrying the pie to the oven.

4. Use the doneness test given in each recipe and be sure to remove the pie from the oven as soon as it tests done. Overcooking the custard causes tiny bubbles to form around the edge, and the filling may separate when the pie is cut.

Basic Custard Pie

Some folks think that nothing tops off dinner
like a silky-smooth slice of plain custard pie dusted with nutmeg.

4 eggs	2½ c. milk, scalded
¾ c. sugar	Unbaked 9″ pie shell
¼ tsp. salt	with fluted edge
1 tsp. vanilla	¼ tsp. ground nutmeg

Beat eggs slightly in bowl, using a rotary beater. Add sugar, salt, vanilla and milk, beating until well blended. Pour into unbaked pie shell and sprinkle with nutmeg.

Bake in 450° oven 20 minutes. Reduce temperature to 350° and bake 15 minutes more, or until a knife inserted halfway between the center and edge comes out clean. Cool on rack. Makes 6 to 8 servings.

Creamy Custard Pie

This velvety-rich custard was a blue-ribbon winner.
It's delicately flavored with vanilla and ground nutmeg.

4 eggs	3 c. milk, scalded
½ c. sugar	Unbaked 9″ pie shell
¼ tsp. salt	with fluted edge
1 tsp. vanilla	Ground nutmeg

Beat eggs slightly in bowl, using a rotary beater. Add sugar, salt, vanilla and milk, beating until well blended. Pour into unbaked pie shell and sprinkle with nutmeg.

Bake in 450° oven 10 minutes. Reduce temperature to 325° and bake 30 to 40 minutes more, or until a knife inserted halfway between the center and edge comes out clean. Cool on rack. Makes 6 to 8 servings.

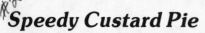

Speedy Custard Pie

Bakes in just 15 minutes in an extra-hot oven.
This is one of our favorite custard pie recipes.

4 eggs	2½ c. milk, scalded
½ c. sugar	Unbaked 9″ pie shell
¼ tsp. salt	with fluted edge
1½ tsp. vanilla	Ground nutmeg

Beat eggs slightly in bowl, using a rotary beater. Add sugar, salt, vanilla and milk, beating until well blended. Pour into unbaked pie shell and sprinkle with nutmeg.

Bake in 475° oven 5 minutes. Reduce temperature to 425° and bake 10 minutes more, or until a knife inserted halfway between the center and edge comes out clean. Cool on rack. Makes 6 to 8 servings.

Low-Calorie Custard Pie

A smooth and tasty custard pie made with skim milk
and baked in a shell with fewer calories than usual. You'll love it!

4 eggs	Unbaked Calorie-reduced
½ c. sugar	Pie Shell with fluted edge
¼ tsp. salt	(see Index)
2½ c. skim milk	Ground nutmeg
1½ tsp. vanilla	

Beat eggs slightly in bowl, using a rotary beater. Add sugar, salt, skim milk and vanilla, beating until well blended. Pour into unbaked Calorie-reduced Pie Shell and sprinkle with nutmeg.

Bake in 450° oven 20 minutes. Reduce temperature to 350° and bake 15 minutes more, or until a knife inserted halfway between the center and edge comes out clean. Cool on rack. Makes 8 servings.

Slip-Slide Custard Pie

First the filling is baked in a pie plate;
after it cools, it's gently eased into a baked pie shell.

4 eggs	1 tsp. vanilla
½ c. sugar	Ground nutmeg
½ tsp. salt	Baked 9″ pie shell
2½ c. milk, scalded	

Beat eggs slightly in bowl, using a rotary beater. Add sugar, salt, milk and vanilla, beating until well blended. Pour into greased 9″ pie plate and sprinkle with nutmeg. Place pie plate in shallow baking pan.

Set baking pan in 350° oven. Pour enough hot water into baking pan to come halfway up side of pie plate. Bake 30 minutes, or until a knife inserted halfway between the center and edge comes out clean. Cool on rack until lukewarm, about 45 minutes.

Carefully pull custard away from pie plate, using a small spatula. Gently shake pie plate to loosen custard. Tilt plate over baked pie shell, with far edge of custard just above far edge of pie shell. Slip the custard into pie shell, pulling the plate back toward you until the custard filling is in the shell. Let custard settle into place. Makes 6 to 8 servings.

Easy Lemon Custard Pie

Just the right size for a small family—a tart,
lemon-flavored version of a basic custard, baked in an 8″ shell.

3 eggs
¾ c. sugar
1 tsp. grated lemon rind
¼ tsp. salt
¾ c. water

⅓ c. lemon juice
Unbaked 8″ pie shell
   with fluted edge
Ground nutmeg

    Beat eggs slightly in bowl, using a rotary beater. Add sugar, lemon rind, salt, water and lemon juice, beating until well blended. Pour into unbaked pie shell and sprinkle with nutmeg.

    Bake in 400° oven 20 minutes. Reduce temperature to 250° and bake 10 minutes more, or until a knife inserted halfway between the center and edge comes out clean. Cool on rack. Makes 6 servings.

Lemon Sponge Pie

An old-time favorite from Pennsylvania Dutch country
that separates into two layers as it bakes. Unusually delicious.

2 c. sugar
1 tblsp. flour
1 tblsp. corn meal
4 eggs
¼ c. butter or regular
   margarine, melted

¼ c. milk
¼ c. lemon juice
2 tblsp. grated lemon rind
Unbaked 9″ pie shell

    Combine sugar, flour and corn meal in bowl. Add eggs, butter, milk, lemon juice and lemon rind. Beat until smooth and well blended, using a rotary beater. Pour into unbaked pie shell.

    Bake in 350° oven 40 minutes, or until golden brown. Cool on rack. Makes 6 to 8 servings.

Creamy Buttermilk Pie

Buttermilk is used instead of regular milk in this
recipe, and the result is marvelous: it tastes like cheesecake.

2 eggs	½ tsp. grated lemon rind
1 c. sugar	2 c. buttermilk
¼ c. flour	Unbaked 9″ pie shell
2 tblsp. butter or	Ground nutmeg
regular margarine, melted	

Beat eggs slightly, using a rotary beater. Add sugar, flour, butter, lemon
rind and buttermilk, beating until well blended. Pour into unbaked pie
shell and sprinkle with nutmeg.

Bake in 425° oven 10 minutes. Reduce temperature to 325° and
bake 25 minutes more, or until a knife inserted halfway between the
center and edge comes out clean. Cool on rack. Makes 6 to 8 servings.

Crusty Coconut Pie

A Louisiana farm woman told us that her mother
always made this chewy coconut pie for family gatherings.

½ c. milk	1 c. sugar
1 (3½-oz.) can flaked	3 eggs
coconut (1⅓ c.)	1 tsp. vanilla
¼ c. butter or	Unbaked 9″ pie shell
regular margarine	

Combine milk and coconut in bowl; set aside.

Cream together butter and sugar in another bowl until light and fluffy,
using an electric mixer at medium speed. Add eggs, one at a time, beating
well after each addition. Blend in vanilla. Stir in coconut-milk mixture and
pour into unbaked pie shell.

Bake in 350° oven 30 minutes, or until almost set in the center and
crust is golden brown. Cool on rack. Makes 6 to 8 servings.

Orange-Coconut Pie

A Kentucky farmer's wife sent us the recipe
for this great coconut-custard pie flavored with orange juice.

¼ c. butter or	1 c. flaked coconut
regular margarine	½ c. orange juice
¾ c. sugar	1 tsp. grated orange rind
3 eggs	Unbaked 8" pie shell

Cream together butter and sugar in bowl until light and fluffy, using an electric mixer at medium speed. Add eggs, one at a time, beating well after each addition. Stir in coconut, orange juice and orange rind. Pour into unbaked pie shell.

Bake in 350° oven 40 minutes, or until a knife inserted halfway between the center and edge comes out clean. Cool on rack. Makes 6 servings.

Spicy Candied Fruit Pie

Candied fruit lovers are sure to like this variation
of a basic custard pie—it's extra-sweet and flavorful.

1 tblsp. flour	2 eggs
½ tsp. ground cinnamon	1 c. light corn syrup
¼ tsp. salt	½ c. brown sugar, packed
¼ tsp. ground nutmeg	2 tblsp. butter or regular
⅛ tsp. ground cloves	margarine, melted
1 c. mixed candied fruit	1 tsp. grated orange rind
½ c. chopped toasted	1 tsp. grated lemon rind
almonds	¼ c. rum or orange juice
¼ c. raisins	Unbaked 9" pie shell

Combine flour, cinnamon, salt, nutmeg and cloves in bowl; mix well. Stir in candied fruit, almonds and raisins; toss to coat.

Beat eggs in bowl until blended, using a rotary beater. Add corn syrup, brown sugar, butter, orange rind and lemon rind; beat until blended. Slowly add rum, blending well. Stir in fruit mixture and pour into unbaked pie shell.

Bake in 400° oven 15 minutes. Reduce temperature to 350° and bake 30 minutes more, or until crust is golden brown and filling is set. Cool on rack. Makes 6 to 8 servings.

Cranberry-Walnut Pie

Terrific for the holidays, when there's so little time
for baking. Coarsely chopped walnuts provide the crunchiness.

3 eggs
1 c. light corn syrup
⅔ c. sugar
2 tblsp. butter or regular
   margarine, melted
⅛ tsp. salt

1 c. fresh or frozen
   cranberries, chopped
¾ c. coarsely chopped
   walnuts
1 tblsp. grated orange rind
Unbaked 9″ pie shell

Beat eggs in bowl until well blended, using a rotary beater. Add corn
syrup, sugar, butter and salt; beat until blended. Gently stir in cranberries,
walnuts and orange rind. Turn into unbaked pie shell.

Bake in 350° oven 1 hour, or until a knife inserted halfway between
center and edge comes out clean. Cool on rack. Makes 6 to 8 servings.

Whipped Prune Custard Pie

A New Jersey farm woman used a recipe from her grandmother's
kitchen to develop this updated version made with a blender.

1⅓ c. pitted prunes
1 c. water
3 eggs, separated
½ c. sugar
4 tsp. flour
1 c. milk

1 tblsp. butter or
   regular margarine
Unbaked 9″ pie shell
¼ tsp. cream of tartar
½ tsp. vanilla
6 tblsp. sugar

Combine prunes and water in 2-qt. saucepan. Cook over high heat until mixture comes to a boil. Reduce heat to low and simmer 2 minutes.
Remove from heat. Cover and cool to room temperature. Drain prunes.

Combine egg yolks, ½ c. sugar, flour, milk, butter and cooked prunes
in blender jar. Blend until smooth and pour into unbaked pie shell.

Bake in 425° oven 10 minutes. Reduce temperature to 325° and
bake 35 minutes more, or until set.

To make meringue, beat egg whites, cream of tartar and vanilla in bowl
until foamy, using an electric mixer at high speed. Gradually add 6 tblsp.
sugar, 1 tblsp. at a time, beating well after each addition. Continue beating
until stiff, glossy peaks form when beaters are slowly lifted.

Spoon some of the meringue around edge of filling. Spread meringue
so it touches inner edge of crust all around, using back of a spoon. Heap
remaining meringue in center. Push out gently to meet meringue border.

Bake in 350° oven 10 minutes, or until meringue is lightly browned.
Cool on rack. Makes 6 to 8 servings.

Rich Pineapple Pie

A Georgia homemaker shared this recipe; her family
has enjoyed her pineapple custard pies for many years.

½ c. butter or
   regular margarine
1 c. sugar
4 eggs
2 tblsp. corn meal
2 tblsp. flour

1 (8¼-oz.) can crushed
   pineapple
1 tsp. vanilla
Unbaked Egg Pastry Pie
   Shell (see Index)

Cream together butter and sugar in bowl until light and fluffy, using an electric mixer at medium speed. Add eggs, one at a time, beating well after each addition. Stir in corn meal, flour, pineapple and vanilla. Pour into unbaked Egg Pastry Pie Shell.

Bake in 350° oven 35 minutes, or until knife inserted halfway between center and edge comes out clean. Cool on rack. Makes 6 to 8 servings.

Pineapple-Oatmeal Pie

This pie won a ribbon at a Pennsylvania fair. It combines
oats, coconut, raisins and pineapple in a brown sugar-flavored filling.

3 eggs
1 c. brown sugar, packed
⅔ c. sugar
2 tblsp. butter or regular
   margarine, melted
1 tsp. vanilla
⅔ c. quick-cooking oats

⅔ c. flaked coconut
1 c. raisins
1 (8¼-oz.) can crushed
   pineapple
Unbaked 9" pie shell

Beat eggs until thick and lemon-colored, using an electric mixer at high speed. Gradually add brown sugar and sugar, beating well after each addition. Blend in butter and vanilla. Stir in oats, coconut, raisins and undrained pineapple. Pour into unbaked pie shell.

Bake in 350° oven 50 minutes, or until filling is set. Cool on rack. Makes 6 to 8 servings.

Creamy Pumpkin Pie

Win compliments at your next Thanksgiving dinner when you
serve this creamy-smooth pumpkin pie with four different spices.

1 (16-oz.) can mashed
   pumpkin (2 c.)
1 c. evaporated milk
½ c. light or dark
   corn syrup
½ c. brown sugar, packed
3 eggs

1½ tsp. ground cinnamon
½ tsp. salt
½ tsp. ground ginger
½ tsp. ground nutmeg
⅛ tsp. ground cloves
Unbaked 9" pie shell

   Combine pumpkin, evaporated milk, corn syrup, brown sugar, eggs,
cinnamon, salt, ginger, nutmeg and cloves in bowl. Beat until smooth, using an electric mixer at medium speed. Pour into unbaked pie shell.
   Bake in 425° oven 15 minutes. Reduce temperature to 350° and
bake 30 to 35 minutes longer, or until a knife inserted near the center
comes out clean. Cool on rack. Makes 6 to 8 servings.

Brown Sugar Pumpkin Pie

Brown sugar enriches the flavor of this basic pumpkin pie.
Enjoy it all year 'round and serve with a crown of whipped cream.

1½ c. cooked or canned
   mashed pumpkin
1 c. brown sugar, packed
1 tsp. ground cinnamon
1 tsp. ground nutmeg

½ tsp. ground allspice
3 eggs
1 c. evaporated milk
Unbaked 9" pie shell

   Combine pumpkin, brown sugar, cinnamon, nutmeg and allspice in
bowl; mix well. Add eggs and evaporated milk. Beat until smooth, using a
rotary beater. Pour into unbaked pie shell.
   Bake in 425° oven 15 minutes. Reduce temperature to 350° and
bake 35 to 45 minutes more, or until a knife inserted in the center comes
out clean. Cool on rack. Makes 6 to 8 servings.

Pumpkin Meringue Pie

The women in one Wisconsin family have handed down
this recipe for several generations—it's served every Thanksgiving.

1½ c. cooked or canned
    mashed pumpkin
½ c. sugar
1 tsp. ground cinnamon
¼ tsp. ground nutmeg
¼ tsp. ground cloves

½ tsp. salt
3 eggs, separated
1 c. evaporated milk
Unbaked 9″ pie shell
⅛ tsp. salt
6 tblsp. sugar

Combine pumpkin, ½ c. sugar, cinnamon, nutmeg, cloves and ½ tsp. salt in bowl; mix well. Add egg yolks, stirring until well blended. Gradually blend in evaporated milk. Pour into unbaked pie shell.

Bake in 400° oven 35 minutes, or until a knife inserted halfway between the center and edge comes out clean. Remove pie from oven. Increase temperature to 425°.

To make meringue, beat egg whites and ⅛ tsp. salt in bowl until foamy, using an electric mixer at high speed. Gradually add 6 tblsp. sugar, 1 tblsp. at a time, beating well after each addition. Continue beating until stiff, glossy peaks form when beaters are slowly lifted.

Spoon some of the meringue around edge of warm pie. Spread meringue so it touches inner edge of crust all around, using back of a spoon. Heap remaining meringue in center. Push out gently to meet meringue border.

Bake in 425° oven 5 minutes, or until meringue is lightly browned. Cool on rack. Makes 6 to 8 servings.

Tawny Pumpkin Pie

A classic pumpkin pie lightly spiced with cinnamon
and sugar and flavored with just a dash of vanilla.

1¼ c. cooked or canned	½ tsp. salt
mashed pumpkin	2 tblsp. water
¾ c. sugar	2 eggs
1 tsp. flour	½ tsp. vanilla
1 tsp. ground cinnamon	1 c. evaporated milk
¼ tsp. ground ginger	Unbaked 9″ pie shell

Combine pumpkin, sugar, flour, cinnamon, ginger, salt and water in bowl; mix well. Add eggs, vanilla and evaporated milk. Beat until smooth, using a rotary beater. Pour into unbaked pie shell.

Bake in 425° oven 15 minutes. Reduce temperature to 350° and bake 45 minutes more, or until a knife inserted halfway between the center and edge comes out clean. Cool on rack. Makes 6 to 8 servings.

Low-Calorie Pumpkin Pie

Every calorie counts! But you can still serve pie
for dessert—this one is made with evaporated skimmed milk.

1 (16-oz.) can mashed	½ tsp. salt
pumpkin (2 c.)	2 egg
¾ c. sugar	1 (13-oz.) can evaporated
1½ tsp. ground cinnamon	skimmed milk
½ tsp. ground ginger	Unbaked 9″ Calorie-reduced
½ tsp. ground nutmeg	Pie Shell with fluted edge
½ tsp. ground allspice	(see Index)
½ tsp. ground cloves	

Combine pumpkin, sugar, cinnamon, ginger, nutmeg, allspice, cloves and salt in bowl; mix well. Add eggs and evaporated skimmed milk. Beat until smooth, using a rotary beater. Pour into unbaked Calorie-reduced Pie Shell.

Bake in 425° oven 15 minutes. Reduce temperature to 350° and bake 45 minutes more, or until a knife inserted in the center comes out clean. Cool on rack. Makes 8 servings.

Pumpkin-Apple Pie

Two autumn fruits baked in one delicious pie:
a layer of apple filling under a classic pumpkin topping.

⅓ c. brown sugar, packed
1 tblsp. cornstarch
½ tsp. ground cinnamon
¼ tsp. salt
⅓ c. water
2 tblsp. butter or
   regular margarine
3 c. thinly sliced,
   pared apples
1 egg

⅓ c. sugar
¾ c. cooked or canned
   mashed pumpkin
½ tsp. ground cinnamon
¼ tsp. ground ginger
⅛ tsp. ground cloves
¼ tsp. salt
¾ c. evaporated milk
Unbaked 9″ pie shell

Combine brown sugar, cornstarch, ½ tsp. cinnamon and ¼ tsp. salt in 2-qt. saucepan. Stir in water and butter. Cook over medium heat, stirring constantly, until mixture comes to a boil. Add apples; cook 4 minutes more. Remove from heat.

Combine egg, sugar, pumpkin, ½ tsp. cinnamon, ginger, cloves, ¼ tsp. salt and evaporated milk in bowl. Beat until blended, using a rotary beater.

Pour apple mixture into unbaked pie shell. Carefully spoon an even layer of pumpkin mixture over apple mixture.

Bake in 425° oven 10 minutes. Reduce temperature to 375° and bake 40 minutes more, or until filling is set around the edge. Cool on rack. Makes 6 to 8 servings.

Mincemeat-Pumpkin Pie

An unusual holiday pie—sure to appeal to those
who just can't decide between mincemeat and pumpkin.

1 c. cooked or canned
   mashed pumpkin
½ c. brown sugar, packed
¾ tsp. ground cinnamon
¾ tsp. ground nutmeg

½ tsp. salt
3 eggs
½ c. heavy cream
1 c. prepared mincemeat
Unbaked 9″ pie shell

Combine pumpkin, brown sugar, cinnamon, nutmeg and salt in bowl; mix well. Add eggs and heavy cream. Beat until smooth, using a rotary beater. Stir in mincemeat. Pour into unbaked pie shell.

Bake in 425° oven 35 minutes, or until filling is set. Cool slightly on rack. Serve warm. Makes 6 to 8 servings.

Molasses-topped Pumpkin Pie

If you like both pecan and pumpkin pie, here's a tempting combination—creamy pumpkin topped with a chewy layer of pecans.

1 (16-oz.) can mashed pumpkin (2 c.)	⅔ c. evaporated milk
¼ c. sugar	Unbaked 9" pie shell with fluted edge
2 eggs	Molasses Topping (recipe follows)
1 tsp. ground pumpkin pie spice	½ c. chopped pecans
1 tsp. ground cinnamon	

Combine pumpkin, sugar, eggs, pumpkin pie spice, cinnamon and evaporated milk in bowl. Beat until smooth, using an electric mixer at low speed. Pour into unbaked pie shell.

Bake in 425° oven 10 minutes. Reduce temperature to 350° and bake 15 minutes more. Meanwhile, prepare Molasses Topping.

Remove pie from oven. Pour Molasses Topping over all and sprinkle with pecans. Return pie to oven and bake 35 minutes more, or until custard is set. Cool on rack. Makes 6 to 8 servings.

Molasses Topping: Beat 2 eggs in bowl until foamy, using an electric mixer at medium speed. Add ½ c. dark corn syrup, 2 tblsp. brown sugar (packed), 2 tblsp. molasses, 1 tsp. vanilla, 1 tblsp. flour and ¼ tsp. salt. Beat until smooth, using an electric mixer at low speed.

Pumpkin-Pecan Pie

The pecan topping is extra-crunchy because after it's
sprinkled over the filling, it's placed under the broiler for just a minute.

1 (16-oz.) can mashed
  pumpkin (2 c.)
¾ c. sugar
1 tsp. ground cinnamon
½ tsp. ground ginger
¼ tsp. ground cloves
½ tsp. salt

2 eggs
1 (13-oz.) can evaporated
  milk
Unbaked 9″ pie shell
Crunchy Pecan Topping
  (recipe follows)

Combine pumpkin, sugar, cinnamon, ginger, cloves and salt in bowl;
mix well. Add eggs and evaporated milk. Beat until smooth, using a
rotary beater. Pour into unbaked pie shell.

Bake in 425° oven 15 minutes. Reduce temperature to 350° and
bake 45 minutes more, or until a knife inserted halfway between the
center and edge comes out clean. Cool on rack.

Prepare Crunchy Pecan Topping and sprinkle over cooled pie.

Place under broiler, 5 inches from source of heat, until mixture begins
to bubble, about 1 minute. Cool on rack. Makes 6 to 8 servings.

Crunchy Pecan Topping: Combine 3 tblsp. soft butter or regular margarine, ⅔ c. brown sugar (packed) and ⅔ c. coarsely chopped pecans in
bowl. Mix until crumbly, using a fork.

Butternut Squash Pie

In some sections of the country, people prefer squash pie
to pumpkin. Great served just plain or with whipped cream.

2 lb. butternut squash,
  cooked, drained and
  mashed (1¾ c.)
1 c. sugar
½ tsp. salt
½ tsp. ground cinnamon
¼ tsp. ground nutmeg

¼ tsp. ground ginger
1 tblsp. butter or regular
  margarine, melted
2 eggs
1½ c. milk
Unbaked 9″ pie shell

Combine squash, sugar, salt, cinnamon, nutmeg, ginger and butter in
bowl; mix well. Add eggs and milk. Beat until smooth, using a rotary
beater. Pour into unbaked pie shell.

Bake in 425° oven 45 minutes, or until a knife inserted halfway between the center and edge comes out clean. Cool on rack. Makes 6 to 8
servings.

Festive Pumpkin Pie

Cheesecake-lovers will be pleased with this version
of a basic pumpkin pie spread with a layer of sweetened sour cream.

1 (8-oz.) pkg. cream cheese, softened	1 c. cooked or canned mashed pumpkin
¾ c. brown sugar, packed	1 c. milk
1 tsp. ground cinnamon	1 tsp. vanilla
½ tsp. ground ginger	Unbaked 9″ pie shell with fluted edge
½ tsp. salt	
¼ tsp. ground cloves	1 c. dairy sour cream
3 eggs	2 tblsp. sugar

Cream together cream cheese, brown sugar, cinnamon, ginger, salt and cloves in bowl until light and fluffy, using an electric mixer at medium speed. Add eggs, one at a time, beating well after each addition. Blend in pumpkin, milk and vanilla. Pour into unbaked pie shell.

Bake in 375° oven 45 to 50 minutes, or until a knife inserted halfway between the center and edge comes out clean.

Blend together sour cream and sugar in bowl. Spread over top of warm pie.

Return pie to oven and bake 3 to 5 minutes, or just until topping is set. Cool on rack.

Cover and chill in refrigerator before serving. Makes 6 to 8 servings.

Lemon Chess Pie

A southern favorite brought to this country from England.
The buttery-rich custard filling has a nut-brown topping.

4 eggs	1 tsp. corn meal
2 c. sugar	1 tsp. flour
½ c. lemon juice	⅛ tsp. salt
½ c. butter or regular margarine, melted	Unbaked 9″ pie shell

Beat eggs in bowl until well blended, using an electric mixer at high speed. Gradually add sugar, beating well after each addition. Add lemon juice, butter, corn meal, flour and salt. Beat well, using low speed. Pour into unbaked pie shell.

Bake in 350° oven 40 minutes, or until top is browned. Cool on rack. Makes 6 to 8 servings.

Golden Lemon Chess Pie

This simple, lemon-flavored pie is a super dessert
after a light meal—and best of all, it's a breeze to make.

2 c. sugar
1 tblsp. flour
1 tblsp. corn meal
4 eggs
¼ c. milk

¼ c. butter or regular
margarine, melted
¼ c. lemon juice
2 tblsp. grated lemon rind
Unbaked 9" pie shell

Combine sugar, flour, and corn meal in bowl. Add eggs, milk, butter, lemon juice and lemon rind. Beat until smooth and well blended, using a rotary beater. Pour into unbaked pie shell.

Bake in 350° oven 40 minutes, or until golden brown. Cool on rack. Makes 6 to 8 servings.

Chocolate Chess Pie

"My family cheers every time I serve this for dessert,"
a Texas woman wrote us. A meltingly delicious chocolate chess pie.

2 c. sugar
2 tblsp. cornstarch
4 eggs
1 (8-oz.) can chocolate-
flavored syrup

¼ c. milk
¼ c. butter or regular
margarine, melted
Unbaked 9" pie shell
with fluted edge

Combine sugar, cornstarch, eggs, chocolate-flavored syrup, milk and butter in bowl. Beat until smooth, using an electric mixer at medium speed. Pour into unbaked pie shell.

Bake in 350° oven 55 minutes, or until center is set. Cool on rack. Makes 6 to 8 servings.

California Chess Pie

Created in one of our country's richest agricultural
regions—a classic chess pie just loaded with raisins and walnuts.

½ c. butter or
regular margarine
¾ c. sugar
¼ tsp. salt
3 eggs

¾ c. chopped walnuts
¾ c. chopped raisins
1 tsp. vanilla
Unbaked 9" pie shell

Cream together butter, sugar and salt in bowl until light and fluffy, using an electric mixer at medium speed. Add eggs, one at a time, beating well after each addition. Stir in walnuts, raisins and vanilla. Pour into unbaked pie shell.

Bake in 425° oven 10 minutes. Reduce temperature to 325° and bake 30 minutes more, or until filling is set. Cool on rack. Makes 6 to 8 servings.

Raisin-Pecan Pie

The filling separates into three layers as it bakes:
custard on the bottom, a raisin-pecan layer and a thin meringue top.

½ c. raisins	½ c. butter or regular
1 c. water	margarine, melted
3 eggs	½ c. chopped pecans
1 c. sugar	Unbaked 9″ pie shell
2 tblsp. yellow corn meal	

Combine raisins and water in small saucepan. Cook over high heat until mixture comes to a boil. Reduce heat to low and simmer 5 minutes. Drain raisins and let cool.

Combine eggs, sugar and corn meal in bowl. Beat 2 minutes, using an electric mixer at medium speed. Blend in butter. Stir in pecans and raisins and pour into unbaked pie shell.

Bake in 375° oven 40 to 45 minutes, or until top is golden brown. Cool on rack. Makes 6 to 8 servings.

Old-fashioned Vinegar Pie

A midwestern specialty. This particular recipe is more than
100 years old, and just as popular as ever in one farm family.

½ c. butter or	3 eggs
regular margarine	1 tsp. vanilla
1¼ c. sugar	Unbaked 8″ pie shell
2 tblsp. vinegar	

Cream together butter and sugar in bowl until light and fluffy, using an electric mixer at medium speed. Add vinegar, eggs and vanilla; beat well. Pour into unbaked pie shell.

Bake in 350° oven 45 minutes, or until a knife inserted halfway between the center and edge comes out clean. Cool on rack. Makes 6 to 8 servings.

Shoofly Pie

A new version of an old-fashioned favorite—
made with flour and butter and lots of brown sugar.

1⅓ c. unsifted flour
¾ c. dark brown sugar,
   packed
½ tsp. salt
⅓ c. butter or regular
   margarine

½ tsp. baking soda
⅓ c. hot water
⅓ c. dark corn syrup
Unbaked 9″ pie shell
¼ tsp. ground cinnamon

Combine flour, brown sugar and salt in bowl. Cut in butter until crumbly, using a pastry blender. Set aside.

Stir baking soda into hot water in another bowl. Stir in corn syrup. Pour corn syrup mixture into unbaked pie shell. Sprinkle crumb mixture evenly over top and dust with cinnamon.

Bake in 400° oven 15 minutes. Reduce temperature to 350° and bake 30 minutes more, or until top is well browned. Cool slightly on rack. Serve warm. Makes 6 to 8 servings.

Amish Vanilla Pie

When Easterners migrated westward, many of them carried
their favorite recipes with them. This is from a Kansas farm wife.

½ c. brown sugar, packed
1 tblsp. flour
¼ c. dark corn syrup
1½ tsp. vanilla
1 egg, beaten
1 c. water
1 c. flour

½ c. brown sugar, packed
½ tsp. cream of tartar
½ tsp. baking soda
⅛ tsp. salt
¼ c. butter or
   regular margarine
Unbaked 9″ pie shell

Combine ½ c. brown sugar, 1 tblsp. flour, corn syrup, vanilla and egg in 2-qt. saucepan. Gradually stir in water. Cook over medium heat, stirring constantly, until mixture boils and thickens. Remove from heat. Cool to room temperature.

Combine 1 c. flour, ½ c. brown sugar, cream of tartar, baking soda and salt in bowl. Cut in butter until mixture is crumbly, using a pastry blender.

Pour cooled mixture into unbaked pie shell and sprinkle with crumb mixture.

Bake in 350° oven 40 minutes, or until golden brown. Cool on rack. Makes 6 to 8 servings.

Cheesecake-lovers will appreciate
Chocolate Cheese Swirl Pie (p. 169),
a simply elegant pie that can be
stirred up and baked in almost no
time. It also can be microwaved
in just 7 minutes.

A winning combination of
apples and Cheddar cheese in one
great-tasting pie, Apple Pie in
Cheddar Crust (p. 29) will please
anyone who likes down-to-earth,
old-fashioned apple pie.

Pecan pies have been popular ever
since they were first created
in the South, and Savannah Pecan
Pie (p. 153) is no exception.
It's loaded with pecans and
sweetened with dark corn syrup.

Cheese-Spinach Quiche (p. 257)
makes a perfect main dish for
either lunch or supper. Its
velvety-smooth custard is rich with
grated Parmesan cheese and seasoned
with parsley and sage.

Basic Pecan Pie

Chopped pecans in a smooth, sweet filling and whole
pecan halves forming a crunchy topping. Doubly delicious!

1 tblsp. butter or
   regular margarine
1 c. sugar
3 eggs
1 c. dark corn syrup

1 tsp. vanilla
1 c. chopped pecans
Unbaked 9" pie shell
1 c. pecan halves

Cream together butter and sugar in bowl until light and fluffy, using an electric mixer at medium speed. Add eggs, one at a time, beating well after each addition. Add corn syrup and vanilla; beat well. Stir in chopped pecans and pour into unbaked pie shell. Arrange pecan halves on top.

Bake in 350° oven 45 minutes, or until filling is set. Cool on rack. Makes 6 to 8 servings.

Special Pecan Pie

A North Carolina farm woman told us that she has to admit
her friends and relatives think her pecan pie is "out of this world."

3 eggs
¾ c. sugar
½ c. light corn syrup
⅛ tsp. salt
1 tblsp. butter or regular
   margarine, melted

1 tblsp. vinegar
1 tsp. vanilla
1½ c. coarsely chopped
   pecans
Unbaked 9" pie shell

Combine eggs, sugar, corn syrup, salt, butter, vinegar and vanilla in bowl. Beat until well blended, using an electric mixer at medium speed. Stir in 1 c. of the pecans and pour into unbaked pie shell. Sprinkle with remaining ½ c. pecans.

Bake in 350° oven 45 minutes, or until a knife inserted halfway between the center and edge comes out clean. Cool on rack. Makes 6 to 8 servings.

First-Prize Pecan Pie

Just one bite of this super-rich pecan pie,
and you'll know why it's won several county fair ribbons.

3 eggs
½ c. dark corn syrup
½ c. light corn syrup
½ c. sugar
½ c. butter or regular
   margarine, melted

½ tsp. vanilla
½ c. chopped pecans
Unbaked 9″ pie shell
½ c. pecan halves

Combine eggs, dark corn syrup, light corn syrup, sugar, butter and vanilla in bowl. Beat until well blended, using an electric mixer at medium speed. Stir in ½ c. chopped pecans and pour into unbaked pie shell. Arrange pecan halves on top.

Bake in 375° oven 40 minutes, or until filling is set. Cool on rack. Makes 6 to 8 servings.

Heirloom Molasses Pies

An old-fashioned favorite that turns out two pies!
Perfect for toting to church suppers, family reunions or picnics.

4 eggs, separated
1 c. sugar
½ c. light molasses
½ c. light corn syrup
1 tblsp. flour

¼ tsp. ground cinnamon
2 c. milk
2 unbaked 9″ pie shells
1½ c. chopped pecans
Sweetened whipped cream

Beat egg yolks in bowl until thick and lemon-colored, using an electric mixer at high speed. Gradually add sugar, molasses, corn syrup, flour and cinnamon, beating well after each addition. Then slowly blend in milk.

Beat egg whites in another bowl until stiff peaks form, using an electric mixer at high speed. Gradually blend egg whites into molasses mixture, using low speed. Pour half in each unbaked pie shell and sprinkle with pecans.

Bake in 350° oven 50 minutes, or until filling is set. Cool on racks.

To serve, top with puffs of sweetened whipped cream. Makes 2 pies, 6 to 8 servings each.

Pecan Pie

If you like a rich-flavored pecan pie, but don't
care for molasses, try this recipe made with dark corn syrup.

3 eggs	1 c. dark corn syrup
1 c. sugar	1 c. pecan halves
1/8 tsp. salt	Unbaked 9" pie shell
3 tblsp. butter or regular	
margarine, melted	

Combine eggs, sugar, salt, butter and corn syrup in bowl. Beat until well blended, using an electric mixer at medium speed. Stir in pecan halves and pour into unbaked pie shell.

Bake in 400° oven 10 minutes. Reduce temperature to 350° and bake 30 minutes more, or until a knife inserted halfway between the center and edge comes out clean. Cool on rack. Makes 6 to 8 servings.

Savannah Pecan Pie

Pecan pie was invented in the South, where pecans are so
abundant that people used to bake them into pies just to use them up!

3 eggs	6 tblsp. butter or regular
1 c. dark corn syrup	margarine, melted
2/3 c. brown sugar, packed	1 c. pecan halves
1/8 tsp. salt	Unbaked 9" pie shell

Beat eggs in bowl until blended, using a rotary beater. Add corn syrup, brown sugar, salt and butter; beat until blended. Stir in pecans and pour into unbaked pie shell.

Bake in 350° oven 50 minutes, or until a knife inserted halfway between the center and edge comes out clean. Cool on rack. Makes 6 to 8 servings.

Chocolate Chip-Pecan Pie

A Missouri woman sent us this out-of-the-ordinary pecan pie
that tastes like a rich chocolate chip cookie baked in a pie crust.

½ c. semisweet chocolate
   pieces
Unbaked 8″ pie shell
2 eggs
¾ c. dark corn syrup

½ c. sugar
¼ c. butter or regular
   margarine, melted
¼ tsp. salt
¾ c. pecan halves

Sprinkle chocolate pieces over bottom of unbaked pie shell. Freeze at least 1 hour.

Combine eggs, corn syrup, sugar, butter and salt in bowl. Beat until well blended, using an electric mixer at medium speed. Stir in pecans. Pour over chocolate pieces in pie shell.

Bake in 375° oven 50 minutes, or until custard is set. Cool on rack. Makes 6 servings.

Chocolate Pecan Pie

"We think this pie is twice as good as regular pecan,"
a Georgia homemaker told us. "And it's so easy to make."

¾ c. sugar
½ tsp. salt
1 c. light corn syrup
3 (1-oz.) squares
   unsweetened chocolate,
   melted and cooled

3 tblsp. butter or regular
   margarine, melted
3 eggs
1 tsp. vanilla
1 c. chopped pecans
Unbaked 9″ pie shell

Combine sugar, salt, corn syrup, cooled chocolate, butter, eggs and vanilla in bowl. Beat until well blended, using an electric mixer at medium speed. Stir in pecans and turn into unbaked pie shell.

Bake in 375° oven 35 minutes, or until set. (Pie will be puffy when it comes out of oven and will sink while cooling.) Cool on rack. Makes 6 to 8 servings.

Extra-Rich Chocolate Pecan Pie

This Farm Journal favorite was sent to us almost 25 years ago
by a farm woman in Louisiana, and it's still requested today.

1 (6-oz.) pkg. semisweet	1 c. sugar
chocolate pieces	2 tblsp. flour
⅔ c. evaporated milk	¼ tsp. salt
2 tblsp. butter or	1 tsp. vanilla
regular margarine	1 c. chopped pecans
2 eggs, slightly beaten	Unbaked 9" pie shell

Combine chocolate pieces, evaporated milk and butter in small
saucepan. Cook over low heat, stirring constantly, until mixture is smooth
and creamy.

Combine eggs, sugar, flour, salt, vanilla and pecans in bowl; mix well.
Gradually stir chocolate mixture into egg mixture and pour into unbaked
pie shell.

Bake in 375° oven 40 minutes, or until filling is set. Cool on rack.
Makes 6 to 8 servings.

Fake Pecan Pie

This economical pie tastes like a pecan pie,
but it's made with crunchy nuggets of cereal instead of nuts.

¾ c. crunchy nut-like	3 tblsp. butter or regular
cereal nuggets	margarine, melted
½ c. warm water	1 tsp. vanilla
3 eggs	⅛ tsp. salt
¾ c. sugar	Unbaked 9" pie shell
1 c. dark corn syrup	Sweetened whipped cream

Combine cereal and warm water in bowl. Let stand until water is absorbed.

Beat together eggs and sugar in bowl until well blended, using an electric mixer at medium speed. Beat in corn syrup, butter, vanilla and salt;
blend well. Stir in cereal mixture and pour into unbaked pie shell.

Bake in 350° oven 50 minutes, or until filling is puffy. Cool on rack.

To serve, top with puffs of sweetened whipped cream. Makes 6 to 8
servings.

Imitation Pecan Pie

Toasted rice cereal adds the crunchiness of pecans
to this unusual pie. Looks and tastes like the real thing.

3 eggs
1 c. sugar
¾ c. light corn syrup
¼ c. butter or regular
   margarine, melted

¼ tsp. salt
1½ c. toasted rice cereal
Unbaked 9″ pie shell
Sweetened whipped cream

Beat eggs in bowl until foamy, using an electric mixer at high speed. Add sugar, corn syrup, butter and salt. Beat until smooth, using low speed. Stir in rice cereal and pour into unbaked pie shell.

Bake in 375° oven 40 minutes, or until a knife inserted halfway between the center and edge comes out clean. Cool on rack.

To serve, top with puffs of sweetened whipped cream. Makes 6 to 8 servings.

English Walnut Pie

A pecan-like pie made with light corn syrup,
white sugar and chopped walnuts. A blue-ribbon winner!

3 eggs
⅓ c. sugar
¼ tsp. salt
1½ c. light corn syrup

1 tsp. vanilla
1½ c. chopped walnuts
Unbaked 9″ pie shell

Beat together eggs, sugar and salt in bowl until blended, using an electric mixer at medium speed. Add corn syrup and vanilla, blending thoroughly. Stir in walnuts and pour into unbaked pie shell.

Bake in 400° oven 10 minutes. Reduce temperature to 350° and bake 35 minutes more, or until filling is set. Cool on rack. Makes 6 to 8 servings.

Walnut-Rum Pie

You can make this pie with either rum or rum flavoring—
just substitute ¼ cup of rum for the rum flavoring and water.

¼ c. butter or
  regular margarine
¾ c. dark corn syrup
¾ c. sugar
1 tblsp. cornstarch
1 tsp. rum flavoring

¼ c. water
3 eggs
1 c. coarsely chopped
  walnuts
Unbaked 9" pie shell

Melt butter in 2-qt. saucepan over low heat. Stir in corn syrup and sugar.

Combine cornstarch, rum flavoring and water in small bowl. Add cornstarch mixture to butter mixture. Cook over medium heat, stirring constantly, until mixture comes to a boil. Cook 1 minute more. Remove from heat.

Beat eggs in bowl until blended, using a rotary beater. Gradually add hot mixture to eggs, a little at a time, beating well after each addition. Stir in walnuts and pour into unbaked pie shell.

Bake in 350° oven 45 minutes, or until filling is set around the edge and center is slightly soft. Cool on rack. Makes 6 to 8 servings.

Tennessee Peanut Pie

If your family likes pecan pie, try this peanut pie
as a change of pace. Melt-in-your-mouth filling with a crunchy peanut top.

3 eggs
1 c. dark corn syrup
1 c. sugar
2 tblsp. butter or regular
  margarine, melted

⅛ tsp. salt
1 tsp. vanilla
1 c. chopped peanuts
Unbaked 9" pie shell

Combine eggs, corn syrup, sugar, butter, salt and vanilla in bowl. Beat until blended, using an electric mixer at high speed. Stir in peanuts and pour into unbaked pie shell.

Bake in 400° oven 15 minutes. Reduce temperature to 350° and bake 35 minutes more, or until filling is set around edge and the center is slightly soft. Cool on rack. Makes 6 to 8 servings.

Prizewinning Peanut Pie

When you serve this pie, cut it into thin wedges—
it's extra-rich and tastes very much like a pecan pie.

1½ c. light corn syrup	3 eggs
½ c. sugar	1 c. salted peanuts
¼ c. butter or	½ tsp. vanilla
regular margarine	Unbaked 9″ pie shell

Combine corn syrup, sugar and butter in 2-qt. saucepan. Cook over medium heat until mixture comes to a boil. Beat eggs slightly in bowl. Slowly pour hot mixture into slightly beaten eggs, stirring constantly. Stir in peanuts and vanilla and pour into unbaked pie shell.

Bake in 350° oven 45 minutes, or until filling is set. Cool on rack. Makes 8 servings.

Peanutty Coconut Pie

A rich, gooey pie made with salted peanuts and coconut.
This pie can be made in a snap and it's perfect for bake sales.

2 eggs	½ c. chopped salted
¼ c. butter or regular	peanuts
margarine, melted	½ c. flaked coconut
½ c. sugar	Unbaked 9″ pie shell
1½ c. dark corn syrup	with fluted edge
1 tsp. vanilla	

Beat together eggs, butter and sugar in bowl until well blended, using an electric mixer at medium speed. Beat in corn syrup and vanilla, blending well. Stir in peanuts and coconut and pour into unbaked pie shell.

Bake in 400° oven 15 minutes. Reduce temperature to 350° and bake 30 minutes more, or until filling is set. Cool on rack. Makes 6 to 8 servings.

Peanut-Coconut Pie

A winner at a New Mexico county fair, generously made
with four eggs, a cup of peanuts and a cup of flaked coconut.

4 eggs	1 c. chopped salted peanuts
1 c. light corn syrup	1 c. flaked coconut
¾ c. sugar	Unbaked 9″ pie shell

Beat eggs in bowl until thick and lemon-colored, using an electric mixer
at high speed. Gradually add corn syrup and sugar, beating well after
each addition. Stir in peanuts and coconut and pour into unbaked pie
shell.

Bake in 350° oven 40 minutes, or until filling is set around the edge
and center is soft. Cool on rack. Makes 6 to 8 servings.

Macaroon Pie

Tastes like a chewy macaroon cookie filled with coconut
and sliced almonds. Great whether you serve it warm or cold.

3 eggs	⅛ tsp. salt
1 c. light corn syrup	1 (3½-oz.) can flaked
½ c. sugar	coconut (1⅓ c.)
2 tblsp. butter or regular	1 c. sliced almonds
margarine, melted	Unbaked 9″ pie shell
¼ tsp. almond extract	

Beat eggs in bowl until blended, using a rotary beater. Add corn syrup,
sugar, butter, almond extract and salt; beat until blended. Stir in coconut
and almonds and pour into unbaked pie shell.

Bake in 350° oven 50 to 55 minutes, or until a knife inserted halfway
between the center and edge comes out clean. Cool on rack. Makes 6 to
8 servings.

Chocolate-Peanut Pie

The filling bakes into layers: a deep chocolate,
custard-like base with a crunchy peanut topping. Scrumptious!

2 (1-oz.) squares
   unsweetened chocolate
¼ c. butter or regular
   margarine
3 eggs
¾ c. sugar
½ c. brown sugar, packed

½ c. milk
¼ c. light corn syrup
1½ tsp. vanilla
1 c. coarsely chopped
   salted peanuts
Unbaked 9″ pie shell

Combine chocolate and butter in saucepan. Place over low heat until melted. Remove from heat; cool slightly.

Beat eggs in bowl until blended, using a rotary beater. Add sugar, brown sugar, milk, corn syrup, vanilla and chocolate mixture; beat until blended. Stir in peanuts and pour into unbaked pie shell.

Bake in 350° oven 45 to 50 minutes, or until a knife inserted halfway between the center and edge comes out clean. Cool on rack. Makes 6 to 8 servings.

Chocolate-Almond Pie

So good, it tastes like a great big chocolate bar
with almonds. Even better when topped with a scoop of ice cream.

3 eggs
¾ c. light corn syrup
⅓ c. sugar
3 tblsp. butter or regular
   margarine, melted
2 (1-oz.) squares
   unsweetened chocolate,
   melted and cooled

1 tsp. vanilla
½ tsp. almond extract
1 c. slivered almonds
Unbaked 9″ pie shell

Beat eggs in bowl until blended, using a rotary beater. Add corn syrup, sugar, butter, chocolate, vanilla and almond extract; beat until blended. Stir in almonds and pour into unbaked pie shell.

Bake in 400° oven 15 minutes. Reduce temperature to 350° and bake 30 minutes more, or until a knife inserted halfway between the center and edge comes out clean. (Filling should be slightly less set at center than around edge.) Cool on rack. Makes 6 to 8 servings.

Chocolate-Coconut-Pecan Pie

Has all the flavor of a German chocolate cake
baked in a pie shell. A grand finale for a festive meal.

1 (4-oz.) pkg. sweet cooking chocolate	¼ c. milk
⅓ c. butter or regular margarine	1½ tblsp. cornstarch
	1 tsp. vanilla
1 c. sugar	½ c. chopped pecans
¾ c. light corn syrup	½ c. flaked coconut
3 eggs	Unbaked 9" pie shell with fluted edge

Melt chocolate in top of double boiler over hot water. Add butter and sugar. Heat until butter melts. Stir in corn syrup. Remove from heat and cool.

Beat eggs in bowl until well blended, using a rotary beater. Add milk, cornstarch and vanilla; beat until blended. Stir egg mixture into cooled chocolate mixture. Stir in pecans and coconut and pour into unbaked pie shell.

Bake in 400° oven 10 minutes. Reduce temperature to 300° and bake 50 minutes more, or until pie is set around the edge. Cool on rack. Makes 6 to 8 servings.

German Chocolate Pies

"I'm enclosing my family's choice pie," wrote a North Carolina
farm woman. "This recipe makes two very rich and delicious pies."

3 c. sugar	1 tsp. vanilla
7 tblsp. baking cocoa	2 c. flaked coconut
1 (13-oz.) can evaporated milk	1 c. chopped pecans
4 eggs, beaten	2 unbaked 9" pie shells
½ c. butter or regular margarine, melted	

Combine sugar and baking cocoa in bowl. Stir in evaporated milk, eggs, butter and vanilla, blending well. Stir in coconut and pecans and turn into two unbaked pie shells.

Bake in 350° oven 40 minutes, or until set around the edges. Cool on racks. Makes 2 pies, 6 to 8 servings each.

Caribbean Fudge Pie

A real chocolate-lover's pie that's sinfully rich!
It has a creamy fudge filling beneath a brownie-like top.

¼ c. butter or regular margarine	2 tsp. instant coffee powder
¾ c. brown sugar, packed	1 tsp. rum flavoring
3 eggs	¼ c. flour
1 (12-oz.) pkg. semisweet chocolate pieces, melted and cooled	1 c. chopped walnuts
	Unbaked 9" pie shell
	Walnut halves

Cream together butter and brown sugar in bowl until light and fluffy, using an electric mixer at medium speed. Add eggs, one at a time, beating well after each addition.

Add cooled chocolate, coffee powder and rum flavoring, blending well. Stir in flour and chopped walnuts and turn into unbaked pie shell. Arrange walnut halves in circle around edge of pie.

Bake in 375° oven 25 minutes, or until set around the edge. Cool on rack. Makes 6 to 8 servings.

Chocolate-Nut-Toffee Pie

This chocolate pie with a crushed toffee topping
looks and tastes like a specialty from a fine French restaurant.

1¼ c. sugar	2 eggs
⅓ c. baking cocoa	1 c. chopped walnuts
2 tblsp. flour	Unbaked 9" pie shell
½ tsp. salt	Toffee (recipe follows)
½ c. light corn syrup	1 c. heavy cream, whipped
1 (5⅓-oz.) can evaporated milk	

Combine sugar, baking cocoa, flour and salt in bowl. Beat in corn syrup and evaporated milk, using an electric mixer at medium speed. Add eggs, one at a time, beating well after each addition. Stir in walnuts and turn into unbaked pie shell.

Bake in 350° oven 55 minutes, or until center is set. Cool on rack.

Meanwhile, prepare Toffee and cool completely. Crush Toffee into small pieces, using a rolling pin. Spread whipped cream over top of pie and sprinkle with Toffee pieces. Makes 6 to 8 servings.

Toffee: Combine ½ c. sugar, 1 tblsp. light corn syrup, 2 tblsp. evaporated milk, 2 tblsp. butter or regular margarine and ⅛ tsp. salt in 1-qt. heavy saucepan. Cook over low heat, stirring often, until mixture is a deep amber color and reaches 280° on candy thermometer. Pour into well-buttered 8″ square baking pan.

Crunchy Chocolate Pie

Has a texture resembling pecan pie, with a chewy topping
of coconut and pecans over a smooth chocolate custard filling.

2 eggs	¾ c. milk
1½ c. sugar	1 tsp. vanilla
3 tblsp. baking cocoa	¾ c. flaked coconut
½ c. butter or regular	½ c. chopped pecans
margarine, melted	Unbaked 9″ pie shell

Combine eggs, sugar, baking cocoa, butter, milk and vanilla in bowl. Beat until well blended, using an electric mixer at medium speed. Stir in coconut and pecans and pour into unbaked pie shell.

Bake in 350° oven 50 minutes, or until top is crusty. Cool on rack. Makes 6 to 8 servings.

Double-Fudge Brownie Pie

Here's one we created in Farm Journal's own Test Kitchens—
a pie that tastes like a super-rich, super-fudgy brownie in a crust.

½ c. butter or	1 tsp. vanilla
regular margarine	⅓ c. flour
4 (1-oz.) squares	¼ tsp. salt
unsweetened chocolate	¾ c. coarsely chopped
¾ c. brown sugar, packed	walnuts
¼ c. water	Unbaked 9″ pie shell
2 eggs, separated	12 walnut halves

Melt together butter and chocolate in saucepan over low heat. Remove from heat; cool slightly.

Add brown sugar, water, egg yolks and vanilla to chocolate mixture; beat well with a spoon. Stir in flour and salt. Set aside.

Beat egg whites in bowl until stiff peaks form, using an electric mixer at high speed. Fold egg whites into chocolate mixture. Then fold in chopped walnuts and pour into unbaked pie shell. Arrange walnut halves around edge of pie.

Bake in 350° oven 40 minutes, or until set around the edge. Cool on rack. Makes 6 to 8 servings.

Crustless Fudge Pie

"My family enjoys this rich, chewy pie;
it bakes its own magic crust," a New York woman told us.

½ c. butter or
   regular margarine
2 (1-oz.) squares
   unsweetened chocolate
3 eggs

1 c. sugar
1 tsp. vanilla
¼ c. flour
½ c. chopped pecans

Combine butter and chocolate in 2-qt. saucepan. Melt over low heat. Remove from heat.

Beat together eggs, sugar and vanilla in bowl until thick and lemon-colored, using an electric mixer at high speed. Stir in flour. Add chocolate mixture, blending well. Stir in pecans and pour into greased 9" pie plate.

Bake in 350° oven 30 minutes, or until no imprint remains when touched lightly with finger. Cool on rack. Makes 6 to 8 servings.

Glazed Blueberry Cream Cheese Pie

Guests are sure to love this cheesecake-type pie
topped with glazed fresh blueberries. A summertime treat!

2 (3-oz.) pkg. cream cheese,
   softened
½ c. light corn syrup
1 tblsp. cornstarch
¼ c. milk

1 egg
1 tsp. vanilla
Unbaked 8" pie shell
Fruit Glaze (recipe follows)
1 pt. fresh blueberries

Beat cream cheese in bowl until smooth, using an electric mixer at medium speed. Gradually add corn syrup, beating until smooth.

Combine cornstarch and milk in small bowl; mix well. Stir cornstarch mixture into cream cheese mixture. Beat in egg and vanilla. Pour into unbaked pie shell.

Bake in 350° oven 45 minutes, or until a knife inserted in the center comes out clean. Cool on rack.

Prepare Fruit Glaze.

Arrange blueberries over top of pie. Spoon Fruit Glaze over blueberries.

Cover and chill in refrigerator until glaze is set. Makes 6 servings.

Fruit Glaze: Combine 1½ tblsp. cornstarch, 1 tblsp. sugar and dash of salt in small saucepan. Gradually stir in 2 tblsp. lemon juice, ⅓ c. water and ⅓ c. light corn syrup. Cook over medium heat, stirring occasionally, until mixture comes to a boil. Remove from heat. Cool slightly.

Chocolate-Cherry Pie

A Colorado ranch wife combined her husband's two
favorite flavors in order to perfect this unusual custard pie.

1 c. sugar
¼ c. baking cocoa
¼ c. flour
1 (16-oz.) can tart red
   cherries in water
1 egg, beaten
2 tblsp. butter or regular
   margarine, melted

¼ tsp. almond flavoring
Unbaked 9" pie shell
¼ c. flour
¼ c. sugar
3 tblsp. butter or
   regular margarine

Combine 1 c. sugar, baking cocoa, ¼ c. flour and undrained cherries in
large bowl. Add egg, 2 tblsp. melted butter and almond flavoring. Mix until blended, using a spoon. Pour into unbaked pie shell.

Combine ¼ c. flour and ¼ c. sugar in bowl. Cut in 3 tblsp. butter until
mixture is crumbly, using a pastry blender. Sprinkle over pie filling.

Bake in 400° oven 40 minutes, or until crust is golden brown. Cool on
rack. Makes 6 to 8 servings.

Funny Cake Pie

Is it a cake or is it a pie? You decide;
it's made with yellow cake batter and a fudge sauce baked in a pie shell.

1 c. sifted flour
1 tsp. baking powder
¼ tsp. salt
¾ c. sugar
¼ c. cooking oil
1 egg
½ c. milk
½ tsp. vanilla

2 (1-oz.) squares
   unsweetened chocolate
2 tblsp. butter or
   regular margarine
½ c. sugar
½ c. warm water
½ tsp. vanilla
Unbaked 9" pie shell

Sift together flour, baking powder and salt into bowl. Add ¾ c. sugar,
oil, egg, milk and ½ tsp. vanilla. Beat 2 minutes, using an electric mixer at
medium speed.

Melt together chocolate and butter in small saucepan over low heat.
Remove from heat. Stir in ½ c. sugar, warm water and ½ tsp. vanilla.
Cool well.

Pour chocolate mixture into unbaked pie shell. Spoon cake batter on
top and spread evenly with a metal spatula.

Bake in 350° oven 50 minutes, or until cake tester or wooden pick inserted in center comes out clean. Cool on rack. Makes 6 to 8 servings.

Raspberry Cheese Pie

A dairy farmer's wife created this splendid cheese pie
made with cream cheese, sour cream and heavy cream. Terrific!

1 (8-oz.) pkg. cream cheese, softened	2 (10-oz.) pkg. frozen raspberries, thawed
½ c. dairy sour cream	Water
⅓ c. sugar	3 tblsp. cornstarch
2 eggs	½ c. heavy cream, whipped
Unbaked 9″ pie shell	

Combine cream cheese and sour cream in bowl. Beat until smooth and fluffy, using an electric mixer at medium speed. Add sugar and eggs, blending well. Pour into unbaked pie shell.

Bake in 375° oven 35 minutes, or until a knife inserted in the center comes out clean. Cool on rack.

Cover and chill in refrigerator 1 hour.

Meanwhile, drain raspberries, reserving juice. Add enough water to juice to make ¾ c. Blend together cornstarch and ¾ c. juice in 2-qt. saucepan. Cook over medium heat, stirring constantly, until mixture comes to a boil. Cook 1 minute more. (Mixture will be very thick.) Remove from heat. Stir in raspberries. Cool to room temperature.

Fold whipped cream into cooled raspberry mixture. Spread over chilled cream cheese layer.

Chill in refrigerator 2 to 3 hours. Makes 6 to 8 servings.

Peach Cheese Pie

Not hard to make, and a real company-pleaser
with its pretty topping of peach slices arranged in a circle.

1 (8-oz.) pkg. cream cheese, softened	1 (29-oz.) can sliced peaches
2 eggs	1 tblsp. cornstarch
½ c. sugar	¼ c. sugar
2 tblsp. milk	1 tsp. lemon juice
1 tsp. vanilla	¼ tsp. almond extract
Unbaked 9″ pie shell	Maraschino cherries

Beat cream cheese in bowl until smooth, using an electric mixer at medium speed. Gradually add eggs, ½ c. sugar, milk and vanilla, beating well after each addition. Pour into unbaked pie shell.

Bake in 375° oven 30 minutes, or until set. Cool on rack.

Drain peaches, reserving 1 c. juice. Combine cornstarch and ¼ c. sugar in small saucepan. Gradually stir in reserved peach juice, lemon juice and almond extract. Cook over medium heat, stirring constantly, until mixture boils and thickens. Remove from heat.

Arrange peaches in a circle, petal-fashion, on top of filling. Garnish with maraschino cherries. Spoon glaze over fruit.

Cover and chill in refrigerator 1 hour, or until set. Makes 6 to 8 servings.

Cherry Cheese Pie

A young Kansas girl sent us this recipe—she says
it's her father's favorite pie. One bite and you'll know why.

Brown Sugar Graham Crust
  (recipe follows)
1 (8-oz.) pkg. cream cheese,
  softened
1 (3-oz.) pkg. cream cheese,
  softened
½ c. sugar

½ tsp. vanilla
2 egg whites, stiffly beaten
1 (16-oz.) can tart red
  cherries in water
Red food coloring
¼ c. sugar
1 tblsp. cornstarch

Prepare Brown Sugar Graham Crust and set aside.

Beat cream cheese in bowl until smooth, using an electric mixer at medium speed. Gradually add ½ c. sugar and vanilla, blending well. Fold beaten egg whites into cream cheese mixture. Pour into Brown Sugar Graham Crust.

Bake in 325° oven 25 minutes, or until filling is set. Cool on rack.

Drain cherries, reserving ½ c. juice. Combine reserved cherry juice, a few drops food coloring, ¼ c. sugar and cornstarch in 2-qt. saucepan. Cook over medium heat, stirring constantly, until mixture boils and thickens. Remove from heat; cool slightly.

Arrange cherries over cheese filling. Spoon glaze over cherries.

Cover and chill in refrigerator before serving. Makes 6 to 8 servings.

Brown Sugar Graham Crust: Combine 1½ c. graham cracker crumbs (about 20 graham crackers), ¼ c. brown sugar (packed), and ⅓ c. butter or regular margarine (melted) in bowl. Mix thoroughly, using a fork. Press into bottom and up sides of 9″ pie plate.

Strawberry Cheese Pie

Made with an easy graham cracker crust, cream cheese
and frozen strawberries, so you can enjoy it all year 'round.

2 (8-oz.) pkg. cream cheese,
  softened
3 eggs
⅔ c. sugar
⅛ tsp. vanilla

10" Graham Cracker
  Crust (see Index)
Strawberry Glaze
  (recipe follows)

Beat cream cheese in bowl until smooth, using an electric mixer at medium speed. Add eggs, one at a time, beating well after each addition. Add sugar and vanilla, beating well. Pour into Graham Cracker Crust.

Bake in 325° oven 50 minutes, or until center appears set. Cool on rack.

Prepare Strawberry Glaze. Spread Strawberry Glaze over cooled pie. Cover and chill in refrigerator. Makes 8 to 10 servings.

Strawberry Glaze: Drain 1 (10-oz.) pkg. frozen strawberries (thawed), reserving liquid. Combine reserved liquid and 1 tblsp. cornstarch in 2-qt. saucepan. Stir in strawberries. Cook over medium heat, stirring constantly, until mixture boils and thickens. Remove from heat. Stir in a few drops of red food coloring. Cool to room temperature.

Golden Treasure Pie

A two-layer treat, with pineapple on the bottom
and a smooth mixture of cottage cheese, eggs and milk on top.

2 (8½-oz.) cans
  crushed pineapple
½ c. sugar
2 tblsp. cornstarch
2 tblsp. water
⅔ c. sugar
1 tblsp. butter or
  regular margarine
¼ c. flour

1 c. creamed small-curd
  cottage cheese
1 tsp. vanilla
½ tsp. salt
2 eggs, slightly beaten
1¼ c. milk
Unbaked 10" pie shell

Combine undrained pineapple, ½ c. sugar, cornstarch and water in small saucepan. Cook over medium heat, stirring constantly, until mixture comes to a boil. Cook 1 minute more. Remove from heat and cool to room temperature.

Combine ⅔ c. sugar and butter in bowl. Beat until blended, using an electric mixer at medium speed. Add flour, cottage cheese, vanilla and salt; beat until smooth. Add eggs, one at a time, beating well after each addition. Beat in milk.

Pour pineapple mixture into unbaked pie shell. Gently pour cottage cheese mixture over pineapple layer, being careful not to disturb first layer.

Bake in 450° oven 15 minutes. Reduce temperature to 325° and bake 45 minutes more, or until a knife inserted halfway between the center and edge comes out clean. Cool on rack. Makes 8 to 10 servings.

Chocolate Cheese Swirl Pie

You have a choice of two cooking methods when you mix up this extra-smooth pie. It bakes in 25 minutes and microwaves in 5.

4 (3-oz.) pkg. cream cheese, softened	9″ Graham Cracker Crust (see Index)
½ c. sugar	½ c. semisweet chocolate pieces
2 eggs	
1½ tsp. vanilla	

Beat cream cheese in bowl until smooth, using an electric mixer at medium speed. Gradually add sugar, eggs and vanilla, beating well. Pour into Graham Cracker Crust.

Melt chocolate pieces in small saucepan over low heat. Drop melted chocolate by teaspoonfuls over pie. Swirl chocolate through cream cheese filling, using a fork.

Bake in 325° oven 20 to 25 minutes, or until center appears set. Cool on rack.

Cover and chill in refrigerator. Makes 8 servings.

Microwave Method: Prepare cream cheese mixture and pour into Graham Cracker Crust as for oven method. Place chocolate pieces in small glass bowl. Microwave (high setting) 1½ minutes to melt. Drop melted chocolate by teaspoonfuls evenly on pie and swirl through filling, using a fork. Microwave (high setting) 5 minutes, or until center appears set, giving pie plate a quarter turn after every minute. Cool on rack. Cover and chill in refrigerator.

Date Delight Pie

A New Jersey woman's invention, featuring a creamy
cheese filling topped with chopped dates and walnuts.

1 (8-oz.) pkg. pitted dates, finely chopped	1 (8-oz.) pkg. cream cheese, softened
½ c. dark corn syrup	¼ c. light corn syrup
¾ c. water	1 egg
¼ c. chopped walnuts	1 tsp. vanilla
2 tblsp. butter or regular margarine	Unbaked 9" pie shell
1 tsp. vanilla	Sweetened whipped cream

Combine dates, dark corn syrup and water in 2-qt. saucepan. Cook over medium heat, stirring occasionally, until mixture comes to a boil. Cook 8 to 10 minutes more, or until thick. Remove from heat. Stir in walnuts, butter and 1 tsp. vanilla. Cool completely.

Combine cream cheese, light corn syrup, egg and 1 tsp. vanilla in bowl. Beat until smooth, using an electric mixer at medium speed. Pour into unbaked pie shell. Gently spread date mixture on top.

Bake in 375° oven 35 to 40 minutes, or until edge of filling is set and crust is lightly browned. Cool on rack.

Cover and chill in refrigerator before serving.

To serve, top with sweetened whipped cream. Makes 6 to 8 servings.

Cherry Cheese Tarts

"Whenever there's a meeting or company coming,
my friends request this dessert," wrote a Michigan homemaker.

Vanilla Wafer Shells (recipe follows)	1 egg
	2 tsp. lemon juice
1 (8-oz.) pkg. cream cheese, softened	1 tsp. vanilla
	1½ c. canned cherry pie filling
⅓ c. sugar	

Prepare Vanilla Wafer Shells.

Cream together cream cheese and sugar in bowl until light and fluffy, using an electric mixer at medium speed. Add egg, lemon juice and vanilla; beat well. Spoon into Vanilla Wafer Shells.

Bake in 375° oven 15 minutes, or until filling is set. Cool on racks.

Top each with cherry pie filling.

Cover and chill in refrigerator before serving. Makes 12 tarts.

Vanilla Wafer Shells: Combine 1 c. vanilla wafer crumbs and 3 tblsp. butter or regular margarine (melted) in bowl; mix well. Press into bottoms of 12 paper-lined 2½" muffin-pan cups.

6 Refrigerated and Frozen Pies

Some occasions call for a spectacular dessert, one that's as extravagant-looking as it is good-tasting. Whether you're planning a bridal or baby shower, graduation, anniversary or birthday party, one of the pies in this chapter is sure to fit the celebration.

Savvy farm and ranch hostesses often turn to refrigerated and frozen pies for fabulous desserts that can be made in advance and whisked out at dessert time. Many country homemakers have two sets of recipes for dependable, make-ahead party pies: one to use when preparation time is short, and a set of traditional recipes made "from scratch." You'll find both types in this collection of 75 recipes—citrus-flavored chiffons wreathed with puffs of whipped cream; cheesecake fantasies decorated with glazed fruit; delicate, fluffy pies so low in calories that even the most dedicated dieter can enjoy them; wickedly rich chocolate creations; and all kinds of ice cream spectaculars with cookie, meringue and pastry shells.

When you want a light, refreshing finale to a heavy meal, a chiffon pie is the perfect choice. Because chiffon pies are such favorites, we've chosen 29 party-perfect recipes to open this chapter. The flavors run the gamut, from lemon and chocolate and apricot to raspberry, butterscotch, pumpkin and peanut butter. Some of the classic chiffon fillings are teamed with interesting pie crusts: the tangy lime-green filling of our new Heavenly Lime Pie is mounded into a crisp meringue shell; Orange Cloud Pie is nestled in a cookie-like, orange-flavored pastry shell; and Apricot Chiffon Pie contrasts billows of delicate, almond-scented filling with a spicy gingersnap crust.

Win over the chocolate fans on your guest list with any

one of two dozen refrigerated and frozen pies. You can choose from dark, fudgy mousse fillings, chocolate-flavored pie shells and light, fluffy cream fillings, some blended with mint, marshmallows or peanut butter.

For a fancy pie that's not difficult to make, work a little magic with marshmallows. Our marshmallow-based pies make elegant, easy desserts, and best of all, most need only a few ingredients. An Oklahoma cook's quick recipe for Chocolate Marshmallow Pie is made by blending marshmallows, milk, whipped cream and chocolate in a graham cracker crust. Another dramatic pie that's a snap to make is Florida's classic Key Lime Pie, with its gelatin-based filling in a graham cracker crust.

You can enjoy the rich, refreshing combination of fresh fruit and cheese in one of these colorful pies: Glazed Apple Cheese Pie, Two-tiered Strawberry Pie and French Blueberry Pie, each made with ripe fruit atop a layer of cream cheese in a flaky pastry shell.

When you want to dazzle your guests but have little time to prepare dessert, plan to make a frozen pie. We've included 17 choices, and they can be frozen as long as four weeks; just remove from the freezer about 15 minutes before serving to soften enough for cutting. Our new recipe for Ice Cream 'n' Pretzel Pie features a pretzel pie shell spread with melted chocolate and then heaped high with gobs and gobs of fudge-swirled vanilla ice cream. Classic desserts were the basis for some of our other new ice cream creations, such as Banana Split Pie and Baked Alaska Pie, a frozen fantasy of vanilla and chocolate ice cream layered with orange sherbet and quickly baked under a blanket of meringue.

Every pie in this chapter is a show-stopper, and each one can be made at your convenience several hours or several weeks before the big event.

How to Make Perfect Chiffon Pies

Here is the basic method for making a chiffon pie:

1. Combine the gelatin with other ingredients and heat as recipe directs until the gelatin dissolves and the liquid is clear. The gelatin must be completely dissolved for the mixture to thicken evenly.

2. Pour the hot gelatin mixture into a metal bowl and chill in the refrigerator or in another bowl of iced water. Metal helps the mixture cool because it conducts the heat to the outside more quickly than other materials.

3. Chill the gelatin mixture until it has the consistency of unbeaten egg whites. Then remove from the refrigerator or bowl of iced water and let stand at room temperature while you beat the egg whites; this will prevent the gelatin from becoming too thick.

4. Beat the egg whites in another bowl until foamy. Add the sugar very gradually, beating at high speed, until the mixture forms stiff, glossy peaks that stand up straight and don't lop over when you raise the beaters. Rub some of the mixture between your fingers to see whether the sugar is dissolved. If the texture feels grainy, continue beating until it's smooth.

5. Check the gelatin mixture by lifting a spoonful and dropping it back into the bowl; it should form a soft mound on top. If it doesn't, chill the mixture until it thickens and test it again.

6. To fold the gelatin mixture into the egg white mixture, cut down through the mixture with a rubber spatula, scraping across the bottom of the bowl. Then bring the spatula up and over, close to the surface. Repeat this circular down-up-and-over motion until the two mixtures are blended.

7. If your recipe contains heavy cream, whip it in another bowl until stiff peaks form. The peaks should mound slightly when the beaters are raised. Fold the egg white-gelatin mixture into the whipped cream.

8. Chill the filling until it mounds well when spooned, and turn it into a baked pie shell. Cover with plastic wrap or waxed paper and chill several hours or overnight until set.

Lemon Chiffon Pie

The tangy lemon flavor of this extra-high chiffon pie
comes from lemon juice, lemon rind and lemon-flavored gelatin.

⅔ c. sugar	1 (3-oz.) pkg. lemon-
½ tsp. salt	flavored gelatin
6 tblsp. lemon juice	⅔ c. boiling water
2 tsp. grated lemon rind	½ tsp. cream of tartar
6 eggs, separated	⅔ c. sugar
	Baked 10″ pie shell

Stir together ⅔ c. sugar and salt in top of double boiler. Stir in lemon juice, lemon rind and slightly beaten egg yolks. Cook over simmering water, stirring constantly, until mixture coats a metal spoon, 7 to 10 minutes.

Dissolve lemon gelatin in boiling water in a metal bowl. Stir hot yolk mixture into dissolved gelatin. Place bowl of gelatin mixture in a bowl filled with iced water. Stir gently until mixture is the consistency of unbeaten egg whites.

Remove bowl from water and immediately beat egg whites and cream of tartar in bowl until foamy, using an electric mixer at high speed. Gradually add ⅔ c. sugar, 1 tblsp. at a time, beating well after each addition. Continue beating until stiff, glossy peaks form when beaters are slowly lifted.

When gelatin mixture mounds slightly when dropped from a spoon, fold into egg white mixture.

Chill in refrigerator until mixture mounds well when spooned. Turn into baked pie shell.

Chill in refrigerator 3 hours, or until set. Makes 8 to 10 servings.

Lemon-plus Pie

There's just a hint of orange in this lemon chiffon pie.
Decorated with Marshmallow Petals, it's a pretty springtime dessert.

1 env. unflavored gelatin	1 tsp. grated lemon rind
¼ c. cold water	⅔ c. sugar
4 eggs, separated	⅔ c. heavy cream, whipped
½ c. lemon juice	Baked 9″ pie shell
3 tblsp. orange juice	Marshmallow Petals
¾ c. sugar	(recipe follows)
¼ tsp. salt	

Sprinkle gelatin over cold water to soften.

Beat egg yolks in top of double boiler until very thick and lemon-colored, using an electric mixer at high speed. Stir in lemon juice, orange juice, ¾ c. sugar and salt. Cook over simmering water, stirring constantly, until mixture coats a metal spoon, about 10 minutes. Remove from heat. Add softened gelatin and lemon rind, stirring until gelatin dissolves.

Chill in refrigerator, stirring occasionally, until mixture is the consistency of unbeaten egg whites.

Remove lemon mixture from refrigerator and immediately beat egg whites in bowl until foamy, using an electric mixer at high speed. Gradually add ⅔ c. sugar, 1 tblsp. at a time, beating well after each addition. Continue beating until stiff, glossy peaks form when beaters are slowly lifted.

Fold whipped cream into egg white mixture.

When lemon mixture mounds slightly when dropped from a spoon, beat until smooth, using an electric mixture at medium speed. Fold whipped cream-egg white mixture into gelatin mixture.

Chill in refrigerator until mixture mounds well when spooned. Turn into baked pie shell.

Chill in refrigerator several hours, or until set.

Prepare Marshmallow Petals while pie is chilling. Before serving, arrange Marshmallow Petals in pairs around the edge of pie. Makes 6 to 8 servings.

Marshmallow Petals: Cut 4 large marshmallows horizontally into 5 slices, using kitchen shears. Dust fingers with confectioners' sugar and twist slices into petal shapes. Coat petals with colored sugar.

Lemon Yogurt Pie

Kind of tangy, and just a little creamier than most other
chiffon pies. Two cups of yogurt make it extra-nutritious, too.

2 env. unflavored gelatin	½ c. lemon juice
1 c. light corn syrup	1 tblsp. grated lemon rind
½ c. water	3 drops yellow food
3 eggs, separated	coloring
2 (8-oz.) containers	Baked 9" pie shell
plain yogurt (2 c.)	Lemon slices

Stir together gelatin, corn syrup, water and slightly beaten egg yolks in small saucepan. Cook over low heat, stirring constantly, until gelatin dissolves. Remove from heat.

Combine yogurt, lemon juice, lemon rind and food coloring in bowl; stir until smooth. Gradually stir hot corn syrup mixture into yogurt mixture; stir until smooth.

Chill in refrigerator, stirring occasionally, until mixture is the consistency of unbeaten egg whites.

Remove yogurt mixture from refrigerator and immediately beat egg whites in bowl until stiff peaks form, using an electric mixer at high speed.

When yogurt mixture mounds slightly when dropped from a spoon, beat until smooth, using an electric mixer at medium speed. Fold gelatin mixture into egg white mixture.

Chill in refrigerator until mixture mounds well when spooned, about 15 minutes. Turn into baked pie shell.

Chill in refrigerator until set, about 3 hours.

To serve, decorate with lemon slices. Makes 6 to 8 servings.

Lemon Velvet Pie

A lightly layered creation with lemon chiffon on the bottom
and a topping that probably will remind you of lemon meringue pie.

1⅓ c. sugar	1 tsp. grated lemon rind
6 tblsp. cornstarch	1 tsp. vanilla
½ tsp. salt	1 tblsp. unflavored gelatin
1½ c. cold water	¼ c. cold water
2 eggs, separated	1 c. light cream
2 tblsp. butter or	Baked 9" pie shell
regular margarine	1 c. heavy cream, whipped
⅓ c. lemon juice	

Combine sugar, cornstarch and salt in 2-qt. saucepan. Gradually stir in 1½ c. cold water. Cook over medium heat, stirring constantly, until mixture thickens and mounds when dropped from a spoon. Stir a small amount of hot mixture into slightly beaten egg yolks. Immediately pour egg yolk mixture back into remaining hot mixture, blending well. Cook over low heat 2 minutes more, stirring constantly. Remove from heat. Gently stir in butter, lemon juice, lemon rind and vanilla. Remove 1 c. of the filling; set aside to cool at room temperature.

Soften gelatin in ¼ c. cold water 5 minutes. Add gelatin mixture to remaining hot filling and stir until dissolved. Gradually stir in light cream. Cool slightly.

When gelatin mixture begins to thicken, beat egg whites in bowl until stiff, glossy (but not dry) peaks form, using an electric mixer at high speed. Fold egg whites into gelatin mixture. Pour mixture into baked pie shell.

Chill in refrigerator 15 minutes.

Carefully spread reserved 1 c. filling on top of pie and chill in refrigerator until set.

To serve, decorate top of pie with puffs of whipped cream. Makes 6 to 8 servings.

Lemon-Lime Chiffon Pie

A new, slimmed-down recipe for a light chiffon pie that's made with nonfat dry milk, a thin meringue shell, and a little less sugar.

1 env. unflavored gelatin	3 egg whites
½ c. water	⅛ tsp. cream of tartar
3 tblsp. lemon juice	½ c. sugar
2 tblsp. lime juice	⅓ c. nonfat dry milk
½ tsp. grated lemon rind	⅛ tsp. cream of tartar
½ tsp. grated lime rind	⅓ c. iced water
3 to 4 drops yellow food	2-Egg White Meringue Pie
coloring	Shell (see Index)

Combine gelatin and ½ c. water in small saucepan. Cook over low heat, stirring constantly, until gelatin dissolves. Remove from heat. Stir in lemon juice, lime juice, lemon rind, lime rind and food coloring and pour into a metal bowl.

Chill in refrigerator, stirring occasionally, until mixture is the consistency of unbeaten egg whites.

Remove lemon-lime mixture from refrigerator and immediately beat egg whites and ⅛ tsp. cream of tartar in bowl until foamy, using an electric mixer at high speed. Gradually add sugar, 1 tblsp. at a time, beating well after each addition. Continue beating until stiff, glossy peaks form when beaters are slowly lifted.

Combine dry milk, ⅛ tsp. cream of tartar and ⅓ c. iced water in chilled bowl. Beat until soft peaks form, using an electric mixer at high speed. Fold egg white mixture into whipped milk.

When lemon-lime mixture mounds slightly when dropped from a spoon, fold into egg white mixture.

Chill in refrigerator until mixture mounds well when spooned. Turn into 2-Egg White Meringue Pie Shell.

Chill in refrigerator 3 hours, or until set. Makes 8 servings.

Heavenly Lime Pie

A pretty pastel pie that looks inviting and tastes as refreshing as it looks; just right for when you want an elegant dessert, but nothing heavy.

½ c. sugar
1 env. unflavored gelatin
½ c. water
⅓ c. lime juice
3 eggs, separated
2 tsp. grated lime rind
3 drops green food
   coloring

⅓ c. sugar
1 c. heavy cream, whipped
3-Egg White Meringue Pie
   Shell (see Index)
Sweetened whipped cream
1 lime, thinly sliced

Stir together ½ c. sugar and gelatin in small saucepan. Stir in water, lime juice and slightly beaten egg yolks. Cook over medium heat, stirring constantly, until sugar and gelatin dissolve. Remove from heat. Stir in lime rind and food coloring and pour mixture into a metal bowl.

Chill in refrigerator, stirring occasionally, until mixture is the consistency of unbeaten egg whites.

Remove lime mixture from refrigerator and immediately beat egg whites in bowl until foamy, using an electric mixer at high speed. Gradually add ⅓ c. sugar, 1 tblsp. at a time, beating well after each addition. Continue beating until stiff, glossy peaks form when beaters are slowly lifted.

When lime mixture mounds slightly when dropped from a spoon, fold into egg white mixture. Fold egg white mixture into whipped cream.

Chill in refrigerator until mixture mounds well when spooned. Turn into 3-Egg White Meringue Pie Shell.

Chill in refrigerator 8 hours, or until set.

To serve, decorate with puffs of sweetened whipped cream and lime slices. Makes 6 to 8 servings.

Fluffy Fruit Pie

Delightfully fruity and very colorful, with bright slices of maraschino cherries dotting the pineapple-and-orange filling.

1 (8¼-oz.) can crushed
   pineapple
¼ c. red maraschino
   cherry juice
1 (3-oz.) pkg. orange-
   flavored gelatin

½ c. sugar
1 c. evaporated milk, chilled
1½ tsp. lemon juice
¼ c. sliced red maraschino
   cherries
Baked 9″ pie shell

Combine undrained pineapple and maraschino cherry juice in 2-qt. saucepan. Cook over medium heat, stirring constantly, until mixture comes to a boil. Add orange gelatin, stirring until gelatin is dissolved. Remove from heat. Stir in sugar and pour mixture into a large metal bowl.

Chill in refrigerator until mixture mounds slightly when dropped from a spoon, about 30 minutes.

Combine chilled evaporated milk and lemon juice in chilled bowl. Beat until stiff peaks form, using an electric mixer at high speed. Fold whipped evaporated milk mixture into chilled gelatin mixture. Fold in maraschino cherries. Turn into baked pie shell.

Chill in refrigerator until set. Makes 6 to 8 servings.

Orange Chiffon Pie

To highlight the tart orange flavor of the filling, a thin layer of unsweetened whipped cream is spread over the top just before serving.

1 env. unflavored gelatin	4 eggs, separated
¼ c. cold water	1 tblsp. grated orange rind
½ c. sugar	½ c. sugar
½ tsp. salt	Baked 9″ pie shell
½ c. orange juice	½ c. heavy cream, whipped
1 tblsp. lemon juice	

Sprinkle gelatin over cold water to soften.

Combine ½ c. sugar and salt in top of double boiler. Stir in orange juice, lemon juice and slightly beaten egg yolks. Cook over simmering water, stirring constantly, until mixture coats a metal spoon, about 5 to 8 minutes. Remove from heat. Add orange rind and softened gelatin, stirring until gelatin dissolves.

Chill in refrigerator, stirring occasionally, until mixture is the consistency of unbeaten egg whites.

Remove orange mixture from refrigerator and immediately beat egg whites in bowl until foamy, using an electric mixer at high speed. Gradually add ½ c. sugar, 1 tblsp. at a time, beating well after each addition. Continue beating until stiff, glossy peaks form when beaters are slowly lifted.

When orange mixture mounds slightly when dropped from a spoon, fold into egg white mixture.

Chill in refrigerator until mixture mounds well when spooned. Turn into baked pie shell.

Chill in refrigerator 3 hours, or until set.

To serve, spread whipped cream over pie. Makes 6 to 8 servings.

Orange Cloud Pie

Heaped into a buttery orange crust, the filling for this new pie has a light, creamy texture. The flavor is both rich and delicious.

Orange Pie Shell
  (recipe follows)
½ c. sugar
1 env. unflavored gelatin
1 c. orange juice
3 tblsp. lemon juice
3 eggs, separated
1 tblsp. grated orange rind

12 drops yellow food
  coloring
2 drops red food coloring
⅓ c. sugar
1 c. heavy cream, whipped
1 orange, peeled and cut
  into sections

Prepare Orange Pie Shell and set aside.

Stir together ½ c. sugar and gelatin in small saucepan. Stir in orange juice, lemon juice and slightly beaten egg yolks. Cook over medium heat, stirring constantly, until sugar and gelatin dissolve. Remove from heat. Stir in orange rind and yellow and red food coloring and pour into a metal bowl.

Chill in refrigerator, stirring occasionally, until mixture is the consistency of unbeaten egg whites.

Remove orange mixture from refrigerator and immediately beat egg whites in bowl until foamy, using an electric mixer at high speed. Gradually add ⅓ c. sugar, 1 tblsp. at a time, beating well after each addition. Continue beating until stiff, glossy peaks form when beaters are slowly lifted.

When orange mixture mounds slightly when dropped from a spoon, fold into egg white mixture. Fold egg white-orange mixture into whipped cream.

Chill in refrigerator until mixture mounds well when spooned. Turn into Orange Pie Shell.

Chill in refrigerator 8 hours, or until set.

To serve, arrange orange sections around edge of pie. Makes 6 to 8 servings.

Orange Pie Shell: Combine 1 c. sifted flour, 3 tblsp. sugar and 1 tsp. grated orange rind in bowl. Cut in ½ c. butter or regular margarine until coarse crumbs form, using a pastry blender. Press mixture into bottom and up sides of 9″ pie plate. Bake in 375° oven 13 minutes, or until golden. Cool on rack.

Orange Blossom Pie

This chiffon pie is a little different because the filling
is made with quick-cooking tapioca. The topping is a sprinkle of coconut.

2 c. milk	2 eggs, separated
½ c. quick-cooking tapioca	1 c. heavy cream, whipped
½ c. sugar	Baked 9" pie shell
⅛ tsp. salt	½ c. toasted, flaked
1 tsp. grated orange rind	coconut*

Heat milk in top of double boiler.

Combine tapioca, sugar and salt in small bowl. Stir tapioca mixture into hot milk. Cook over boiling water, stirring constantly, until mixture begins to thicken, about 4 minutes. Stir in orange rind. Cook 15 minutes more, stirring occasionally. (Mixture is very thick.)

Beat egg yolks slightly, using a fork. Stir a small amount of hot mixture into egg yolks. Immediately pour yolk mixture back into remaining hot mixture, blending thoroughly. Cook 1 minute more. Remove from heat. Let mixture cool at room temperature.

Beat egg whites in bowl until stiff but not dry peaks form, using an electric mixer at high speed. Fold egg whites into slightly cooled pudding mixture. Fold in whipped cream. Turn into baked pie shell. Sprinkle with toasted coconut.

Chill in refrigerator until set. Makes 6 to 8 servings.

*Note: To toast coconut, place coconut in 8" square baking pan. Bake in 350° oven 7 to 10 minutes, stirring once, or until coconut is toasted.

Orange-Lemon Chiffon Pie

A sunny citrus pie with the fresh flavors of lemon and orange,
blended in just the right proportions to bring out the best of each.

½ c. sugar
1 env. unflavored gelatin
Dash of salt
4 eggs, separated
½ c. orange juice
⅓ c. lemon juice

¼ c. water
½ tsp. grated orange rind
½ tsp. grated lemon rind
⅓ c. sugar
Baked 9" pie shell
Sweetened whipped cream

Combine ½ c. sugar, gelatin and salt in 2-qt. saucepan. Beat together
egg yolks, orange juice, lemon juice and water in bowl, using a rotary
beater. Add yolk mixture to gelatin mixture; blend well. Cook over
medium heat, stirring constantly, until mixture comes to a boil and gelatin
is dissolved. Remove from heat. Stir in orange rind and lemon rind and
pour into a metal bowl.

Chill in refrigerator until mixture is partially set.

Beat egg whites in bowl until foamy, using an electric mixer at high
speed. Gradually add ⅓ c. sugar, 1 tblsp. at a time, beating well after each
addition. Continue beating until stiff, glossy peaks form when beaters are
slowly lifted. Fold gelatin mixture into egg white mixture. Spoon mixture
into baked pie shell.

Chill in refrigerator until set.

To serve, decorate with sweetened whipped cream. Makes 6 to 8 servings.

Spring Daffodil Pie

A whole cupful of heavy cream is whipped and folded
into the pale, lemon-orange filling to make it rich and creamy.

1 env. unflavored gelatin
¼ c. cold water
3 egg yolks
1 c. sugar
½ c. milk
¼ tsp. salt
¾ c. fresh orange juice

¼ c. lemon juice
1 tsp. grated orange rind
½ tsp. grated lemon rind
1 c. heavy cream, whipped
Baked 9" pie shell
Sweetened whipped cream
Pastel candy mints

Sprinkle gelatin over cold water to soften; let stand 5 minutes.

Beat egg yolks slightly, using a fork.

Combine egg yolks, sugar, milk and salt in small saucepan; mix well.
Cook over medium heat, stirring constantly, until mixture comes to a boil.
Remove from heat.

Add softened gelatin, stirring until dissolved. Stir in orange juice, lemon juice, orange rind and lemon rind and pour into a metal bowl.

Chill in refrigerator until mixture mounds slightly when dropped from a spoon.

Fold whipped cream into thickened gelatin mixture. Pour mixture into baked pie shell.

Chill in refrigerator several hours, or until set.

To serve, decorate pie with puffs of sweetened whipped cream and pastel candy mints. Makes 6 to 8 servings.

Pink Grapefruit Pies

This recipe makes enough for a party—two pies, 20 servings—
and each tangy wedge is studded with sections of pink grapefruit.

2 large pink grapefruit	Red food coloring
Water	1 (13-oz.) can evaporated
1 env. unflavored gelatin	milk, chilled
2 eggs, separated	¼ c. lemon juice
½ c. sugar	¼ tsp. cream of tartar
¼ tsp. salt	¼ c. sugar
½ tsp. grated lemon rind	2 baked 10″ pie shells

Peel grapefruit with a sharp knife, removing all of the white membrane. Cut into sections over bowl, catching juice in bowl. Set grapefruit sections aside. Add enough water to juice to make 1 c.

Sprinkle gelatin over ½ c. of the grapefruit juice to soften. Combine egg yolks, ½ c. sugar, salt, lemon rind and remaining ½ c. grapefruit juice in small saucepan. Beat until blended, using a rotary beater. Cook over low heat, stirring constantly, until mixture coats a metal spoon. Remove from heat. Add softened gelatin and stir until dissolved. Add a few drops food coloring to tint mixture a delicate pink and pour into a metal bowl.

Chill in refrigerator until mixture mounds slightly when dropped from a spoon.

Beat chilled evaporated milk in chilled bowl until it begins to thicken, using an electric mixer at high speed. Gradually add lemon juice and beat until stiff peaks form. Fold gelatin mixture into whipped evaporated milk.

Beat egg whites and cream of tartar in another bowl until foamy, using an electric mixer at high speed. Gradually add ¼ c. sugar, 1 tblsp. at a time, beating well after each addition. Continue beating until stiff, glossy peaks form when beaters are slowly lifted. Fold egg white mixture into gelatin mixture. Then fold in whipped evaporated milk and grapefruit sections. Pour mixture evenly into two baked pie shells.

Chill in refrigerator 2 to 3 hours, or until set. Makes 2 pies, 10 servings each.

Apricot Chiffon Pie

A brand new combination—a spicy gingersnap crust,
fresh apricot quarters and a creamy, almond-flavored filling.

Gingersnap Crust	*2 tsp. vanilla*
(recipe follows)	*½ tsp. almond extract*
1 env. plus 1 tsp.	*¼ tsp. cream of tartar*
unflavored gelatin	*⅓ c. sugar*
¼ c. cold water	*1 c. heavy cream, whipped*
½ c. sugar	*8 fresh apricots, peeled*
2 tblsp. cornstarch	*and cut into quarters*
2 c. milk	*3 tblsp. apricot preserves*
2 eggs, separated	

Prepare Gingersnap Crust and set aside.

Sprinkle gelatin over cold water to soften.

Combine ½ c. sugar and cornstarch in 2-qt. saucepan. Gradually add milk, stirring well. Cook over medium heat, stirring constantly, until mixture boils and thickens, about 15 minutes. Cook 1 minute more. Remove from heat.

Beat egg yolks slightly, using a fork. Stir a small amount of hot mixture into egg yolks. Immediately pour yolk mixture back into remaining hot mixture, blending thoroughly. Cook 2 minutes more over low heat, stirring constantly. Remove from heat. Gently stir in softened gelatin, vanilla and almond extract and pour into a metal bowl. Place bowl in bowl of iced water. Stir until mixture mounds slightly when dropped from a spoon.

Remove from iced water and immediately beat egg whites and cream of tartar in bowl until foamy, using an electric mixer at high speed. Gradually add ⅓ c. sugar, 1 tblsp. at a time, beating well after each addition. Continue beating until stiff, glossy peaks form when beaters are slowly lifted.

Fold whipped cream into egg white mixture. Then fold in custard mixture.

Chill in refrigerator until mixture mounds well when spooned. Turn into Gingersnap Crust.

Chill in refrigerator 2 hours, or until set.

Arrange apricot quarters around edge of pie.

Heat apricot preserves in small saucepan over medium heat until preserves begin to bubble around edge. Carefully spoon hot preserves over apricots.

Chill in refrigerator at least 1 hour before serving. Makes 6 to 8 servings.

Gingersnap Crust: Combine 1½ c. finely crushed gingersnaps and ⅓ c. butter or regular margarine (melted) in bowl; mix well. Press mixture into bottom and up sides of 9″ pie plate. Chill in refrigerator until set.

Raspberry Chiffon Pie

Just three tablespoons of sugar are needed to sweeten
the fluffy pink filling of this pie, made with frozen berries.

1 (10-oz.) pkg. frozen
  raspberries, thawed
1 env. unflavored gelatin
3 egg whites
$1/_8$ tsp. cream of tartar
3 tblsp. sugar

$1/_3$ c. nonfat dry milk
$1/_3$ c. iced water
$1/_8$ tsp. cream of tartar
2-Egg White Meringue Pie
  Shell (see Index)

Drain raspberries, reserving juice. Place juice in small saucepan.
Sprinkle gelatin over juice. Let stand 5 minutes to soften. Cook over low
heat, stirring constantly, until gelatin dissolves. Remove from heat. Stir in
raspberries and pour into a metal bowl.

Chill in refrigerator, stirring occasionally, until mixture is the consistency of unbeaten egg whites.

Remove mixture from refrigerator and immediately beat egg whites
and cream of tartar in bowl until foamy, using an electric mixer at high
speed. Gradually sugar, 1 tblsp. at a time, beating well after each addition.
Continue beating until stiff, glossy peaks form when beaters are slowly
lifted.

Beat nonfat dry milk, iced water and $1/_8$ tsp. cream of tartar in chilled
bowl until soft peaks form, using an electric mixer at high speed, about 5
minutes. When raspberry mixture mounds slightly when dropped from a
spoon, fold milk mixture into egg white mixture. Then fold in raspberry
mixture. Spoon into 2-Egg White Meringue Pie Shell.

Chill in refrigerator until set, about 3 hours. Makes 8 servings.

Pineapple Chiffon Pie

A new recipe for an extra-creamy chiffon pie that's truly beautiful
with its garnish of pineapple slices, coconut and puffs of whipped cream.

1 env. unflavored gelatin
$1/_4$ c. cold water
2 tblsp. sugar
2 tblsp. cornstarch
$1 1/_2$ c. pineapple juice
2 eggs, separated
$1/_2$ c. cream of coconut
$1/_4$ tsp. cream of tartar
3 tblsp. sugar

$1/_2$ c. heavy cream, whipped
$1/_2$ c. flaked coconut
Baked 9" pie shell
  with fluted edge
1 (8-oz.) can sliced
  pineapple, drained
Sweetened whipped cream
Flaked coconut

Sprinkle gelatin over cold water to soften.

Combine 2 tblsp. sugar and cornstarch in 2-qt. saucepan. Gradually
add pineapple juice, stirring well. Cook over medium heat, stirring con-

stantly, until mixture comes to a boil. Cook 1 minute more. Remove from heat.

Beat egg yolks slightly, using a fork. Stir a small amount of hot mixture into egg yolks. Immediately pour yolk mixture back into remaining hot mixture, blending thoroughly. Cook 2 minutes more over low heat, stirring constantly. Remove from heat. Add cream of coconut and softened gelatin, stirring until gelatin dissolves. Pour into a metal bowl.

Chill in refrigerator until mixture mounds slightly when dropped from a spoon.

Remove gelatin mixture from refrigerator and immediately beat egg whites and cream of tartar in bowl until foamy, using an electric mixer at high speed. Gradually add 3 tblsp. sugar, 1 tblsp. at a time, beating well after each addition. Continue beating until stiff, glossy peaks form when beaters are slowly lifted.

Fold whipped cream into egg white mixture. Then fold in gelatin mixture and ½ c. coconut.

Chill in refrigerator until mixture mounds well when spooned. Turn into baked pie shell.

Chill in refrigerator 3 hours, or until set.

To serve, cut pineapple slices in half and arrange around edge of pie. Top pineapple with puffs of sweetened whipped cream and sprinkle with coconut. Makes 6 to 8 servings.

Pumpkin Chiffon Pie

A chiffon pie with the all-American flavor of pumpkin,
topped with whipped cream and spiced with a sprinkle of nutmeg.

⅓ c. brown sugar, packed	2 eggs, separated
1 env. unflavored gelatin	¾ c. cooked, mashed pumpkin,
1 tsp. ground cinnamon	fresh or canned
¼ tsp. ground allspice	¼ c. sugar
¼ tsp. salt	Baked 9″ pie shell
¾ c. evaporated milk	Sweetened whipped cream
¼ c. water	Ground nutmeg

Stir together brown sugar, gelatin, cinnamon, allspice and salt in top of double boiler. Stir in evaporated milk, water, slightly beaten egg yolks and pumpkin. Beat until smooth, using a rotary beater. Cook over simmering water, stirring constantly, until mixture thickens, 5 to 7 minutes. Remove from heat.

Place double boiler top in bowl of iced water. Stir gently until mixture cools to room temperature.

Remove from iced water and immediately beat egg whites in bowl until foamy, using an electric mixer at high speed. Gradually add sugar, 1 tblsp. at a time, beating well after each addition. Continue beating until stiff, glossy peaks form when beaters are slowly lifted.

When pumpkin mixture mounds slightly when dropped from a spoon, fold into egg white mixture.

Chill in refrigerator until mixture mounds well when spooned. Turn into baked pie shell.

Chill in refrigerator until set.

To serve, decorate pie with puffs of sweetened whipped cream and sprinkle with nutmeg. Makes 6 to 8 servings.

Spicy Pumpkin Chiffon Pie

The light, airy filling is spiced with cinnamon, nutmeg
and cloves; brown sugar and dark corn syrup are the sweeteners.

2 env. unflavored gelatin
½ c. cold water
1½ c. cooked, mashed
    pumpkin, fresh or canned
½ c. dark corn syrup
⅓ c. brown sugar, packed
1 tsp. ground cinnamon
½ tsp. salt

½ tsp. ground ginger
⅛ tsp. ground cloves
3 eggs, separated
1½ c. evaporated milk
½ c. dark corn syrup
9″ Graham Cracker Crust
    (see Index)

Sprinkle gelatin over cold water to soften.

Combine pumpkin, ½ c. corn syrup, brown sugar, cinnamon, salt, ginger, cloves and slightly beaten egg yolks in 2-qt. saucepan. Blend in evaporated milk. Cook over medium heat, stirring constantly, until mixture comes to a boil. Remove from heat. Add softened gelatin, stirring until dissolved. Pour into a metal bowl.

Chill in refrigerator until mixture mounds when dropped from a spoon, about 2½ hours.

Remove pumpkin mixture from refrigerator and immediately beat egg whites in bowl until soft peaks form when beaters are slowly lifted, using an electric mixer at high speed. Gradually add ½ c. corn syrup, 1 tblsp. at a time, beating well after each addition. Continue beating until stiff, glossy peaks form when beaters are slowly lifted. Fold egg white mixture into pumpkin mixture.

Chill in refrigerator until mixture is very thick and almost set. Turn into Graham Cracker Crust.

Chill in refrigerator 2 hours, or until set. Makes 6 to 8 servings.

Butterscotch Chiffon Pie

A Mississippi cook sent the recipe for this pie;
it's delicately flavored and topped with a cloud of whipped cream.

¾ c. brown sugar, packed
1 env. unflavored gelatin
½ c. milk
¼ c. water
3 eggs, separated

¼ c. sugar
1 tblsp. vanilla
Baked 9″ pie shell
Sweetened whipped cream

Combine brown sugar and gelatin in 2-qt. saucepan. Stir in milk, water
and slightly beaten egg yolks. Cook over medium heat, stirring constantly, until sugar and gelatin dissolve. Pour into a metal bowl.

Chill in refrigerator, stirring occasionally, until mixture is the consistency of unbeaten egg whites.

Remove brown sugar mixture from refrigerator and immediately beat
egg whites in bowl until foamy, using an electric mixer at high speed.
Gradually add sugar, 1 tblsp. at a time, beating well after each addition.
Continue beating until stiff, glossy peaks form when beaters are slowly
lifted. Beat in vanilla.

When gelatin mixture mounds slightly when spooned, fold into egg
white mixture.

Chill in refrigerator until mixture mounds well when spooned. Turn into baked pie shell.

Chill in refrigerator 3 hours, or until set.

To serve, spread sweetened whipped cream over pie. Makes 6 to 8
servings.

Peanut Butter Chiffon Pie

A pretzel crust and a creamy peanut butter filling
will delight children with two of their favorite flavors.

Pretzel Crumb Pie Shell
  (recipe follows)
¼ c. sugar
1 env. unflavored gelatin
¼ tsp. salt

1 c. milk
2 eggs, separated
½ c. creamy peanut butter
¼ c. sugar
1 c. heavy cream, whipped

Prepare Pretzel Crumb Pie Shell and set aside.

Stir together ¼ c. sugar, gelatin and salt in 2-qt. saucepan. Stir in milk
and slightly beaten egg yolks. Cook over medium heat, stirring constantly, until mixture comes to a boil. Reduce heat to low and cook 5 minutes.
Remove from heat. Add peanut butter, stirring until blended. Pour into a
metal bowl.

Place bowl of peanut butter mixture in bowl filled with iced water. Stir
gently until mixture is the consistency of unbeaten egg whites.

Remove bowl from water and immediately beat egg whites until foamy, using an electric mixer at high speed. Gradually add ¼ c. sugar, 1 tblsp. at a time, beating well after each addition. Continue beating until stiff, glossy peaks form when beaters are slowly lifted.

When peanut butter mixture mounds slightly when dropped from a spoon, fold in egg white mixture. Then fold in whipped cream.

Chill in refrigerator until mixture mounds well when spooned. Turn into Pretzel Crumb Pie Shell.

Chill in refrigerator 3 hours, or until set. Makes 6 to 8 servings.

Pretzel Crumb Pie Shell: Combine ¾ c. crushed pretzels, 3 tblsp. sugar and 6 tblsp. butter or regular margarine (melted) in bowl; mix well. Press crumb mixture evenly into bottom and up sides of 9″ pie plate. Bake in 350° oven 8 minutes. Cool on rack.

Coffee Chiffon Pie

Just 120 calories in each serving of coffee-flavored filling mounded into a crisp meringue shell. And it tastes heavenly.

2½ tsp. instant coffee powder
1 env. unflavored gelatin
¾ c. water
3 egg whites
⅛ tsp. cream of tartar
½ c. sugar

1 tsp. vanilla
⅓ c. nonfat dry milk
⅛ tsp. cream of tartar
⅓ c. iced water
2-Egg White Meringue Pie
  Shell (see Index)

Combine coffee powder and gelatin in small saucepan. Stir in ¾ c. water. Cook over medium heat, stirring constantly, until coffee and gelatin dissolve. Remove from heat. Pour into a metal bowl.

Chill in refrigerator, stirring occasionally, until mixture is the consistency of unbeaten egg whites.

Remove coffee mixture from refrigerator and immediately beat egg whites and ⅛ tsp. cream of tartar in bowl until foamy, using an electric mixer at high speed. Gradually add sugar, 1 tblsp. at a time, beating well after each addition. Continue beating until stiff, glossy peaks form when beaters are slowly lifted. Beat in vanilla.

Combine dry milk, ⅛ tsp. cream of tartar and ⅓ c. iced water in chilled bowl. Beat until soft peaks form, using an electric mixer at high speed. Fold egg white mixture into whipped milk.

When coffee mixture mounds slightly when dropped from a spoon, fold into egg white-whipped milk mixture.

Chill in refrigerator until mixture mounds well when spooned. Turn into 2-Egg White Meringue Pie Shell.

Chill in refrigerator 3 hours, or until set. Makes 8 servings.

Minty Refrigerator Pie

This chiffon version of the classic grasshopper pie
is served in a pastry shell and topped with shaved chocolate.

1 env. unflavored gelatin
¼ c. cold water
¼ c. creme de cacao
¼ c. creme de menthe
2 c. heavy cream, whipped
1 egg white

Dash of salt
2 tblsp. sugar
¼ c. light corn syrup
Baked 9″ pie shell
1 (1-oz.) square semisweet
  chocolate, shaved

Sprinkle gelatin over cold water to soften.

Combine creme de cacao and creme de menthe in small saucepan.
Cook over low heat until mixture comes to a boil. Remove from heat.
Add softened gelatin, stirring until dissolved. Cool at room temperature
until lukewarm.

Fold gelatin mixture into whipped cream.

Chill in refrigerator while preparing egg white mixture.

Beat egg white and salt in bowl until foamy, using an electric mixer at
high speed. Gradually add sugar, 1 tblsp. at a time, beating well after each
addition. Continue beating until mixture is smooth and glossy. Gradually
add corn syrup, 1 tblsp. at a time, beating well after each addition. Continue beating until stiff, glossy peaks form when beaters are slowly lifted.
Fold egg white mixture into whipped cream-gelatin mixture.

Chill in refrigerator until mixture mounds well when spooned. Turn into baked pie shell.

Chill in refrigerator several hours, or until set.

To serve, decorate with shaved chocolate. Makes 6 to 8 servings.

Peppermint Chiffon Pie

A fluffy pink peppermint filling in a chocolate cookie crust
is a combination that's popular with children as well as older folks.

1 (10½-oz.) pkg.
  miniature marshmallows
1 c. milk
¾ tsp. peppermint extract
8 drops red food coloring
3 egg whites
⅓ c. sugar

1 c. heavy cream, whipped
Chocolate Cookie Crust
  (see Index)
Sweetened whipped cream
Chocolate Leaves
  (recipe follows)

Cook marshmallows and milk in 3-qt. saucepan over medium heat, stirring constantly, until marshmallows are melted. Remove from heat. Stir in peppermint extract and food coloring. Pour into a metal bowl.

Chill in refrigerator until mixture begins to thicken, stirring occasionally.

Remove peppermint mixture from refrigerator and immediately beat egg whites in bowl until foamy, using an electric mixer at high speed. Gradually add sugar, 1 tblsp. at a time, beating well after each addition. Continue beating until stiff, glossy peaks form when beaters are slowly lifted.

Fold peppermint mixture into egg white mixture. Fold egg white-peppermint mixture into whipped cream.

Chill in refrigerator until mixture mounds well when spooned. Turn into Chocolate Cookie Crust.

Chill in refrigerator 8 hours, or until set.

Prepare Chocolate Leaves while pie is chilling.

To serve, pipe sweetened whipped cream around edge of pie or decorate with puffs of sweetened whipped cream. Decorate with Chocolate Leaves. Makes 6 to 8 servings.

Chocolate Leaves: Melt ½ c. semisweet chocolate pieces in small saucepan over low heat. Spread chocolate thinly over waxed paper-lined baking sheet. Let stand at room temperature until set. Cut into leaf shapes, using a small cookie cutter or sharp knife.

Chocolate Marshmallow Pie

From Oklahoma, a pie with just the right amount of chocolate to give it a good flavor and still be light enough for warm weather.

30 large marshmallows	1 (1-oz.) square
½ c. milk	unsweetened chocolate
1 c. heavy cream,	9" Graham Cracker Crust
whipped	(see Index)

Combine marshmallows and milk in top of double boiler. Heat over simmering water, stirring occasionally, until marshmallows are melted. Remove from heat. Cool well.

Fold marshmallow mixture into whipped cream. Coarsely grate chocolate. Fold chocolate into whipped cream mixture. Turn into Graham Cracker Crust.

Chill in refrigerator 2 hours, or until set. Makes 6 to 8 servings.

White Christmas Pie

This snowy white chiffon pie has a hint of almond;
it's decorated with coconut, whipped cream and maraschino cherries.

1 env. unflavored gelatin
¼ c. cold water
½ c. sugar
4 tblsp. flour
½ tsp. salt
1½ c. milk
¾ tsp. vanilla
¼ tsp. almond extract
½ c. heavy cream, whipped

3 egg whites
¼ tsp. cream of tartar
½ c. sugar
1½ c. flaked coconut
Baked 9" pie shell
Sweetened whipped cream
Red and green maraschino
    cherries

Sprinkle gelatin over cold water to soften.

Combine ½ c. sugar, flour and salt in 2-qt. saucepan. Gradually add milk, stirring well. Cook over medium heat, stirring constantly, until mixture comes to a boil. Cook 1 minute more. Remove from heat. Add softened gelatin, vanilla and almond extract, stirring until gelatin dissolves. Pour into a metal bowl. Cool at room temperature until mixture is partially set.

Fold whipped cream into custard mixture.

Beat egg whites and cream of tartar in bowl until foamy, using an electric mixer at high speed. Gradually add ½ c. sugar, 1 tblsp. at a time, beating well after each addition. Continue beating until stiff, glossy peaks form when beaters are slowly lifted. Fold whipped cream-custard mixture into egg white mixture. Fold in 1 c. of the coconut.

Chill in refrigerator until mixture mounds well when spooned. Turn into baked pie shell. Sprinkle with remaining ½ c. coconut.

Chill in refrigerator until set.

To serve, decorate with puffs of sweetened whipped cream and red and green maraschino cherries. Makes 6 to 8 servings.

Vanilla Cloud Pies

These light-as-air white pies, topped with a sprinkle
of chocolate cookie crumbs, are ideal to serve at a party.

Chocolate Wafer Crusts (recipe follows)	4 eggs, separated
1 env. plus 1 tsp. unflavored gelatin	1⅓ c. milk
¼ c. cold water	1 tsp. vanilla
⅔ c. sugar	¼ tsp. almond extract
	1 c. heavy cream, whipped

Prepare Chocolate Wafer Crusts, reserving 2 tblsp. of the crumbs for topping.

Sprinkle gelatin over cold water to soften.

Combine sugar and slightly beaten egg yolks in 2-qt. saucepan. Stir in milk. Cook over medium heat, stirring constantly, until mixture thickens and coats a metal spoon, about 5 minutes. Remove from heat. Add softened gelatin, vanilla and almond extract, stirring until gelatin dissolves. Pour into a metal bowl. Place bowl in larger bowl filled with iced water. Gently stir until mixture is cooled.

Remove from iced water and immediately beat egg whites in bowl until stiff peaks form, using an electric mixer at high speed. Fold egg whites into cooled custard mixture. Fold whipped cream into egg white-custard mixture. Chill in refrigerator until mixture mounds well when spooned. Pour filling evenly into Chocolate Wafer Crusts. Sprinkle each with reserved crumbs.

Chill in refrigerator until set. Makes 2 pies, 6 to 8 servings each.

Chocolate Wafer Crusts: Crush 1 (8½-oz.) pkg. chocolate wafers into fine crumbs. Reserve 2 tblsp. crumbs for topping. Combine remaining crumbs and ½ c. butter or regular margarine (melted) in bowl; mix well. Press mixture evenly into bottom and up sides of 2 (9″) pie plates. Bake in 375° oven 6 to 8 minutes, or until set. Cool on racks.

Chocolate Chiffon Pie

Sent to us by a Texas farm woman, this pie is light as a cloud, but it has a good strong chocolate flavor and a creamy texture.

1 env. unflavored gelatin
3 tblsp. cold water
1 (6-oz.) pkg. semisweet
   chocolate pieces
½ c. milk
⅓ c. sugar
½ tsp. salt
1 c. milk

3 eggs, separated
1 tsp. vanilla
¼ tsp. cream of tartar
⅓ c. sugar
Baked 9″ pie shell
   with fluted edge
Sweetened whipped cream
Chocolate jimmies

Sprinkle gelatin over cold water to soften.

Combine chocolate pieces and ½ c. milk in 2-qt. saucepan. Cook over low heat until chocolate melts. Stir until smooth. Remove from heat. Stir in ⅓ c. sugar, salt, 1 c. milk and slightly beaten egg yolks. Cook over low heat, stirring constantly, until mixture is slightly thickened. Remove from heat. Add softened gelatin and vanilla, stirring until gelatin dissolves. Pour into a metal bowl.

Chill in refrigerator, stirring occasionally, until mixture is the consistency of unbeaten egg whites.

Remove chocolate mixture from refrigerator and immediately beat egg whites and cream of tartar in bowl until foamy, using an electric mixer at high speed. Gradually add ⅓ c. sugar, 1 tblsp. at a time, beating well after each addition. Continue beating until stiff, glossy peaks form when beaters are slowly lifted.

When chocolate mixture mounds slightly when dropped from a spoon, fold into egg white mixture.

Chill in refrigerator until mixture mounds well when spooned. Turn into baked pie shell.

Chill in refrigerator 1 hour, or until set.

To serve, top with puffs of sweetened whipped cream and sprinkle with chocolate jimmies. Makes 6 to 8 servings.

Divine Triple-Chocolate Pie

The chocolate filling is poured into a chocolate pie shell
and decorated with whipped cream and even more chocolate.

Chocolate Pie Shell
  (recipe follows)
1/4 c. sugar
1 env. unflavored gelatin
1/4 tsp. salt
1 c. milk
3 eggs, separated
3 (1-oz.) squares
  unsweetened chocolate,
  cut up

1/2 tsp. vanilla
1/4 tsp. cream of tartar
1/4 c. sugar
1 c. heavy cream, whipped
Sweetened whipped cream
1/2 (1-oz.) square
  semisweet chocolate

Prepare Chocolate Pie Shell and set aside.

Stir together 1/4 c. sugar, gelatin and salt in 2-qt. saucepan. Stir in milk and slightly beaten egg yolks. Add 3 squares unsweetened chocolate. Cook over low heat, stirring constantly, until chocolate melts and gelatin dissolves. Remove from heat. Stir in vanilla.

Chill in refrigerator, stirring occasionally, until mixture is the consistency of unbeaten egg whites.

Remove chocolate mixture from refrigerator and immediately beat egg whites and cream of tartar in bowl until foamy, using an electric mixer at high speed. Gradually add 1/4 c. sugar, 1 tblsp. at a time, beating well after each addition. Continue beating until stiff, glossy peaks form when beaters are slowly lifted.

When chocolate mixture mounds slightly when dropped from a spoon, beat until smooth, using an electric mixer at medium speed. Fold egg white mixture into chocolate mixture. Then fold in whipped cream.

Chill in refrigerator until mixture mounds well when spooned. Turn into Chocolate Pie Shell.

Chill in refrigerator 2 hours, or until set.

To serve, decorate pie with puffs of sweetened whipped cream. Grate semisweet chocolate and sprinkle over puffs of whipped cream. Makes 6 to 8 servings.

Chocolate Pie Shell: Stir together 1 c. sifted flour and 1/4 tsp. salt in bowl. Cut in 1/3 c. shortening until coarse crumbs form, using a pastry blender. Add 1/2 (1-oz.) square semisweet chocolate (grated) and 2 tblsp. cold water, tossing with a fork until dough forms. Press dough firmly into a ball. Roll out dough on floured surface to 13" circle. Loosely fit dough into 9" pie plate. Trim edge to 1" beyond rim of pie plate. Fold under edge of crust and form a ridge. Flute edge. Prick entire surface of pie shell with a fork. Bake in 400° oven 12 minutes, or until golden brown. Cool on rack.

Black Bottom Pie

A classic recipe—a layer of dark chocolate and a layer of mild, rum-flavored custard capped with whipped cream and grated chocolate.

1 env. unflavored gelatin
3 tblsp. cold water
½ c. sugar
2 tblsp. cornstarch
¼ tsp. salt
2 c. milk
2 eggs, separated
2 tsp. rum flavoring or
   3 tblsp. rum
¼ tsp. cream of tartar

⅓ c. sugar
1 (1-oz.) square
   unsweetened chocolate,
   melted and cooled
¼ tsp. vanilla
Vanilla Wafer Crumb Crust
   (see Index)
1 c. heavy cream, whipped
Grated semisweet chocolate

Sprinkle gelatin over cold water to soften.

Combine ½ c. sugar, cornstarch and salt in 2-qt. saucepan. Stir in milk and slightly beaten egg yolks. Cook over medium heat, stirring constantly, until mixture comes to a boil. Remove from heat. Remove 1 c. custard mixture and set aside. Add softened gelatin and rum flavoring to remaining custard mixture, stirring until gelatin dissolves. Pour into a metal bowl.

Chill in refrigerator until mixture mounds slightly when dropped from a spoon.

Remove custard mixture from refrigerator and immediately beat egg whites and cream of tartar in bowl until foamy, using an electric mixer at high speed. Gradually add ⅓ c. sugar, 1 tblsp. at a time, beating well after each addition. Continue beating until stiff, glossy peaks form when beaters are slowly lifted. Fold custard mixture into egg white mixture.

Chill in refrigerator until mixture mounds well when spooned.

Blend together melted chocolate, vanilla and 1 c. reserved custard mixture. Spread over bottom of Vanilla Wafer Crumb Crust. Spread egg white-custard mixture over chocolate layer.

Chill in refrigerator 3 hours, or until set.

To serve, spread whipped cream over pie and decorate with grated chocolate. Makes 6 to 8 servings.

Light Chocolate Chiffon Pie

We created this chiffon pie for those chocolate-lovers
who have to count calories, but everyone else will enjoy it, too.

1 env. unflavored gelatin	1/8 tsp. cream of tartar
1/4 c. cold water	1 tblsp. sugar
1/3 c. semisweet	1/2 c. nonfat dry milk
chocolate pieces	1/2 c. iced water
1/4 c. water	1/8 tsp. cream of tartar
1 tsp. vanilla	9" Graham Cracker
2 egg whites	Crust (see Index)

Sprinkle gelatin over 1/4 c. cold water to soften.

Combine chocolate pieces and 1/4 c. water in top of double boiler. Cook over simmering water until chocolate melts. Add softened gelatin, stirring until dissolved. Remove from heat. Stir in vanilla.

Chill in refrigerator, stirring occasionally, until mixture is the consistency of unbeaten egg whites.

Remove chocolate mixture from refrigerator and immediately beat egg whites and 1/8 tsp. cream of tartar in bowl until foamy, using an electric mixer at high speed. Add 1 tblsp. sugar, beating until stiff, glossy peaks form when beaters are slowly lifted.

Beat together nonfat dry milk, 1/2 c. iced water and 1/8 tsp. cream of tartar in chilled bowl until soft peaks form, using an electric mixer at high speed, about 5 minutes. Fold egg white mixture into whipped milk. When chocolate mixture mounds slightly when dropped from a spoon, fold into egg white-milk mixture.

Chill in refrigerator until mixture mounds well when spooned. Turn into Graham Cracker Crust.

Chill in refrigerator until set, about 3 hours. Makes 8 servings.

Marbled Chocolate Rum Pie

The mousse-like chocolate filling of this pie, swirled
with whipped cream, tastes like vanilla and chocolate ice cream.

1/4 c. sugar	1/2 c. sugar
1 env. unflavored gelatin	1 c. heavy cream
1/8 tsp. salt	1/4 c. sugar
1 c. milk	1 tsp. vanilla
1/4 c. light rum	Baked 9" pie shell
2 eggs, separated	
1 (12-oz.) pkg. semisweet	
chocolate pieces	

Stir together ¼ c. sugar, gelatin and salt in top of double boiler. Stir in milk, rum and slightly beaten egg yolks. Cook over simmering water, stirring constantly, until sugar and gelatin dissolve, about 7 minutes. Remove from heat. Add chocolate pieces, stirring until melted.

Chill in refrigerator, stirring occasionally, until mixture is the consistency of unbeaten egg whites.

Remove chocolate mixture from refrigerator and immediately beat egg whites in bowl until foamy, using an electric mixer at high speed. Gradually add ½ c. sugar, 1 tblsp. at a time, beating well after each addition. Continue beating until stiff, glossy peaks form when beaters are slowly lifted.

When chocolate mixture mounds slightly when dropped from a spoon, fold into egg white mixture.

Chill in refrigerator until mixture mounds well when spooned.

Combine heavy cream, ¼ c. sugar and vanilla in chilled bowl. Beat until soft peaks form, using an electric mixer at high speed.

Alternate spoonfuls of chocolate mixture and whipped cream in baked pie shell. Swirl with a spoon to give marbled effect.

Chill in refrigerator until set. Makes 6 to 8 servings.

German Chocolate Mallow Pie

An Iowa homemaker shared this recipe for her favorite special-occasion dessert—it's simple to make and looks elegant.

2 oz. sweet cooking
   chocolate (½ bar)
35 large marshmallows
¾ c. milk
1 c. heavy cream

1 tsp. vanilla
9" Graham Cracker Crust
   (see Index)
Sweetened whipped cream
Chocolate curls

Combine chocolate, marshmallows and milk in top of double boiler. Heat over simmering water, stirring occasionally, until marshmallows and chocolate are melted. Remove from heat; cool well.

Whip heavy cream with vanilla in chilled bowl until soft peaks form, using an electric mixer at high speed. Fold chocolate mixture into whipped cream. Pour into Graham Cracker Crust.

Chill in refrigerator 3 hours, or until set.

To serve, decorate with sweetened whipped cream and chocolate curls. Makes 6 to 8 servings.

Chocolate Candy Pie

It's hard to believe that something as rich and luscious
as this creamy milk-chocolate pie can be so simple to make.

25 large marshmallows	*1 (8-oz.) milk chocolate*
½ c. milk	*almond bar*
1 c. heavy cream, whipped	*Baked 9″ pie shell*

Combine marshmallows and milk in top of double boiler. Heat over simmering water, stirring occasionally, until marshmallows are melted. Remove from heat. Cool completely.

Fold cooled marshmallow mixture into whipped cream. Coarsely grate chocolate bar. Fold chocolate into whipped cream mixture. Turn into baked pie shell.

Chill in refrigerator 2 hours, or until set. Makes 6 to 8 servings.

Orange Marshmallow Pie

There are just two steps to making this easy filling:
melt the marshmallow mixture and fold in the cream, and it's done.

Orange Pastry Shell	*6 tblsp. orange juice*
(recipe follows)	*2 tblsp. lemon juice*
1 (10½-oz.) bag	*1 tblsp. grated orange rind*
miniature marshmallows	*2 c. heavy cream, whipped*

Prepare Orange Pastry Shell and set aside.

Combine marshmallows, orange juice and lemon juice in top of double boiler. Heat over simmering water, stirring occasionally, until marshmallows are melted and mixture is smooth. Remove from heat. Stir in orange rind. Cool to lukewarm.

Fold whipped cream into cooled filling. Turn into Orange Pastry Shell. Chill in refrigerator until set. Makes 6 to 8 servings.

Orange Pastry Shell: Combine 1½ c. sifted flour, 1 tblsp. sugar, ½ tsp. salt, 1 tsp. grated orange rind and ⅓ c. ground almonds in bowl. Cut in ½ c. shortening until mixture forms coarse crumbs, using a pastry blender. Sprinkle 4 to 5 tblsp. orange juice over crumb mixture, a little at a time, mixing with a fork until dough forms. Press dough firmly into a ball. Roll out pastry on floured surface to 13″ circle. Line 9″ pie plate with pastry. Trim edge to 1″ beyond rim of pie plate. Fold under edge of crust and form a ridge. Flute edge. Prick bottom and sides of crust with a fork. Bake in 400° oven 12 minutes, or until golden brown. Cool on rack.

Prune Marshmallow Pie

The mocha-flavored marshmallow filling is flecked
with chopped, cooked prunes. A different combination, and a good one.

20 large marshmallows
¾ c. milk
2 tsp. instant coffee powder
⅛ tsp. salt
½ tsp. chocolate extract

1 c. heavy cream, whipped
1 c. finely chopped, cooked
  prunes
Baked 8″ pie shell
  with fluted edge

Combine marshmallows, milk, coffee powder and salt in 2-qt. saucepan. Heat over low heat, stirring constantly, until marshmallows are melted. Remove from heat. Stir in chocolate extract and pour into a metal bowl.

Chill in refrigerator until mixture thickens slightly. Fold whipped cream and prunes into chocolate mixture. Pour into baked pie shell.

Chill in refrigerator 4 to 6 hours, or until set. Makes 6 servings.

Marshmallow Cream Peach Pie

This peachy marshmallow and cream pie is so easy
that even a child can make it with just a little help from an adult.

18 large marshmallows
¼ c. milk
1 c. heavy cream, whipped
3 c. diced, pared peaches
  (5 to 6 medium)

9″ Graham Cracker Crust
  (see Index)

Combine marshmallows and milk in top of double boiler. Heat over simmering water, stirring occasionally, until marshmallows are melted. Remove from heat. Cool at room temperature until mixture begins to set.

Beat marshmallow mixture until smooth, using a rotary beater. Fold marshmallow mixture into whipped cream. Then fold in peaches. Pour into Graham Cracker Crust.

Chill in refrigerator until set. Makes 6 to 8 servings.

Lemon Cheese Pie

Meringue folded into the cream cheese filling makes this lemon-flavored pie light and airy. Just right for a light dessert.

¾ c. sugar
¼ c. cornstarch
1 c. water
2 eggs, separated
⅓ c. lemon juice

1 tsp. grated lemon rind
1 (3-oz.) pkg. cream cheese, softened
¼ c. sugar
Baked 9" pie shell

Combine ¾ c. sugar and cornstarch in 2-qt. saucepan. Gradually add water, stirring well. Beat egg yolks slightly, using a fork. Stir egg yolks into cornstarch mixture. Cook over low heat, stirring constantly, until mixture comes to a boil. Cook 1 minute more. Remove from heat. Gently stir in lemon juice and lemon rind.

Beat cream cheese in bowl until smooth, using an electric mixer at medium speed. Gradually stir cream cheese into egg yolk mixture.

Beat egg whites in another bowl until foamy, using an electric mixer at high speed. Gradually add ¼ c. sugar, 1 tblsp. at a time, beating well after each addition. Continue beating until stiff, glossy peaks form when beaters are slowly lifted. Fold egg white mixture into cream cheese mixture. Turn into baked pie shell.

Chill in refrigerator 3 hours, or until firm. Makes 6 to 8 servings.

Glazed Apple Cheese Pie

A fruit and cheese pie with the apples sliced nice and thick, then arranged over the cream cheese and glazed with their own syrup.

2 (3-oz.) pkg. cream cheese, softened
2 tblsp. sugar
½ tsp. grated lemon rind
Baked 9" pie shell
1 c. water
½ c. sugar

1 tblsp. lemon juice
4 medium apples, pared, cored and cut into eighths
1 tblsp. cornstarch
1 tblsp. water
⅛ tsp. ground nutmeg

Combine cream cheese, 2 tblsp. sugar and lemon rind in bowl. Beat until smooth and creamy, using an electric mixer at medium speed. Spread cream cheese mixture evenly over bottom of baked pie shell.

Chill in refrigerator 30 minutes.

Meanwhile, combine 1 c. water, ½ c. sugar and lemon juice in 12" skillet. Cook over high heat until mixture comes to a boil. Add apples. Reduce heat to low and simmer, uncovered, 8 to 10 minutes, or until tender, turning and basting apples frequently. Remove apples from syrup and set aside.

Combine cornstarch, 1 tblsp. water and nutmeg in bowl; stir until blended. Stir into syrup. Cook over medium heat, stirring constantly, until mixture boils. Cook 1 minute more. Remove from heat.

Arrange apples on top of cream cheese layer. Pour warm glaze evenly over apples.

Chill in refrigerator at least 2 hours before serving. Makes 6 to 8 servings.

Two-tiered Strawberry Pie

A lovely springtime dessert of fresh whole strawberries
in a grenadine sauce spooned over a filling of cream cheese.

1 (3-oz.) pkg. cream cheese,
  softened
½ c. sifted confectioners'
  sugar
½ tsp. vanilla
¼ tsp. almond extract
½ c. heavy cream, whipped
Baked 9″ pie shell

⅓ c. sugar
2 tblsp. cornstarch
⅓ c. water
⅓ c. grenadine syrup
1 tblsp. lemon juice
1 pt. fresh strawberries,
  hulled

Beat cream cheese in bowl until smooth, using an electric mixer at medium speed. Gradually add confectioners' sugar, vanilla and almond extract, beating until smooth and creamy. Fold whipped cream into cream cheese mixture and spread over bottom of baked pie shell.

Chill in refrigerator several hours.

Combine sugar and cornstarch in 2-qt. saucepan. Gradually stir in water, grenadine syrup and lemon juice. Cook over medium heat, stirring constantly, until mixture is thick and clear. Remove from heat; cool to room temperature.

Stir strawberries into cornstarch mixture. Spoon strawberry mixture over top of chilled cheese layer.

Chill in refrigerator until serving time. Makes 8 servings.

Glazed Strawberry Cream Pie

This pie needs no flavoring—three cupfuls of fresh strawberries
make their own syrup, and the naturally good fruit flavor comes through.

Golden Baked Pie Shell
  (recipe follows)
3 c. sliced fresh strawberries
1½ c. sifted confectioners'
  sugar
2 (3-oz.) pkg. cream cheese,
  softened

1 tsp. vanilla
1 c. heavy cream, whipped
Water
2 tsp. cornstarch
3 drops red food coloring
1 drop yellow food
  coloring

Prepare Golden Baked Pie Shell and set aside.

Combine strawberries and ½ c. of the sifted confectioners' sugar in bowl. Let stand 30 minutes.

Beat cream cheese in bowl until smooth, using an electric mixer at medium speed. Gradually add remaining 1 c. confectioners' sugar, beating until smooth and creamy. Beat in vanilla. Fold cream cheese mixture into whipped cream. Turn into pie shell.

Chill in refrigerator.

Drain strawberries, reserving juice. Add enough water to juice to make ⅓ c. Combine ⅓ c. juice, cornstarch, red and yellow food coloring in small saucepan. Cook over medium heat, stirring constantly, until mixture boils and thickens.

Remove from heat. Cool slightly. Combine strawberries and cornstarch mixture in bowl; mix gently. Spoon strawberry mixture over filling.

Chill in refrigerator at least 2 hours before serving. Makes 6 to 8 servings.

Golden Baked Pie Shell: Combine 1¼ c. sifted flour and ¼ c. sugar in bowl. Cut in ½ c. butter or regular margarine until fine crumbs form, using a pastry blender. Knead with hands until dough forms. Press dough into bottom and up sides of 9" pie plate. Bake in 325° oven 25 minutes, or until golden brown. Cool on rack.

French Blueberry Pie

Blueberries and more blueberries—a double-decker pie
with a base of lemon-flavored cream cheese in a pastry shell.

2 (3-oz.) pkg. cream cheese, softened
2 tblsp. milk
1 tsp. grated lemon rind
Baked 9" pie shell
2 pt. fresh blueberries

1 tblsp. lemon juice
⅛ tsp. salt
Water
1 c. sugar
2 tblsp. cornstarch

Beat cream cheese in bowl until smooth, using an electric mixer at medium speed. Gradually add milk and lemon rind, beating well. Spread cream cheese mixture evenly in bottom of baked pie shell.

Sprinkle half of the blueberries over cream cheese layer.

Mash remaining blueberries. Stir in lemon juice and salt. Add enough water to blueberry mixture to make 1½ c.

Combine sugar and cornstarch in small saucepan. Stir in blueberry mixture. Cook over medium heat, stirring constantly, until mixture comes to a boil. Cook 2 minutes more. Remove from heat; cool to lukewarm.

Spoon blueberry sauce over blueberries in pie shell.

Chill in refrigerator several hours before serving. Makes 8 servings.

Raspberry Ribbon Pie

There's a red ribbon of raspberries running through the rich, cream cheese filling of this easy-to-make pie.

1 (3-oz.) pkg. raspberry-
　flavored gelatin
¼ c. sugar
1¼ c. boiling water
1 (10-oz.) pkg. frozen
　raspberries
1 tblsp. lemon juice
1 (3-oz.) pkg. cream cheese,
　softened

⅓ c. sifted confectioners'
　sugar
1 tsp. vanilla
1 c. heavy cream
9″ Graham Cracker Crust
　(see Index)

Dissolve raspberry gelatin and sugar in boiling water in bowl. Add raspberries and stir until thawed. Stir in lemon juice.

Chill in refrigerator until mixture is very thick or almost set.

Combine cream cheese, confectioners' sugar and vanilla in bowl. Beat until smooth and creamy, using an electric mixer at medium speed.

Gradually add heavy cream, beating until soft peaks form, using an electric mixer at high speed. Spread half of the cream cheese mixture over the bottom of Graham Cracker Crust. Carefully spoon half of the raspberry mixture over cream cheese layer. Repeat layers.

Chill in refrigerator until set. Makes 6 to 8 servings.

Chocolate Cheese Pie

Very rich—a superb blend of chocolate and cream cheese
with a velvet-smooth texture in a chocolate graham cracker crust.

Chocolate Graham Crust
 (recipe follows)
1 (6-oz.) pkg. semisweet
 chocolate pieces
1 (8-oz.) pkg. cream cheese,
 softened

¾ c. brown sugar, packed
⅛ tsp. salt
1 tsp. vanilla
2 eggs, separated
1 c. heavy cream, whipped

Prepare Chocolate Graham Crust and set aside.

Melt chocolate pieces in top of double boiler over hot water. Remove from heat and cool 10 minutes.

Beat cream cheese in bowl until smooth, using an electric mixer at medium speed. Gradually add ½ c. of the brown sugar, salt and vanilla, blending well. Add egg yolks, one at a time, beating well after each addition. Beat in cooled chocolate.

Beat egg whites in another bowl until foamy, using an electric mixer at high speed. Gradually add remaining ¼ c. brown sugar, 1 tblsp. at a time, beating well after each addition. Continue beating until stiff, glossy peaks form when beaters are slowly lifted.

Fold chocolate mixture into egg white mixture. Then fold in whipped cream. Turn into Chocolate Graham Crust, reserving one fourth of the mixture for decorating.

Chill pie and reserved mixture in refrigerator until slightly set. Drop reserved mixture in mounds over top of pie, using a spoon.

Chill in refrigerator overnight. Makes 6 to 8 servings.

Chocolate Graham Crust: Combine 1½ c. graham cracker crumbs, ¼ c. brown sugar (packed), ⅛ tsp. ground nutmeg, ⅓ c. butter or regular margarine (melted) and 1 (1-oz.) square unsweetened chocolate (melted and cooled) in bowl. Mix thoroughly. Press mixture into bottom and up sides of 9" pie plate. Chill in refrigerator until firm.

Lemon Angel Pie

Tangy lemon custard blanketed with real whipped cream
in a delicate meringue shell—a combination that's simply heavenly.

¾ c. sugar
3 tblsp. cornstarch
¼ tsp. salt
3 egg yolks
¼ c. water
1 tblsp. butter or
 regular margarine

⅓ c. lemon juice
1¼ tsp. grated lemon rind
3-Egg White Meringue Pie
 Shell (see Index)
1 c. heavy cream, whipped

Combine sugar, cornstarch and salt in 2-qt. saucepan. Beat together egg yolks and water in bowl, using a rotary beater. Add egg yolk mixture to cornstarch mixture, blending well. Cook over medium heat, stirring constantly, until mixture comes to a boil. Cook 1 minute more. Remove from heat. Gently stir in butter, lemon juice and lemon rind. Cool to room temperature.

Spoon cooled lemon filling into 3-Egg White Meringue Pie Shell.

Chill in refrigerator 12 hours or overnight.

To serve, spread whipped cream over pie. Makes 8 servings.

Chocolate-Cinnamon Pie

A crispy thin meringue crust cradles this pie filling
of rich cocoa butter cream lightened with fluffy whipped topping.

½ c. butter or regular margarine	½ c. milk
¾ c. sugar	½ tsp. vanilla
½ c. plus 2 tblsp. baking cocoa	2-Egg White Meringue Pie Shell (see Index)
1 tsp. ground cinnamon	1 (1-oz.) square
2 eggs	semisweet chocolate
1 (2-oz.) env. whipped topping mix	

Cream together butter and sugar in bowl until light and fluffy, using an electric mixer at medium speed. Add baking cocoa and cinnamon; blend well. Add eggs, one at a time, beating well after each addition.

Prepare whipped topping mix with milk and vanilla according to package directions. Fold prepared whipped topping into cocoa mixture. Turn into 2-Egg White Meringue Pie Shell.

Chill in refrigerator 2 hours, or until set.

Cut semisweet chocolate into shavings, using a vegetable peeler.

To serve, sprinkle with chocolate shavings. Makes 6 to 8 servings.

Chocolate-Orange Meringue Pie

Light and colorful, with grated chocolate as a garnish
and a surprise layer of chocolate under the orange custard filling.

Thick Meringue Shell (recipe follows)	2 tblsp. orange juice
½ c. sugar	1 tblsp. lemon juice
½ tsp. salt	2 (1-oz.) milk chocolate bars
4 egg yolks, beaten	1 c. heavy cream, whipped

Prepare Thick Meringue Shell and set aside.

Combine sugar, salt, egg yolks, orange juice and lemon juice in small saucepan. Cook over low heat, stirring constantly, until mixture thickens. Remove from heat. Cool well.

Grate 1 chocolate bar. Sprinkle over bottom of Thick Meringue Shell. Spread half of the whipped cream evenly over chocolate. Cover with cooled filling. Top with remaining whipped cream. Grate remaining chocolate bar and sprinkle on top.

Chill in refrigerator 8 hours or overnight. Makes 6 to 8 servings.

Thick Meringue Shell: Beat 4 egg whites in bowl until foamy, using an electric mixer at high speed. Add ¼ tsp. cream of tartar. Gradually add ¾ c. sugar, beating until stiff, glossy peaks form. Spread meringue in bottom and up sides of well-greased 9" pie plate. Bake in 275° oven 1 hour, or until light beige and crisp to the touch. Turn off heat and leave shell in oven with door open 30 minutes more. Remove from oven and cool on rack.

Cream-filled Meringue Pie

This crisp and nut-like meringue shell, piled high
with a cloud of whipped cream, is the height of simple elegance.

Pecan Meringue Shell	*3 tblsp. sugar*
(recipe follows)	*1 tsp. vanilla*
1½ c. heavy cream	*¼ c. chopped pecans*

Prepare Pecan Meringue Shell and set aside.

Whip heavy cream, sugar and vanilla in chilled bowl until soft peaks form, using an electric mixer at high speed. Spread cream mixture in Pecan Meringue Shell. Sprinkle with pecans.

Chill in refrigerator until serving time. Makes 6 to 8 servings.

Pecan Meringue Shell: Beat 3 egg whites and ½ tsp. cream of tartar in bowl until foamy, using an electric mixer at high speed. Gradually add 1 c. sugar, 1 tblsp. at a time, beating well after each addition. Continue beating until stiff, glossy peaks form. Beat in 2 tsp. vanilla. Fold in ½ c. unsalted soda cracker crumbs and 1 c. ground pecans. Spread meringue mixture in bottom and up sides of well-greased 9" pie plate. Bake in 350° oven 40 minutes, or until delicately browned. Cool on rack.

Snow-capped Chocolate Pie

The wonderful thing about this pie is the crust—it's a deliciously chewy meringue crust made with chocolate and chopped pecans.

3 egg whites	1 c. buttery cracker crumbs
1 tsp. vanilla	½ c. chopped pecans
¾ c. sugar	1 c. heavy cream
1 tsp. baking powder	2 tblsp. sugar
1 (4-oz.) bar sweet cooking chocolate, grated	1 tsp. vanilla

Beat egg whites and 1 tsp. vanilla in bowl until foamy, using an electric mixer at high speed. Gradually add ¾ c. sugar, 1 tblsp. at a time, beating well after each addition. Add baking powder and continue beating until stiff, glossy peaks form.

Reserve 2 tblsp. grated chocolate for topping. Fold remaining grated chocolate, cracker crumbs and pecans into egg white mixture. Spread in bottom and up sides of well-greased 9" pie plate.

Bake in 325° oven 25 minutes, or until lightly browned. Cool on rack.

Whip heavy cream in bowl until it begins to thicken, using an electric mixer at high speed. Gradually add 2 tblsp. sugar and 1 tsp. vanilla, beating until soft peaks form. Turn into meringue shell. Sprinkle with reserved 2 tblsp. grated chocolate.

Chill in refrigerator 6 to 8 hours or overnight. Makes 6 to 8 servings.

Creamy Choco-Nut Pie

This is a good company dessert, because it's pretty, easy to make ahead of time and has a wonderful chocolaty flavor.

1 env. unflavored gelatin	1 tsp. vanilla
1½ c. milk	1 c. heavy cream, whipped
½ c. sugar	Baked 9" pie shell
⅛ tsp. salt	with fluted edge
1 (6-oz.) pkg. semisweet chocolate pieces	Sweetened whipped cream
	Walnut halves

Sprinkle gelatin over milk in 2-qt. saucepan to soften, 5 minutes.

Add sugar, salt and chocolate pieces. Cook over medium heat, stirring constantly, until chocolate is melted. Remove from heat; pour into a metal bowl. Beat until mixture is smooth, using a rotary beater. Stir in vanilla.

Chill in refrigerator until mixture mounds slightly when dropped from a spoon.

Fold chocolate mixture into whipped cream. Turn into baked pie shell.

Chill in refrigerator 3 hours, or until set.

To serve, decorate with puffs of sweetened whipped cream and walnut halves. Makes 6 to 8 servings.

Meringue Crunch Pie

Macaroons, dates and pecans make the crisp meringue shell
for this pie very chewy. It's filled with almond-flavored whipped cream.

1 c. sugar	1 c. chopped pecans
½ tsp. baking powder	10 almond macaroons,
½ tsp. salt	crumbled
3 egg whites	1 c. heavy cream
10 pitted dates, cut up	1 tblsp. sugar
1 tblsp. flour	½ tsp. almond extract

Combine 1 c. sugar, baking powder and salt; mix well.

Beat egg whites in bowl until foamy, using an electric mixer at high speed. Gradually add sugar mixture, 1 tblsp. at a time, beating well after each addition. Continue beating until stiff, glossy peaks form.

Combine dates and flour in bowl; toss to coat. Fold dates, pecans and macaroon crumbs into egg white mixture. Spread in bottom and up sides of well-greased 9″ pie plate.

Bake in 350° oven 30 minutes, or until lightly browned. Cool on rack.

Whip heavy cream in chilled bowl until it begins to thicken, using an electric mixer at high speed. Gradually add 1 tblsp. sugar and almond extract, beating until soft peaks form. Turn into meringue shell.

Chill in refrigerator until serving time. Makes 6 to 8 servings.

Heavenly Chocolate Angel Pie

A special-occasion dessert with layers of cinnamon-flavored
chocolate and whipped cream turned into a pecan meringue shell.

Nutty Meringue Pie Shell	¼ c. water
(recipe follows)	¼ tsp. ground cinnamon
1 (6-oz.) pkg. semisweet	1 c. heavy cream
chocolate pieces	¼ c. sugar
2 egg yolks	½ tsp. vanilla

Prepare Nutty Meringue Pie Shell and set aside.

Melt chocolate pieces in top of double boiler over hot water. Beat egg yolks slightly, using a fork. Add egg yolks, water and cinnamon to chocolate; blend well. Remove from heat; cool slightly.

Spread ½ c. of the chocolate mixture over bottom of Nutty Meringue Pie Shell.

Chill pie shell in refrigerator. Chill remaining chocolate mixture in refrigerator until it begins to thicken.

Whip heavy cream in chilled bowl until it begins to thicken, using an electric mixer at high speed. Gradually add sugar and vanilla, beating until soft peaks form. Spread half of the whipped cream over chocolate layer in pie shell.

Fold remaining chocolate mixture into remaining whipped cream. Spread evenly over whipped cream layer in pie shell.

Chill in refrigerator 4 hours, or until set. Makes 6 to 8 servings.

Nutty Meringue Pie Shell: Combine 2 egg whites, ½ tsp. vinegar, ¼ tsp. ground cinnamon and ¼ tsp. salt in bowl. Beat until foamy, using an electric mixer at high speed. Gradually add ½ c. sugar, 1 tblsp. at a time, beating well after each addition. Continue beating until stiff, glossy peaks form. Fold in ½ c. chopped pecans and ½ tsp. vanilla. Spread meringue in bottom and up sides of well-greased 9" pie plate. Bake in 325° oven 1 hour, or until golden brown. Cool on rack.

Fluffy Chocolate Pie

A North Carolina woman has traced the origin of this
cloud-like chocolate chiffon pie back to the Roaring Twenties.

1 c. evaporated milk	1 tsp. vanilla
1 env. unflavored gelatin	Baked 9" pie shell
¼ c. cold water	1 c. heavy cream
¾ c. sugar	2 tblsp. sugar
½ c. milk	1 tsp. vanilla
⅛ tsp. salt	½ (1-oz.) square
1 egg yolk, beaten	semisweet chocolate,
3 (1-oz.) squares unsweetened	melted and cooled
chocolate, melted and cooled	

Pour evaporated milk into freezer tray. Freeze until partially frozen around edges. Meanwhile, chill small bowl and beaters.

Sprinkle gelatin over cold water to soften; set aside.

Combine ¾ c. sugar, milk and salt in top of double boiler. Cook over simmering water until milk is hot and sugar is dissolved. Stir some of hot mixture into egg yolk. Then stir all of egg yolk mixture into hot milk mixture. Cook 2 minutes over simmering water, stirring constantly. Stir in softened gelatin, 3 squares cooled unsweetened chocolate and 1 tsp. vanilla. Remove from heat.

Chill in refrigerator until mixture thickens and mounds slightly when dropped from a spoon.

Whip partially frozen evaporated milk in chilled bowl until stiff peaks form, using an electric mixer at high speed. Fold chocolate mixture into whipped milk. Turn into baked pie shell.

Chill in refrigerator 2 hours, or until set.

Whip heavy cream in bowl until it begins to thicken. Gradually add 2 tblsp. sugar and 1 tsp. vanilla, beating until soft peaks form. Spread whipped cream over top of pie.

Drizzle ½ oz. cooled semisweet chocolate over whipped cream.

Chill in refrigerator until serving time. Makes 6 to 8 servings.

Luscious Lemon Pie

You don't need to turn on either the range or the oven
to make this simple pie. There's absolutely no cooking!

Chilled Graham Cracker
  Crust (recipe follows)
1 c. heavy cream
1 (6-oz.) can frozen lemonade
  concentrate, thawed

1 (14-oz.) can sweetened
  condensed milk
3 drops yellow food
  coloring

Prepare Chilled Graham Cracker Crust, reserving ⅓ c. crumb mixture
for topping.

Whip heavy cream in chilled bowl until soft peaks form, using an electric mixer at high speed. Slowly add lemonade concentrate, sweetened
condensed milk and food coloring, mixing well. Pour into Chilled
Graham Cracker Crust. Sprinkle with reserved crumbs.

Chill in refrigerator at least 2 hours before serving. Makes 6 to 8 servings.

Chilled Graham Cracker Crust: Combine 1½ c. graham cracker
crumbs, 3 tblsp. sugar and ⅓ c. butter or regular margarine (melted) in
bowl; mix well. Reserve ⅓ c. crumb mixture for topping. Press remaining
crumb mixture into bottom and up sides of 9" pie plate. Chill in refrigerator 1 hour, or until set.

Key Lime Pie

Truly a summertime pie, because you can make the creamy filling
and the graham cracker crust without heating up the kitchen or the cook.

1 env. unflavored gelatin
¾ c. cold water
1 (14-oz.) can sweetened
  condensed milk
½ c. fresh lime juice
1 tsp. grated lime rind

10 drops green food
  coloring
4 drops yellow food
  coloring
9" Graham Cracker Crust
  (see Index)

Sprinkle gelatin over cold water in small saucepan to soften. Let stand
5 minutes. Heat over low heat, stirring constantly, until gelatin is dissolved.

Combine gelatin, sweetened condensed milk, lime juice, lime rind and
green and yellow food coloring in bowl; mix well. Pour into Graham
Cracker Crust.

Chill in refrigerator until set. Makes 6 to 8 servings.

Strawberry Cream Pie

You can serve strawberries and cream any time of year
if you use this recipe, because it calls for frozen strawberries.

1 (10-oz.) bag frozen whole strawberries, thawed	4 drops red food coloring
Water	1 c. heavy cream
¾ c. sugar	1 tsp. sugar
2½ tblsp. cornstarch	1 tsp. vanilla
	Baked 9″ pie shell

Drain strawberries, reserving juice. Add enough water to juice to make 1 c.

Combine ¾ c. sugar and cornstarch in 2-qt. saucepan. Stir in reserved 1 c. juice and red food coloring. Cook over medium heat, stirring constantly, until mixture comes to a boil. Cook 1 minute more. Remove from heat and cool to lukewarm.

Stir in drained strawberries. Chill in refrigerator until mixture begins to thicken.

Whip heavy cream, 1 tsp. sugar and vanilla in bowl until soft peaks form, using an electric mixer at high speed. Spread whipped cream in bottom and up sides of baked pie shell. Pour chilled strawberry mixture into center.

Chill in refrigerator 2 to 3 hours, or until set. Makes 6 to 8 servings.

Open-face Cranberry Pie

A delicious holiday dessert made with cranberry juice
and cranberry sauce and spread with a layer of sweetened sour cream.

¾ c. sugar	1 c. dairy sour cream
1 env. unflavored gelatin	Baked 9″ Graham Cracker
½ tsp. salt	Crust (see Index)
1 c. cranberry juice	2 tblsp. confectioners' sugar
1 (16-oz.) can whole cranberry sauce	

Combine sugar, gelatin and salt in 2-qt. saucepan. Stir in cranberry juice and cranberry sauce. Cook over medium heat, stirring constantly, until mixture comes to a boil. Remove from heat. Pour mixture into a metal bowl.

Chill in refrigerator until mixture mounds slightly when dropped from a spoon.

Fold ½ c. of the sour cream into gelatin mixture. Pour mixture into Graham Cracker Crust. Chill in refrigerator several hours, or until set.

To serve, fold confectioners' sugar into remaining ½ c. sour cream. Spread sour cream mixture over top of pie. Makes 6 to 8 servings.

Elegant Fudge Pie

The Iowa farm woman who sent the recipe for this pie
says that it's so rich, you'll want to cut it into small wedges.

Vanilla Wafer-Pecan Crust
   (recipe follows)
¾ c. butter or
   regular margarine
1 c. sugar
2 (1-oz.) squares unsweetened
   chocolate, melted and cooled

1 tsp. vanilla
3 eggs
1 c. heavy cream
1 tblsp. sugar
½ tsp. vanilla

Prepare Vanilla Wafer-Pecan Crust and set aside.

Cream together butter and 1 c. sugar in bowl until light and fluffy, using
an electric mixer at medium speed. Beat in cooled chocolate and 1 tsp.
vanilla. Add eggs, one at a time, beating 4 minutes after each addition.
Turn into cooled Vanilla Wafer-Pecan Crust.

Chill in refrigerator 2 hours before serving.

To serve, whip heavy cream, 1 tblsp. sugar and ½ tsp. vanilla in chilled
bowl until soft peaks form, using an electric mixer at high speed. Spread
whipped cream evenly over pie. Makes 10 servings.

Vanilla Wafer-Pecan Crust: Combine 1 c. vanilla wafer crumbs (25
wafers), ½ c. finely chopped pecans and ¼ c. butter or regular margarine
(melted) in bowl; mix well. Press crumb mixture into bottom and up sides
of 9″ pie plate. Bake in 300° oven 15 minutes, or until lightly browned.
Cool on rack.

French Chocolate Pie

The best he's ever tasted, says a Missouri farmer.
Surprisingly easy, too—made with convenient frozen whipped topping.

½ c. butter or regular
   margarine, softened
¾ c. sugar
2 (1-oz.) squares
   unsweetened chocolate,
   melted and cooled

2 eggs
2 c. frozen whipped topping,
   thawed
9″ Graham Cracker Crust
   (see Index)

Combine butter, sugar and cooled chocolate in large bowl. Beat until
well blended, using an electric mixer at medium speed, about 1 to 2 minutes. Add eggs, one at a time, beating well after each addition. Fold in
whipped topping. Turn into Graham Cracker Crust.

Chill in refrigerator 4 hours, or until set. Makes 6 to 8 servings.

Bavarian Mint Pie

"Resist the temptation to garnish this pie with whipped cream," warned the Minnesota cook who sent us the recipe—"it's rich enough as is!"

½ c. butter or
   regular margarine
¾ c. sugar
3 eggs
2 (1-oz.) squares
   unsweetened chocolate,
   melted and cooled

1 (4-oz.) bar sweet
   cooking chocolate, melted
   and cooled
¼ tsp. peppermint flavoring
Vanilla Wafer Crumb Crust
   (see Index)
¼ c. chopped pecans

Cream together butter and sugar in bowl until light and fluffy, using an electric mixer at medium speed. Add eggs, one at a time, beating well after each addition. Blend in cooled unsweetened chocolate, cooled sweet cooking chocolate and peppermint flavoring. Turn into Vanilla Wafer Crumb Crust. Sprinkle with pecans.

Chill in refrigerator 3 hours, or until set. Makes 12 servings.

Choco-Mint Pie

Three favorite flavors—chocolate, vanilla and peppermint—
all together in a minty chocolate pie with a vanilla crumb crust.

½ c. butter or
   regular margarine
1½ c. sifted confectioners'
   sugar
2 (1-oz.) squares
   unsweetened chocolate,
   melted and cooled
½ tsp. vanilla

15 drops peppermint extract
2 eggs
Vanilla Wafer Crumb Crust
   (see Index)
1 c. heavy cream
2 tblsp. sugar
1 tsp. vanilla

Cream together butter and confectioners' sugar in bowl until light and fluffy, using an electric mixer at medium speed. Beat in cooled chocolate, vanilla and peppermint extract. Add eggs, one at a time, beating well after each addition. Continue beating until fluffy. Turn mixture into Vanilla Wafer Crumb Crust.

Chill in refrigerator 4 hours, or until set.

To serve, whip heavy cream, sugar and 1 tsp. vanilla in chilled bowl until soft peaks form, using an electric mixer at high speed. Swirl whipped cream over top of pie. Makes 6 to 8 servings.

Frozen Chocolate Cream Pie

An Alabama homemaker shared this easy recipe. You can stir up
the filling in almost no time; then freeze the pie till it's time to serve.

2 c. heavy cream
½ tsp. vanilla
1 c. chocolate-flavored
  syrup

Baked 9" pie shell
¼ c. chopped pecans

Whip heavy cream and vanilla in chilled bowl until soft peaks form, using an electric mixer at high speed. Carefully fold in chocolate-flavored
syrup, ¼ c. at a time. Turn into baked pie shell. Decorate with chopped
pecans.

Freeze until firm. Wrap securely in aluminum foil. Return to freezer
and continue freezing 8 hours or overnight.

Remove from freezer 10 minutes before serving. Makes 6 to 8 servings.

Chocolate Mousse Pie

A sinfully rich, classic dessert served in a pastry shell
and guaranteed to satisfy chocolate-lovers the world over.

4 eggs, separated
1 (6-oz.) pkg. semisweet
  chocolate pieces,
  melted and cooled
1 tsp. vanilla

¼ c. sugar
1 c. heavy cream, whipped
Baked 9" pie shell
  with fluted edge
Sweetened whipped cream

Beat egg yolks in bowl until thick and lemon-colored, using an electric
mixer at high speed. Gradually beat in cooled chocolate and vanilla.

Beat egg whites in another bowl until foamy, using an electric mixer at
high speed. Gradually add sugar, 1 tblsp. at a time, beating well after each
addition. Continue beating until stiff, glossy peaks form when beaters are
slowly lifted. Fold egg white mixture into chocolate mixture. Then fold
chocolate mixture into whipped cream. Turn into baked pie shell.

Freeze until firm. Wrap securely in aluminum foil. Return to freezer
and continue freezing 8 hours or overnight.

Remove from freezer 10 minutes before serving.

To serve, top with puffs of sweetened whipped cream. Makes 8 servings.

Chocolate Ripple Pie

From a New York farm wife, a frozen pie with a filling
delicately ribboned with fudge in a rich and buttery shortbread crust.

Butter Crust
  (recipe follows)
1 (6-oz.) pkg. semisweet
  chocolate pieces
¼ c. light corn syrup
¼ c. water

1 egg white
¼ c. water
1 tsp. vanilla
1 tsp. lemon juice
½ c. sugar
1 c. heavy cream, whipped

Prepare Butter Crust and set aside.

Combine chocolate pieces, corn syrup and ¼ c. water in top of double boiler. Cook over simmering water, stirring constantly, until chocolate is melted. Remove from heat; cool well.

Combine egg white, ¼ c. water, vanilla and lemon juice in bowl. Beat until foamy, using an electric mixer at high speed. Gradually add sugar, beating until soft peaks form, about 4 minutes. Fold whipped cream into egg white mixture. Then fold in two thirds of chocolate mixture.

Spread half of filling mixture in pie shell. Drizzle with one half of remaining chocolate mixture. Cover with remaining filling. Drizzle remaining chocolate mixture on top in parallel lines. To make rippled effect, pull a knife through filling across lines of chocolate at even intervals.

Freeze until firm. Wrap securely in aluminum foil. Return to freezer and continue freezing 8 hours or overnight.

Remove from freezer 10 minutes before serving. Makes 6 to 8 servings.

Butter Crust: Combine 1 c. sifted flour and 2 tblsp. sugar in bowl. Cut in ½ c. butter or regular margarine until fine crumbs form, using a pastry blender. Press mixture into bottom and up sides of 9" pie plate. Bake in 375° oven 13 minutes, or until golden brown. Cool on rack.

Frozen Peppermint Chocolate Pie

Two kinds of chocolate and a sprinkle of crushed peppermint candy have made this pie the special-occasion favorite of one Illinois family.

⅔ c. butter or
  regular margarine
1 c. sugar
3 eggs
2 (1-oz.) squares
  unsweetened chocolate,
  melted and cooled

½ c. semisweet chocolate
  pieces, melted and cooled
9" Graham Cracker Crust
  (see Index)
1 c. heavy cream, whipped
¼ c. crushed peppermint
  stick candy

Cream together butter and sugar in bowl until light and fluffy, using an electric mixer at medium speed. Add eggs, one at a time, beating well after each addition. Blend in both chocolates. Turn into Graham Cracker Crust.

Spread whipped cream over chocolate filling. Sprinkle with peppermint candy.

Freeze until firm. Wrap securely in aluminum foil. Return to freezer and continue freezing 8 hours or overnight.

Remove from freezer 10 minutes before serving. Makes 6 to 8 servings.

Double Chocolate Ice Cream Pie

The pie shell is made of chocolate meringue; the filling
is chocolate ice cream studded with pecans—and morsels of chocolate.

Chocolate Meringue Crust (recipe follows)	1 qt. chocolate ice cream
1 (1-oz.) square semisweet chocolate	½ c. chopped pecans
½ tsp. butter or regular margarine	Sweetened whipped cream

Prepare Chocolate Meringue Crust and set aside.

Melt chocolate and butter in small saucepan over low heat. Remove from heat and cool slightly.

Stir ice cream in bowl until softened, using a spoon or an electric mixer at low speed. Stir in pecans. Slowly add chocolate mixture to ice cream, stirring until chocolate chips form. Spread ice cream mixture in Chocolate Meringue Crust.

Freeze until firm, about 3 hours. Wrap securely in aluminum foil. Return to freezer and continue freezing 8 hours or overnight.

Remove from freezer 10 minutes before serving.

To serve, top with puffs of sweetened whipped cream. Makes 6 to 8 servings.

Chocolate Meringue Crust: Beat together 3 egg whites and ¼ tsp. cream of tartar in bowl until foamy, using an electric mixer at high speed. Gradually add ¾ c. sugar, 1 tblsp. at a time, beating well after each addition. Continue beating until stiff, glossy peaks form. Beat in ¾ tsp. vanilla. Fold in ¼ c. chopped pecans and 1 (1-oz.) square semisweet chocolate (grated). Spread meringue in bottom and up sides of well-greased 9" pie plate. Bake in 275° oven 45 to 50 minutes, or until crisp to the touch. Cool on rack.

Chocolate Peanut Butter Pie

Something for everyone—chocolate and peanut butter, cookies and candy, all blended together and frozen into one scrumptious dessert.

Peanut Butter Cookie Crust
(recipe follows)
⅓ c. semisweet
chocolate pieces
1 tblsp. light corn syrup
1 tblsp. water
⅓ c. creamy peanut
butter

⅓ c. sugar
3 tblsp. light corn syrup
3 tblsp. water
¼ c. chopped peanuts
2 egg whites
2 tblsp. sugar
1 tsp. vanilla
1 c. heavy cream, whipped

Prepare Peanut Butter Cookie Crust and set aside.

Combine chocolate pieces, 1 tblsp. corn syrup and 1 tblsp. water in top of double boiler. Cook over simmering water until chocolate melts and mixture is smooth. Remove from heat; cool well.

Meanwhile, combine peanut butter, ⅓ c. sugar, 3 tblsp. corn syrup and 3 tblsp. water in 2-qt. saucepan. Cook over medium heat, stirring constantly, until sugar is dissolved and mixture is blended. Pour into bowl. Stir in peanuts and cool.

Beat egg whites in bowl until foamy, using an electric mixer at high speed. Gradually add 2 tblsp. sugar, 1 tblsp. at a time, beating well after each addition. Beat in vanilla and continue beating until stiff, glossy peaks form when beaters are slowly lifted. Fold egg white mixture into whipped cream. Then fold in peanut butter mixture.

Pour half of the peanut butter mixture into Peanut Butter Cookie Crust. Drizzle half of the chocolate mixture over filling. Top with remaining filling. Drizzle remaining chocolate in parallel lines over filling. Pull a knife across the lines at 1" intervals.

Freeze until firm. Wrap securely in aluminum foil. Return to freezer and continue freezing 8 hours or overnight.

Remove from freezer 10 minutes before serving. Makes 6 to 8 servings.

Peanut Butter Cookie Crust: Combine 14 peanut butter sandwich cookies (crushed) and 3 tblsp. butter or regular margarine (melted) in bowl; mix well. Press crumb mixture into bottom and up sides of 9" pie plate. Chill in refrigerator until set.

Hard-Hat Ice Cream Pie

On top is a thin, chocolate-candy shell; underneath it
there's a quart of coffee ice cream heaped into a butter cookie crust.

Butter Cookie Crust
  (recipe follows)
1 qt. coffee ice cream
½ c. semisweet
  chocolate pieces

¼ c. butter or
  regular margarine

Prepare Butter Cookie Crust and set aside.

Arrange spoonfuls or scoops of ice cream in Butter Cookie Crust.
Freeze until firm.

Combine chocolate pieces and butter in small saucepan. Cook over
low heat until melted, stirring occasionally. Remove from heat and cool
well.

Spoon cooled chocolate mixture over ice cream. Return pie to freezer
until chocolate sets. Wrap securely in aluminum foil. Return to freezer
and continue freezing 8 hours or overnight.

Remove from freezer 10 minutes before serving. Makes 6 to 8 servings.

Butter Cookie Crust: Combine 1 c. sifted flour and 3 tblsp. sugar in
bowl. Cut in ¼ c. butter or regular margarine until fine crumbs form, using a pastry blender. Press mixture into bottom and up sides of 9″ pie
plate. Bake in 375° oven 13 to 15 minutes, or until golden brown. Cool
on rack.

Banana Split Pie

Almost everyone loves a banana split, and who wouldn't enjoy
this concoction of ice cream and bananas in a meringue-lined pie shell?

3 egg whites	1 tblsp. sugar
¼ tsp. cream of tartar	½ tsp. vanilla
¾ c. sugar	1 qt. strawberry ice cream
¾ tsp. vanilla	½ c. strawberry ice cream
3 tblsp. baking cocoa	topping
Baked 9″ pie shell	2 medium bananas, sliced
1 c. heavy cream	

Beat together egg whites and cream of tartar in bowl until foamy, using
an electric mixer at high speed. Gradually add ¾ c. sugar, 1 tblsp. at a
time, beating well after each addition. Continue beating until stiff, glossy
peaks form. Beat in ¾ tsp. vanilla.

Add cocoa, a little at a time, folding a few strokes after each addition.
Spread meringue in bottom and up sides of baked pie shell.

Bake in 325° oven 25 minutes, or until meringue is set, but still slightly
soft. Cool on rack.

To serve, combine heavy cream, 1 tblsp. sugar and ½ tsp. vanilla in
chilled bowl. Beat until soft peaks form, using an electric mixer at high
speed. Spoon half of the ice cream into meringue-lined pie shell. Top with
strawberry topping. Spoon remaining ice cream over topping. Arrange
bananas on top. Spread sweetened whipped cream over pie. Serve immediately. Makes 6 to 8 servings.

Grasshopper Marshmallow Pie

For carefree entertaining later on, make this festive pie
and tuck it into your freezer. It has a no-bake chocolate cookie crust.

1 (7½-oz.) jar marsh-	1 tblsp. hot water
mallow creme	2 c. heavy cream, whipped
½ tsp. peppermint extract	Chocolate Cookie Crust
16 drops green food	(see Index)
coloring	

Combine marshmallow creme, peppermint extract, food coloring and hot water in bowl. Beat until well blended, using an electric mixer at medium speed.

Fold marshmallow creme mixture into whipped cream. Turn into Chocolate Cookie Crust.

Freeze until firm. Wrap securely in aluminum foil. Return to freezer and continue freezing 8 hours or overnight.

Remove from freezer 10 minutes before serving. Makes 6 to 8 servings.

Baked Alaska Pie

A new variation on a classic—orange sherbet layered over vanilla and chocolate ice cream and topped with delicately browned meringue.

1 pt. chocolate ice cream	4 egg whites
Baked 9" pie shell	¼ tsp. cream of tartar
1 pt. vanilla ice cream	¾ c. sugar
1 pt. orange sherbet	¾ tsp. vanilla

Stir chocolate ice cream in bowl until softened, using a spoon or an electric mixer at low speed. Spread chocolate ice cream over bottom of baked pie shell.

Soften vanilla ice cream. Spread over chocolate layer. Soften orange sherbet and spread over vanilla layer.

Freeze until firm, about 3 hours. Wrap securely in aluminum foil. Return to freezer and continue freezing 8 hours or overnight.

About 15 minutes before serving, beat egg whites and cream of tartar in bowl until foamy, using an electric mixer at high speed. Gradually add sugar, 1 tblsp. at a time, beating well after each addition. Continue beating until stiff, glossy peaks form when beaters are slowly lifted. Beat in vanilla. Spoon some of the meringue around edge of pie. Spread meringue so it touches inner edge of crust all around, using back of a spoon. Heap remaining meringue in center. Push out gently to meet meringue border.

Bake in 475° oven 3 to 4 minutes, or until meringue is lightly browned. Makes 6 to 8 servings.

Coconut Crunch Ice Cream Pie

A tantalizing ice cream pie with a butterscotch-pecan topping
and a crust made with cornflakes, pecans, coconut and brown sugar.

Crunchy Cornflake Crust
  (recipe follows)
1 qt. vanilla ice cream
½ c. heavy cream
2 tsp. sugar

¼ tsp. vanilla
Butterscotch ice cream
  topping
Chopped pecans

Prepare Crunchy Cornflake Crust and set aside.

Stir ice cream in bowl until softened, using a spoon or an electric mixer at low speed. Spread ice cream in Crunchy Cornflake Crust.

Freeze until firm, about 3 hours. Wrap securely in aluminum foil. Return to freezer and continue freezing 8 hours or overnight.

Remove from freezer 10 to 15 minutes before serving.

To serve, combine heavy cream, sugar and vanilla in chilled bowl. Beat until soft peaks form, using an electric mixer at high speed. Spoon butterscotch ice cream topping over pie. Top with puffs of whipped cream and sprinkle with pecans. Makes 6 to 8 servings.

Crunchy Cornflake Crust: Combine ½ c. brown sugar (packed) and ¼ c. butter or regular margarine in small saucepan. Cook over medium heat, stirring occasionally, until butter melts and sugar dissolves. Combine 2½ c. cornflakes (coarsely crushed), ¼ c. chopped pecans, ¼ c. flaked coconut and brown sugar mixture in bowl; mix well. Press mixture into bottom and up sides of greased 9″ pie plate. Chill in refrigerator 15 minutes, or until set.

Ice Cream 'n' Pretzel Pie

The unusual combination of salted pretzels and ice cream,
popular in Philadelphia, was the inspiration for this new recipe.

Pretzel Crust
  (recipe follows)
½ c. semisweet
  chocolate pieces, melted

½ gal. vanilla fudge
  ice cream

Prepare Pretzel Crust. Freeze at least 1 hour.

Spread melted chocolate pieces over bottom of Pretzel Crust.

Freeze 10 minutes, or until chocolate is set.

Spoon or scoop ice cream over chocolate layer.

Freeze until firm. Wrap securely in aluminum foil. Return to freezer and continue freezing 8 hours or overnight.

Remove from freezer 10 to 15 minutes before serving. Makes 6 to 8 servings.

Pretzel Crust: Combine 1½ c. coarsely crushed pretzel rods and ½ c. butter or regular margarine in bowl; mix well. Press mixture into bottom and up sides of 9" pie plate. Freeze at least 1 hour before filling.

Peanutty Ice Cream Pie

Sure to thrill kids of all ages—vanilla ice cream swirled
with peanuts and peanut butter—and it's a snap to make, too.

¼ c. light corn syrup
3 tblsp. peanut butter
⅓ c. chopped peanuts

1 qt. vanilla ice cream
9" Graham Cracker Crust
  (see Index)

Blend together corn syrup and peanut butter in bowl. Stir in peanuts.

Stir ice cream in bowl until softened, using a spoon or an electric mixer at low speed. Spread half of the ice cream in Graham Cracker Crust. Top with half of the peanut butter mixture. Repeat layers. Cut through ice cream with knife to swirl.

Freeze until firm, about 3 hours. Wrap securely in aluminum foil. Return to freezer and continue freezing 8 hours or overnight.

Remove from freezer 10 to 15 minutes before serving. Makes 6 to 8 servings.

Frozen Pumpkin Pie

Just about the richest pumpkin pie we've ever tasted: a mixture of pumpkin, marshmallows and cream over butter pecan ice cream!

1 pt. butter pecan ice cream
Baked 9" Graham Cracker Crust (see Index)
1 c. cooked, mashed pumpkin, fresh or canned
1 c. sugar
½ tsp. salt

½ tsp. ground cinnamon
¼ tsp. ground ginger
¼ tsp. ground nutmeg
½ tsp. vanilla
1½ c. miniature marshmallows
1 c. heavy cream, whipped

Stir ice cream in bowl until softened, using a spoon or an electric mixer at low speed. Spread ice cream in Baked Graham Cracker Crust. Freeze until firm.

Combine pumpkin, sugar, salt, cinnamon, ginger, nutmeg and vanilla in bowl; mix well. Fold in miniature marshmallows and whipped cream. Spoon over ice cream layer.

Freeze until firm. Wrap securely in aluminum foil. Return to freezer and continue freezing 8 hours or overnight.

Remove from freezer 10 minutes before serving. Makes 6 to 8 servings.

Frozen Peach Melba Pie

A regal ice cream and sherbet pie inspired by the classic dessert, with a layer of raspberry sherbet topped off by a purée of fresh peaches.

2 c. sliced, peeled peaches
¾ c. light corn syrup
1 tblsp. lemon juice
1 pt. raspberry sherbet
2 drops red food coloring

9" Graham Cracker Crust (see Index)
1 c. vanilla ice cream
2 drops yellow food coloring
Fresh peach slices

Combine 2 c. peaches, corn syrup and lemon juice in blender jar. Cover and blend until smooth.

Stir raspberry sherbet in bowl until softened, using a spoon or an electric mixer at low speed. Fold in red food coloring and half of the puréed peach mixture. Spread over bottom of Graham Cracker Crust.

Freeze 1 hour, or until firm.

Stir vanilla ice cream in bowl until softened, using a spoon or an electric mixer at low speed. Fold in yellow food coloring and remaining puréed peaches. Pour over raspberry layer.

Freeze until firm. Wrap securely in aluminum foil. Return to freezer and continue freezing 8 hours or overnight.

Remove from freezer 10 to 15 minutes before serving. Decorate with fresh peach slices. Makes 6 to 8 servings.

Strawberry Ice Cream Pie

A very romantic-looking dessert, with a layer of fresh strawberries over vanilla and strawberry ice cream. Even the meringue shell is pink.

Pink Meringue Shell	*3 tblsp. sugar*
(recipe follows)	*1 tsp. vanilla*
1 pt. vanilla ice cream	*1 tblsp. sugar*
1 pt. strawberry ice cream	*2 c. sliced fresh strawberries*
1 c. heavy cream	

Prepare Pink Meringue Shell and set aside.

Stir vanilla ice cream in bowl until softened, using a spoon or an electric mixer at low speed. Spread in bottom of Pink Meringue Shell.

Freeze until firm.

Stir strawberry ice cream in bowl until softened, using a spoon or an electric mixer at low speed. Spread over vanilla ice cream layer.

Freeze until firm.

Whip heavy cream in chilled bowl until it begins to thicken. Gradually add 3 tblsp. sugar, beating until soft peaks form. Beat in vanilla. Spread whipped cream over strawberry ice cream layer.

Sprinkle 1 tblsp. sugar over strawberries; toss to mix. Spoon strawberries over whipped cream.

Freeze until firm. Wrap securely in aluminum foil. Return to freezer and continue freezing 8 hours or overnight.

Remove from freezer 10 minutes before serving. Makes 6 to 8 servings.

Pink Meringue Shell: Beat 4 egg whites and ¼ tsp. cream of tartar in bowl until foamy, using an eletric mixer at high speed. Gradually add 1 c. sugar, 1 tblsp. at a time, beating well after each addition. Add 2 drops red food coloring and continue beating until stiff, glossy peaks form. Spread mixture in bottom and up sides of greased 9″ pie plate, making bottom ¼″ thick and sides 1″ thick. Bake in 275° oven 1 hour, or until light brown and crisp to the touch. Cool on rack.

Peanut Butter Ice Cream Pie

Better than an ice cream parlor sundae! This fudge-topped
ice cream pie has a crust made with peanut butter and rice cereal.

Crunchy Peanut Crust
(recipe follows)
1 qt. vanilla ice cream

Fudge ice cream topping
Sweetened whipped cream
Chopped peanuts

Prepare Crunchy Peanut Crust and set aside.

Stir ice cream in bowl until softened, using a spoon or an electric mixer
at low speed. Spread ice cream into Crunchy Peanut Crust.

Freeze until firm. Wrap securely in aluminum foil. Return to freezer
and continue freezing 8 hours or overnight.

Remove from freezer 10 minutes before serving.

To serve, drizzle ice cream topping over pie, top with puffs of sweetened whipped cream and sprinkle with peanuts. Makes 6 to 8 servings.

Crunchy Peanut Crust: Blend together 1/4 c. chunky peanut butter and
1/4 c. light corn syrup in bowl. Add 2 c. oven-toasted rice cereal, stirring
until all the cereal is coated. Press mixture into bottom and up sides of
greased 9″ pie plate. Chill in refrigerator until set, about 20 minutes.

Lemon Crunch Ice Cream Pie

A new combination that will keep your family guessing—the crunchy
morsels in the filling and topping are made from cornflakes and pecans.

2 tblsp. butter or
regular margarine
1/2 c. crushed cornflakes
1/2 c. chopped pecans
3 tblsp. brown sugar,
packed

1 qt. vanilla ice cream
1/2 (6-oz.) can frozen
lemonade concentrate
9″ Graham Cracker Crust
(see Index)

Melt butter in 10″ skillet over medium heat. Stir in cornflakes, chopped
pecans and brown sugar. Cook, stirring constantly, 5 minutes. Remove
from heat. Remove one fourth of the cornflake mixture and set aside.

Stir ice cream in bowl until softened, using an electric mixer at low
speed. Stir lemonade concentrate and remaining cornflake mixture into
ice cream. Spread ice cream mixture in Graham Cracker Crust. Sprinkle
with reserved cornflake mixture.

Freeze until firm, about 3 hours. Wrap securely in aluminum foil. Return to freezer and continue freezing 8 hours or overnight.

Remove from freezer 10 to 15 minutes before serving. Makes 6 to 8
servings.

7 Savory Main-Dish Pies

Say "pie," and most people think of dessert—yet main-dish pies are an American specialty dating back to colonial days, when thrifty cooks stretched scarce ingredients by wrapping them in flaky pastry.

Today, a savory pie still provides a delicious, nourishing solution to the question of what to serve for lunch or dinner, and the choices are wonderfully abundant: deep-dish chicken pies bubbling with giblet gravy, light and creamy quiches made with fresh garden vegetables, and spicy, sizzling-hot pizza pies. Men like meaty main-dish pies with lots of potatoes and other vegetables, and farm cooks make these pies often during the busy harvesting and planting seasons.

Many of the pies in this chapter can be prepared quickly or frozen until ready to serve, and once you've decided on a main-dish pie, the rest of the meal falls into place: salad and a dessert of ice cream or fruit are all that's needed to round out the menu.

Here's an enticing selection of 60 main-dish pies that have been favorites in farm homes for years. At the beginning of this chapter you'll find recipes for half a dozen robust beef pies, starting with Steak-and-Potato Pie, a big, juicy pie with lots of onions and gravy. An Illinois homemaker's Yorkshire Beef Pie teams leftover cooked beef with an easy popover-like crust that puffs up to surround the lightly seasoned filling of beef and vegetables. Other meat pies combine vegetables and spices with ground beef, pork, chicken, turkey or lamb, some baked in a flaky double-crust pastry and others topped with melted cheese, whipped potatoes or corn bread.

Not every pie is baked in a pastry shell; several have no

crusts at all, and Microwaved Tuna Pie has a soft crust made with spaghetti and eggs and Parmesan cheese. The Iowa farm wife who sent us that recipe likes it best when it's made with layers of tuna and mozzarella, but she says it's also good made with beef, meat loaf or turkey. If you love stuffing as much as one New York farm family does, try Hamburger 'n' Stuffing Pie, a mixture of meat loaf and Cheddar cheese baked in a crust made from stuffing.

For a quick hot meal when you don't have time to fuss, keep a supply of jiffy crust ingredients on hand. Frozen puff pastry can turn leftover chicken into a gourmet treat of chicken turnovers featuring a flavorful blend of chicken and cream cheese. A Kansas farm woman uses refrigerated dinner rolls to make Beef-Biscuit Pie, a double-crust pie made with ground beef and tomato sauce—she says that her family likes it because it tastes just like pizza.

Some main-dish pies are perfect for breakfast or brunch. An Oklahoma woman's recipe for Potato-and-Sausage Quiche has a shell made with shredded potatoes and a cheesy custard dotted with slices of pork sausage. For a lighter meal, there are elegant quiches made with combinations of broccoli, zucchini, mushrooms and cheese, including an Idaho woman's no-crust quiche and a colorful spinach-and-tomato quiche sprinkled with peanuts. For special occasions, there's a recipe that makes two dozen quiches baked in a muffin pan.

Bake a batch of Cornish pasties for a nutritious snack or a meal on the run—there are two recipes in this chapter for these little meat-and-potato pastries, both made with extra-flaky lard pastry. Cornish pasties have been popular in this country since the 1800s, when Midwestern cooks used to tuck them into their husbands' lunch boxes to take with them down into the coal mines; they're simply seasoned, and good hot or cold.

When you crave a pizza, turn to the end of this chapter; we've included half a dozen recipes, each one with a different crust. If you like a pizza with a nice, thick crust, take the time to make a Sicilian Pizza smothered with onion, green pepper, sausage and cheese. Even with its real yeast dough, you can probably make it from scratch faster than a take-out pizza can reach your front door. To help you prepare for those days when there just isn't time to let the dough rise, the recipe for Freeze-Ahead Pizza Crusts yields four prebaked, 12" crusts to stock your freezer.

Next time someone wants to know, "What's for dinner?"—say "pie!"

Steak-and-Potato Pie

A double-crust pie just made for meat-and-potato lovers—
it's filled with cubes of round steak and diced potatoes in a brown gravy.

3 tblsp. flour	1/3 c. cooking oil
1/2 tsp. paprika	2 c. chopped onion
1/8 tsp. pepper	1 3/4 c. beef broth
1/8 tsp. ground ginger	2 c. diced, pared potatoes
1/8 tsp. ground allspice	Pastry for 2-crust 10" pie
1 lb. beef round steak,	1 egg yolk, beaten
cut into 1/2" cubes	1 tblsp. water

Combine flour, paprika, pepper, ginger and allspice in bowl. Dredge beef cubes in flour mixture. Heat oil in 4-qt. Dutch oven over medium-high heat. Brown beef cubes in hot oil, stirring often. When beef begins to brown, stir in onion and cook mixture until well browned. Add beef broth. Bring to a boil; reduce heat to low and cover.

Simmer 1 hour, or until meat is tender. Add potatoes and cook 20 minutes more, or until potatoes are tender. Remove from heat. Let mixture cool while preparing pastry.

Divide pastry almost in half. Roll out larger half on floured surface to 14" circle. Line 10" pie plate with pastry. Trim edge to 1/2" beyond rim of pie plate. Pour slightly cooled beef mixture into pastry-lined pie plate.

Roll out remaining pastry to 12" circle. Cut slits. Place top crust over filling and trim edge to 1" beyond rim of pie plate. Fold top crust under lower crust and form a ridge. Flute edge. Combine egg yolk and water and brush over crust.

Bake in 400° oven 30 minutes, or until crust is golden brown. Let stand 10 minutes before serving. Makes 8 servings.

Savory Beef-Vegetable Pie

Plan to save leftover pot roast and gravy to make this pie.
Peas, carrots, potatoes and cooked beef are the main ingredients.

Pastry for 2-crust 9" pie
½ c. chopped onion
2 tblsp. butter or
   regular margarine
2 c. cubed, cooked beef
   (¾" pieces)
1½ c. cubed, cooked
   potatoes (¾" pieces)

1 c. sliced, cooked carrots
   (½" thick)
1 c. peas, fresh or frozen
1 (10½-oz.) can beef gravy
   or 1¼ c. leftover
   beef gravy
1 egg, beaten

Divide pastry almost in half. Roll out larger half on floured surface to 13" circle. Line 9" pie plate with pastry. Trim edge to ½" beyond rim of pie plate.

Sauté onion in butter in 10" skillet over medium heat until tender. Stir in beef, potatoes, carrots, peas and gravy. Cook over high heat until mixture comes to a boil. Remove from heat. Pour hot beef mixture into pastry-lined pie plate.

Roll out remaining pastry to 11" circle. Cut slits. Place top crust over filling and trim edge to 1" beyond rim of pie plate. Fold top crust under lower crust and form a ridge. Flute edge. Brush crust with beaten egg.

Bake in 400° oven 35 minutes, or until crust is golden brown and filling is bubbly. Let stand 10 minutes before serving. Makes 6 to 8 servings.

Yorkshire Beef Pie

Yorkshire pudding is the easy crust for this pie. As it bakes,
the pudding puffs up around the meat-and-vegetable filling.

3½ c. cut-up, cooked beef
½ c. sliced onion
2 tblsp. cooking oil
1 c. cooked mixed
   vegetables
½ c. canned or leftover
   beef gravy

2 tblsp. butter or
   regular margarine
2 eggs
1 c. milk
1 c. sifted flour
½ tsp. salt
Hot beef gravy

Grind meat in a food grinder, using medium blade; set aside.
Place 9" pie plate in 400° oven.
Cook onion and ground meat in hot oil in 10" skillet over medium heat until meat is lightly browned and onion is tender. Stir in mixed vegetables and ½ c. beef gravy. Remove from heat.

Place butter in hot pie plate. Return to 400° oven for 2 minutes, or until butter melts.

Beat eggs in bowl until frothy, using an electric mixer at high speed. Add milk and beat at medium speed until well blended. Gradually add flour and salt, beating until smooth. Pour mixture into hot pie plate.

Spoon meat mixture over all, spreading to within 1" of edge.

Bake in 400° oven 30 minutes, or until crust is golden brown and puffy. Serve with hot beef gravy. Makes 6 servings.

Meatball-Vegetable Pie

Lots of tiny meatballs make this pie special.
It's a little extra work, but your family will love every mouthful.

Pastry for 2-crust 10" pie	1 egg, slightly beaten
1 lb. ground beef	2 tblsp. milk
¾ c. soft bread crumbs	2 tblsp. cooking oil
¼ c. minced onion	1 (16-oz.) can stewed
2 tblsp. chopped fresh	tomatoes
parsley	1 tblsp. cornstarch
1 tsp. salt	2 beef bouillon cubes
½ tsp. dried marjoram	1 c. frozen peas, thawed
leaves	1 c. sliced, cooked carrots
⅛ tsp. pepper	

Divide pastry almost in half. Roll out larger half on floured surface to 14" circle. Line 10" pie plate with pastry. Trim edge to ½" beyond rim of pie plate.

Combine ground beef, bread crumbs, onion, parsley, salt, marjoram, pepper, egg and milk in bowl. Mix lightly, but well. Divide mixture into fourths. Shape each fourth into 12 tiny meatballs.

Heat cooking oil in 10" skillet over medium heat. Brown meatballs in hot oil. Remove meatballs from skillet as they brown. Drain on paper towels. Drain fat from skillet.

Combine some of liquid from stewed tomatoes with cornstarch. Add cornstarch mixture, stewed tomatoes and bouillon cubes to skillet. Cook over medium heat, stirring constantly, until mixture comes to a boil. Stir in peas and carrots. Remove from heat.

Arrange meatballs in pastry-lined pie plate. Pour hot mixture over all. Roll out remaining pastry to 12" circle. Cut slits. Place top crust over filling and trim edge to 1" beyond rim of pie plate. Fold top crust under lower crust and form a ridge. Flute edge.

Bake in 400° oven 15 minutes. Reduce temperature to 350° and bake 25 minutes more, or until crust is golden brown. Let stand 10 minutes before serving. Makes 8 servings.

Beef-and-Potato Pie

Mounds of whipped potatoes top off a chunky stew of beef
and fresh vegetables, all baked in a casserole. A truly inviting dish.

1½ lb. beef round steak,
   cut into 1" cubes
1 tsp. salt
¼ tsp. pepper
¼ c. flour
4 tblsp. butter or
   regular margarine
½ c. chopped celery
½ c. chopped onion
2 oz. fresh mushrooms,
   sliced

2 c. water
1 c. sliced, cooked
   carrots
½ c. fresh or frozen peas
1 tsp. browning for gravy
1 tsp. chopped fresh parsley
Mashed Potatoes
   (recipe follows)
Paprika

Season beef with salt and pepper. Dredge beef in flour.

Brown beef in melted butter in 10" skillet over medium heat. Add celery, onion, mushrooms and water. Cook over high heat until mixture comes to a boil. Reduce heat to low. Cover and simmer 1 hour 30 minutes, or until beef is tender. Meanwhile, prepare Mashed Potatoes.

Stir carrots, peas and browning for gravy into beef mixture. Pour mixture into 12x8x2" (2-qt.) baking dish. Sprinkle with parsley. Pipe potatoes on top, using a large decorator tip, or drop potatoes in spoonfuls around edges of dish. Sprinkle potatoes with paprika.

Bake in 425° oven 20 minutes, or until hot. Makes 6 servings.

Mashed Potatoes: Cook 1½ lb. pared and quartered potatoes in 1" boiling, salted water 20 to 25 minutes, or until tender. Drain. Mash potatoes until smooth, using a potato masher. Add 4 to 6 tblsp. milk, 3 tblsp. butter or regular margarine, ¼ tsp. salt and a dash of pepper. Beat until light and fluffy.

Cornish Pasties

Plump, golden crescents of flaky pastry filled with beef
and potatoes, mildly spiced. Try serving them with ketchup or chili sauce.

Cornish Pastry
   (recipe follows)
1 lb. beef round or chuck,
   minced
2 c. diced, pared potatoes
1½ c. chopped onion

1 tblsp. Worcestershire
   sauce
2 tsp. salt
⅛ tsp. pepper
1 egg, beaten

Prepare Cornish Pastry and set aside.

Combine beef, potatoes, onion, Worcestershire sauce, salt and pepper in bowl; mix lightly, but well.

Divide pastry into 6 portions. Roll out each portion on floured surface to 7″ circle. Place one sixth of meat mixture on half of each circle. Fold the other half of each circle over meat mixture; press edges together to seal, using the tines of a fork. Cut slits in top of each. Place on ungreased baking sheets and brush with beaten egg.

Bake in 350° oven 45 minutes, or until crust is golden brown and meat mixture is tender. Makes 6 servings.

Cornish Pastry: Combine 3 c. sifted flour and 1½ tsp. salt in bowl. Cut in 1 c. lard until coarse crumbs form, using a pastry blender. Sprinkle 4 to 5 tblsp. iced water over crumb mixture, a little at a time, tossing with a fork until dough forms. Press dough firmly into a ball.

Wisconsin-style Cornish Pasties

A new recipe from a homemaker who lives on a farm
in the old Cornish community of Mineral Point, Wisconsin.

Extra-Flaky Pastry
  (recipe follows)
1¼ lb. beef round steak,
  finely chopped
1 c. diced, pared potatoes
¼ c. chopped onion

1 tblsp. finely chopped
  beef suet
½ tsp. salt
⅛ tsp. pepper
1 egg yolk, beaten
1 tblsp. water

Prepare Extra-Flaky Pastry and set aside.

Combine round steak, potatoes, onion, suet, salt and pepper in bowl. Mix lightly, but well.

Divide pastry into 6 portions. Roll out each portion on floured surface to 9″ circle. Place one sixth of the meat mixture on half of each circle. Fold the other half of each circle over meat mixture; press edges together to seal, using the tines of a fork. Cut slits in top of each. Place on ungreased baking sheets. Blend together egg yolk and water in small bowl and brush each pastry with yolk mixture.

Bake in 400° oven 15 minutes. Reduce temperature to 350° and bake 45 minutes more, or until crust is golden brown and meat is tender. Makes 6 servings.

Extra-Flaky Pastry: Combine 4 c. sifted flour and 2 tsp. salt in bowl. Cut in 1½ c. lard until coarse crumbs form, using a pastry blender. Blend together 2 eggs (beaten) and ¼ c. iced water in bowl. Sprinkle egg mixture over crumb mixture, a little at a time, tossing with a fork until dough forms. Press dough firmly into a ball.

*Savory Main-Dish Pies*_____**233**

Ground Beef-Cheese Pie

So easy to make, this single-crust, family-style pie gets its
extra richness from a custard made with eggs and mayonnaise.

3/4 lb. ground beef
1/2 c. finely chopped
  onion
2 c. shredded Cheddar
  cheese
Unbaked 9" pie shell
  with fluted edge

3/4 c. mayonnaise or
  salad dressing
3/4 c. milk
4 tsp. cornstarch
3 eggs
1/2 tsp. salt
1/8 tsp. pepper

Cook ground beef and onion in 10" skillet over medium heat until well
browned. Remove from heat.

Place hot beef mixture and Cheddar cheese in unbaked pie shell.

Combine mayonnaise, milk, cornstarch, eggs, salt and pepper in bowl.
Beat until smooth, using a rotary beater. Pour egg mixture over beef mixture in pie shell.

Bake in 350° oven 35 minutes, or until golden brown and puffy. Let
stand 10 minutes before serving. Makes 6 to 8 servings.

Pennsylvania Pizza-style Pie

"This recipe resembles pizza, but we think it tastes
a whole lot better than pizza," a Pennsylvania farm woman wrote.

1 lb. ground beef
1/2 c. chopped onion
1 clove garlic, minced
1 (8-oz.) can tomato sauce
1 (6-oz.) can tomato paste
2 tblsp. chopped fresh
  parsley
1 tsp. dried oregano leaves

1/4 tsp. pepper
Unbaked 9" pie shell
  with fluted edge
4 oz. sliced mozzarella
  cheese
1/2 c. grated Parmesan
  cheese

Cook ground beef, onion and garlic in 10" skillet over medium heat
until meat is browned. Drain fat from skillet. Stir in tomato sauce, tomato
paste, parsley, oregano and pepper. Pour meat mixture into unbaked pie
shell.

Bake in 400° oven 15 minutes.

Arrange slices of mozzarella cheese on top of pie. Sprinkle with Parmesan cheese.

Bake 10 minutes more, or until crust is golden brown and cheese is
melted. Let stand 10 minutes before serving. Makes 6 to 8 servings.

Beef-Biscuit Pie

Refrigerated crescent dinner rolls are used to make
the double crust that holds this cheesy beef-and-tomato filling.

2 (8-oz.) pkg. refrigerated
  crescent dinner rolls
1 lb. ground beef
¾ c. chopped onion
1 clove garlic, minced
1 (8-oz.) can tomato sauce
1 (4-oz.) can mushroom
  stems and pieces,
  drained

¼ c. chopped fresh
  parsley
½ tsp. dried oregano leaves
2 eggs
1 egg, separated
6 slices pasteurized
  process American
  cheese
1 tblsp. water

Unroll 1 pkg. crescent rolls on lightly floured surface and press together perforations to seal. Roll out to 12" square. Line 9" pie plate with dough. Trim edge to ½" beyond rim of pie plate.

Cook ground beef, onion and garlic in 10" skillet over medium heat until meat is browned. Stir in tomato sauce, mushrooms, parsley and oregano. Remove from heat.

Combine eggs and egg white in bowl. Beat until blended, using a rotary beater. Pour half of the egg mixture into crescent roll-lined pie plate. Arrange hot beef mixture on top. Top with cheese slices. Pour remaining egg mixture over all.

Roll out remaining pkg. crescent rolls to 12" square. Cut slits. Place top crust over filling and trim edge to 1" beyond rim of pie plate. Fold top crust under lower crust and form a ridge. Flute edge. Slightly beat egg yolk and mix with water in bowl. Brush over crust.

Bake in 350° oven 50 minutes, or until crust is browned. Cover loosely with foil if top begins to get too brown. Let stand 10 minutes before serving. Makes 6 to 8 servings.

Beef-Corn Pie

Keep an extra pound of ground beef in your freezer
and serve this pie on days when you need to make something simple.

2 eggs
1 lb. ground beef
¼ c. soft bread crumbs
¼ c. ketchup
2 tblsp. finely chopped
   onion
1 tsp. chili powder

1 tsp. salt
⅛ tsp. pepper
1 (12-oz.) can Mexican-
   style corn, drained
2 tblsp. soft bread crumbs
½ c. shredded Cheddar
   cheese

Beat 1 of the eggs slightly, using a fork. Combine beaten egg, ground beef, ¼ c. bread crumbs, ketchup, onion, chili powder, salt and pepper in bowl. Mix lightly, but well. Pat meat mixture evenly over bottom and up sides of 9″ pie plate.

Beat remaining egg slightly, using a fork. Combine beaten egg, corn and 2 tblsp. bread crumbs in bowl; mix well. Pour corn mixture into meat-lined pie plate.

Bake in 350° oven 40 minutes, or until corn filling is set. Sprinkle with cheese. Bake 5 minutes more, or until cheese melts. Let stand 10 minutes before serving. Makes 6 servings.

Shepherd's Pie

This new recipe for shepherd's pie blends lots of ground beef
and vegetables in tomato sauce and tops them with whipped potatoes.

6 small all-purpose
   potatoes, pared
   and quartered (1½ lb.)
1½ lb. ground beef
¾ c. chopped onion
½ c. chopped celery
½ c. chopped green
   pepper
1 (15-oz.) can tomato
   sauce
1 (6-oz.) can tomato paste

2 c. cooked mixed
   vegetables
2 c. cooked green beans
1 tsp. dried basil leaves
1 tsp. salt
⅛ tsp. pepper
⅔ c. warm milk
1 egg, beaten
½ tsp. salt
Paprika

Cook potatoes in 3-qt. saucepan in 1″ boiling, salted water until tender, about 20 minutes.

Meanwhile, cook ground beef in 12″ skillet over medium heat until it begins to change color. Add onion, celery and green pepper. Cook until meat is browned and vegetables are tender. Remove from heat. Stir in tomato sauce, tomato paste, mixed vegetables, green beans, basil, 1 tsp. salt and pepper. Pour mixture into greased 2-qt. casserole.

Drain potatoes. Mash until smooth, using a potato masher. Stir in warm milk, beaten egg and 1/2 tsp. salt; mix well. Spoon potato mixture over meat mixture, spreading to cover filling. Sprinkle with paprika.

Bake in 350° oven 30 minutes, or until potatoes are golden brown and filling is bubbly. Makes 6 to 8 servings.

Chili con Carne Pie

Just right for a chilly autumn night—hot and spicy
chili con carne surrounded by golden corn bread dumplings.

1½ lb. ground beef	1 (8-oz.) can tomato sauce
½ c. chopped onion	1 tblsp. chili powder
1 clove garlic, minced	1 tsp. salt
1 (20-oz.) can red kidney	Corn Bread Topping
beans, drained	(recipe follows)
1 (16-oz.) can tomatoes,	¼ c. grated Parmesan
cut up	cheese

Cook ground beef, onion and garlic in 12″ skillet over medium heat until beef is well browned. Drain fat from skillet. Stir in kidney beans, tomatoes, tomato sauce, chili powder and salt. Cook over high heat until mixture comes to a boil. Reduce heat to low and simmer 10 minutes, stirring occasionally.

Meanwhile, prepare Corn Bread Topping.

Pour hot meat mixture into 12x8x2″ (2-qt.) baking dish. Sprinkle with cheese. Spoon Corn Bread Topping around the edges of dish.

Bake in 425° oven 15 minutes, or until Corn Bread Topping is golden brown. Makes 6 servings.

Corn Bread Topping: Sift together ¾ c. yellow corn meal, ¼ c. sifted flour, ½ tsp. salt and 1½ tsp. baking powder. Add 1 egg, ½ c. milk and ¼ c. shortening. Beat just until smooth, about 1 minute, using a rotary beater. (Do not overbeat.) Stir in 1 tblsp. chopped fresh parsley.

Hamburger 'n' Stuffing Pie

"My family loves stuffing," a New York woman told us recently, "so this is one of their favorite hamburger recipes."

Easy Stuffing Crust
   (recipe follows)
1 lb. ground beef
1 c. shredded Cheddar
   cheese
1 egg, beaten
¼ c. ketchup
2 tblsp. chopped
   fresh parsley

2 tblsp. finely chopped
   onion
½ tsp. dried basil
   leaves
¼ tsp. seasoned salt
⅛ tsp. pepper

Prepare Easy Stuffing Crust, reserving 1 c. stuffing mixture for filling.

Combine ground beef, cheese, egg, ketchup, parsley, onion, basil, seasoned salt, pepper and 1 c. reserved stuffing mixture in bowl. Mix lightly, but well. Spoon mixture into Easy Stuffing Crust.

Bake in 350° oven 40 minutes, or until firm. Blot excess fat from surface, using paper towels. Let stand 10 minutes before serving. Makes 6 to 8 servings.

Easy Stuffing Crust: Combine 1 (6-oz.) pkg. chicken flavor stuffing mix and 1¾ c. hot water in bowl; mix well. Measure 1 c. stuffing mixture and reserve for filling. Press remaining mixture into bottom and up sides of 10" pie plate.

Tamale Pie

Whole-kernel corn mingled with ground beef under a corn meal topping. To bring the filling to full flavor, simmer for 20 minutes.

1 lb. ground beef
1 c. chopped onion
½ c. chopped green
   pepper
1 (15-oz.) can tomato sauce
1 (12-oz.) can whole-
   kernel corn, drained
1 clove garlic, minced

1 tblsp. chili powder
1 tsp. salt
Dash of pepper
1½ c. shredded
   pasteurized process
   American cheese
Tamale Pie Topping
   (recipe follows)

Cook ground beef, onion and green pepper in 12" skillet over medium heat until meat is browned. Stir in tomato sauce, corn, garlic, chili powder, salt and pepper. Cook over high heat until mixture comes to a boil. Reduce heat to low. Cover and simmer 20 minutes. Add cheese and stir until melted.

Meanwhile, prepare Tamale Pie Topping.

Pour hot meat mixture into greased 2-qt. casserole. Spoon Tamale Pie Topping over top, spreading to cover meat mixture.

Bake in 375° oven 40 minutes. Makes 6 servings.

Tamale Pie Topping: Combine ¾ c. yellow corn meal, ½ tsp. salt and 2 c. cold water in 2-qt. saucepan. Cook over medium heat, stirring constantly, until mixture thickens. Stir in 1 tblsp. butter or regular margarine.

Tamale Pie Santa Fe

This Mexican-style hamburger pie, topped with a layer of corn meal and a sprinkle of American cheese, is a good budget-stretching recipe.

1½ lb. ground beef	½ tsp. pepper
1 (16-oz.) can tomatoes, cut up	1 (12-oz.) can Mexican-style corn, drained
⅔ c. finely chopped onion	Corn Meal Topping (recipe follows)
1½ tsp. salt	½ c. shredded pasteurized process American cheese
½ tsp. dried oregano leaves	

Cook ground beef in 10″ skillet over medium heat until lightly browned. Drain fat from skillet. Stir in tomatoes, onion, salt, oregano and pepper. Cook over high heat until mixture comes to a boil. Reduce heat to low and simmer 10 minutes or until mixture thickens. Stir in corn. Cook 2 minutes or until hot. Pour mixture into greased 2½-qt. casserole.

Prepare Corn Meal Topping. Drop topping by spoonfuls over hot meat mixture; then spread topping in a thin layer.

Bake in 375° oven 30 minutes. Sprinkle with cheese. Bake 10 to 15 minutes more, or until cheese melts. Makes 8 servings.

Corn Meal Topping: Combine 1 c. yellow corn meal, 2 tsp. salt, ½ tsp. chili powder, 2 tblsp. butter or regular margarine and 2 c. water in 2-qt. saucepan. Cook over medium heat, stirring often, until mixture thickens.

Italian Pie

Tastes a lot like lasagne—a layer of beef and a layer
of cheese, baked in a pie shell and served with spaghetti sauce.

¾ lb. ground beef
⅓ c. chopped onion
½ tsp. dried Italian
　herb seasoning
¼ tsp. salt
⅛ tsp. garlic salt
⅛ tsp. pepper
Unbaked 9" pie shell
2 eggs, slightly beaten

¾ c. creamed, small-curd
　cottage cheese
2 tblsp. chopped fresh
　parsley
½ c. shredded Cheddar
　cheese
1 c. hot spaghetti sauce,
　homemade or canned

Cook ground beef, onion, Italian seasoning, salt, garlic salt and pepper
in 10" skillet over medium heat until meat is browned. Drain fat from skillet. Spoon meat mixture into unbaked pie shell.

Combine eggs, cottage cheese and parsley in bowl; mix well. Spread
cottage cheese mixture over beef mixture.

Bake in 375° oven 15 minutes. Sprinkle with Cheddar cheese.

Bake 10 minutes more, or until crust is golden brown and cheese is
melted. Let stand 10 minutes before serving. Serve with hot spaghetti
sauce. Makes 6 to 8 servings.

Simple Pork Pie

Just what it sounds like—a straightforward recipe
for a savory pork pie made with potatoes, ground pork and seasonings.

Pastry for 2-crust 9" pie
1 lb. ground pork
2 c. diced, cooked potatoes
1 tsp. salt
½ tsp. dried savory leaves

¼ tsp. dried rubbed sage
⅛ tsp. ground cinnamon
⅛ tsp. ground cloves
⅛ tsp. pepper
½ c. water

Divide pastry almost in half. Roll out larger half on floured surface to
13" circle. Line 9" pie plate with pastry. Trim edge to ½" beyond rim of
pie plate.

Brown pork in 10" skillet over medium heat. Drain fat from skillet and
remove skillet from heat. Add potatoes, salt, savory, sage, cinnamon,
cloves, pepper and water. Mix well and turn mixture into pastry-lined pie
plate.

Roll out remaining pastry to 11" circle. Cut slits. Place top crust over

filling and trim edge to 1" beyond rim of pie plate. Fold top crust under lower crust and form a ridge. Flute edge.

Bake in 400° oven 50 minutes, or until crust is golden brown. Let stand 10 minutes before serving. Makes 6 to 8 servings.

Iowa-style Pork Pie

"My kids like to see how many different kinds of vegetables they can find inside this pie," said the cook who sent this recipe.

Meat Pie Pastry
  (recipe follows)
3 tblsp. butter or
  regular margarine
3 tblsp. flour
1½ c. chicken broth
1½ c. cubed, cooked pork
1½ c. cooked mixed
  vegetables

2 tblsp. finely chopped
  onion
½ tsp. dried marjoram
  leaves
¼ tsp. ground ginger
¼ tsp. dry mustard
½ tsp. browning for
  gravy

Prepare Meat Pie Pastry and divide pastry almost in half. Roll out larger half on floured surface to 12" circle. Line 8" pie plate with pastry. Trim edge to ½" beyond rim of pie plate.

Melt butter in 2-qt. saucepan over medium heat. Stir in flour. Cook 1 minute, stirring constantly. Gradually stir in chicken broth. Cook, stirring constantly, until mixture boils and thickens. Stir in pork, mixed vegetables, onion, marjoram, ginger, mustard and browning for gravy. Turn pork mixture into pastry-lined pie plate.

Roll out remaining pastry to 10" circle. Cut slits. Place top crust over filling and trim edge to 1" beyond rim of pie plate. Fold top crust under lower crust and form a ridge. Flute edge.

Bake in 400° oven 40 to 45 minutes, or until crust is golden brown. Let stand 10 minutes before serving. Makes 4 servings.

Meat Pie Pastry: Combine 1½ c. sifted flour and ½ tsp. salt in bowl. Cut in ⅓ c. shortening until coarse crumbs form, using a pastry blender. Sprinkle 4 to 5 tblsp. iced water over crumb mixture, a little at a time, tossing with a fork until dough forms.

Pork-Vegetable Pie

Pork, carrots and green beans, seasoned just so
and wrapped in a flaky, thyme-flavored crust, make a tasty dish.

Thyme-Seasoned Pastry
(recipe follows)
3 tblsp. butter or
regular margarine
1 c. chopped green pepper
1/4 c. chopped onion
3 tblsp. flour
1 tsp. salt
1/4 tsp. ground ginger
1/8 tsp. dry mustard

1/16 tsp. pepper
1 1/4 c. chicken broth
1/4 tsp. browning for gravy
2 1/2 c. cubed, cooked pork
1 c. sliced, cooked carrots
1 1/2 c. cooked cut green
beans
1 egg yolk, beaten
2 tsp. water

Prepare Thyme-Seasoned Pastry and divide pastry almost in half. Roll out larger half on floured surface to 13" circle. Line 9" pie plate with pastry. Trim edge to 1/2" beyond rim of pie plate.

Melt butter in 10" skillet over medium heat. Add green pepper and onion; sauté until tender. Stir in flour, salt, ginger, mustard and pepper. Cook 1 minute, stirring constantly. Gradually stir in chicken broth. Cook, stirring constantly, until mixture boils and thickens. Remove from heat.

Stir in browning for gravy, pork, carrots and green beans. Pour into pastry-lined pie plate.

Roll out remaining pastry to 11" circle. Cut slits. Place top crust over filling and trim edge to 1" beyond rim of pie plate. Fold top crust under lower crust and form a ridge. Flute edge. Combine egg yolk and water in bowl and brush over crust.

Bake in 400° oven 30 to 35 minutes, or until crust is golden brown. Let stand 10 minutes before serving. Makes 6 to 8 servings.

Thyme-Seasoned Pastry: Combine 2 1/3 c. sifted flour, 3/4 tsp. salt and 1/8 tsp. dried thyme leaves in bowl. Cut in 3/4 c. regular margarine until coarse crumbs form, using a pastry blender. Add 6 to 8 tblsp. iced water, a little at a time, tossing with a fork until dough forms.

Fried Ham 'n' Cheese Pies

Delicious little fried pies so versatile that you'll want
to serve them all the time—as a meal, as appetizers, or as snacks.

Flaky Pastry
  (recipe follows)
1 c. ground, fully cooked
  ham
¾ c. shredded Colby or
  Cheddar cheese
2 tblsp. mayonnaise or
  salad dressing

1 tblsp. finely chopped
  onion
Cooking oil
Ketchup
Prepared mustard

Prepare Flaky Pastry and divide pastry in half. Roll out each half on
floured surface to ⅛" thickness. Cut 20 rounds with floured 4" cookie
cutter, rerolling dough as needed.

Combine ham, cheese, mayonnaise and onion in bowl; mix well. Place
a small spoonful of ham mixture on each round of pastry. Moisten edges
with water. Fold each pastry in half over filling and press edges together
to seal, using the tines of a fork.

Pour cooking oil into 12" skillet or electric frypan to a depth of ½".
Heat over medium heat until oil reaches 375°.

Fry pies, five at a time, in hot oil 2 to 3 minutes, or until golden brown,
turning once. Drain on paper towels. Serve warm with ketchup and mustard. Makes 20 small pies.

Flaky Pastry: Combine 3 c. sifted flour and 1½ tsp. salt in bowl. Cut in
1 c. shortening until coarse crumbs form, using a pastry blender. Sprinkle
½ c. iced water over crumb mixture, a little at a time, tossing with a fork
until dough forms. Press dough firmly into a ball.

Cheese-and-Bacon Pie

Great for brunch, this pie uses three breakfast foods—
bacon and eggs in the filling and shredded wheat in the crust.

4 large shredded wheat
* biscuits, crushed (1½ c.)*
3 tblsp. butter or regular
* margarine, melted*
6 strips bacon
2 c. shredded Cheddar
* cheese*

3 eggs
½ tsp. salt
1/16 tsp. pepper
1½ c. milk
Paprika

Combine crushed shredded wheat biscuits and melted butter in bowl; mix well. Press shredded wheat biscuit mixture into bottom and up sides of greased 9″ pie plate and set aside.

Fry bacon in skillet over medium heat until crisp. Remove bacon and drain on paper towels. Crumble bacon.

Sprinkle half of the crumbled bacon over bottom of shredded wheat biscuit shell. Top with 1 c. of the cheese. Arrange remaining bacon on top.

Beat together eggs, salt, pepper and milk in bowl until well blended, using a rotary beater. Pour egg mixture evenly over all. Top with remaining 1 c. cheese and sprinkle with paprika.

Bake in 350° oven 40 minutes, or until golden brown. Let stand 10 minutes before serving. Makes 6 servings.

Savory Sausage-and-Potato Pie

An easy pie to make, from its whipped-potato crust
to the filling made with a can of prepared mushroom gravy.

Potato Crust (recipe follows)
1 lb. bulk pork sausage
½ c. green pepper strips
2 tsp. cornstarch
1 (10½-oz.) can mushroom
* gravy*

1 (12-oz.) can Mexican-
* style corn, drained*
1 c. shredded Cheddar
* cheese*

Prepare Potato Crust and set aside.

Brown pork sausage in 10″ skillet over medium heat and break into chunks, using a spoon. Remove and drain on paper towels. Drain all but 1 tblsp. fat from skillet. Add green pepper to fat in skillet; sauté 5 minutes, or until tender-crisp. Stir in sausage and cornstarch. Add gravy and corn; mix well. Heat thoroughly. Pour hot filling into Potato Crust. Sprinkle with Cheddar cheese.

Bake in 400° oven 25 minutes, or until golden brown. Let stand 10 minutes before serving. Makes 6 to 8 servings.

Potato Crust: Pare 1½ lb. all-purpose potatoes (5 medium). Quarter potatoes and cook in boiling, salted water in 3-qt. saucepan over medium heat 25 minutes, or until tender. Drain well and mash until smooth, using a potato masher. Stir in 1 egg (beaten), ½ c. chopped onion, ½ c. cornflake crumbs and 2 tsp. dried parsley flakes; mix well. Spread mixture evenly over bottom and up sides of greased 10″ pie plate.

Cheesy Lamb Pie

A rich, double-crust pie made with ground lamb, five eggs
and lots of cottage cheese. The top crust is sprinkled with Parmesan.

Pastry for 2-crust 10″ pie	½ tsp. dried oregano leaves
1 lb. ground lamb	½ tsp. garlic salt
5 eggs	⅛ tsp. pepper
1 (16-oz.) container	4 tblsp. butter or
creamed small-curd	regular margarine
cottage cheese	3 tblsp. grated Parmesan
3 tblsp. chopped fresh	cheese
parsley	

Divide pastry almost in half. Roll out larger half on floured surface to 14″ circle. Line 10″ pie plate with pastry. Trim edge to ½″ beyond rim of pie plate.

Cook ground lamb in 10″ skillet over medium heat until browned. Remove from heat. Drain fat from skillet.

Beat eggs in bowl until blended, using a rotary beater. Add cottage cheese, parsley, oregano, garlic salt, pepper and browned lamb; mix well. Turn mixture into pastry-lined pie plate. Dot with 2 tblsp. of the butter.

Roll out remaining pastry to 12″ circle. Cut slits. Place top crust over filling and trim edge to 1″ beyond rim of pie plate. Fold top crust under lower crust and form a ridge. Flute edge.

Melt remaining 2 tblsp. butter in small saucepan over low heat. Brush melted butter over pie and sprinkle with Parmesan cheese.

Place pie in preheated 450° oven. Immediately reduce temperature to 400° and bake 35 minutes, or until crust is golden brown. Let stand 10 minutes before serving. Makes 8 servings.

Country Lamb Pie

A country-style stew of cubed lamb shoulder and vegetables topped with dill-flavored biscuits—a really outstanding pie.

1½ lb. boneless lamb
  shoulder, cut into
  1" cubes
2 tblsp. cooking oil
1 clove garlic, minced
2½ c. water
2½ tsp. salt
¼ tsp. pepper
4 carrots, pared and cut
  into 1" pieces

3 medium potatoes, pared
  and quartered
1 medium onion, sliced
Dill Biscuits
  (recipe follows)
1 (10-oz.) pkg. frozen peas
  (2 c.)
⅓ c. flour
½ c. water

Brown lamb cubes in hot oil in 4-qt. Dutch oven over medium-high heat. Add garlic, 2½ c. water, salt and pepper. Cook over high heat until mixture comes to a boil. Reduce heat to low. Cover and simmer 1½ hours, or until meat is almost tender. Add carrots, potatoes and onion. Cover and simmer 25 minutes more, or until meat and vegetables are tender.

Meanwhile, prepare Dill Biscuits; set aside.

Add peas to lamb mixture. Cook 5 minutes, or until peas can be separated.

Combine flour and ½ c. water in jar. Cover and shake until blended. Stir into meat mixture. Cook over medium heat, stirring constantly, until mixture boils and thickens. Pour hot stew into 3-qt. casserole. Top with Dill Biscuits.

Bake in 425° oven 12 to 15 minutes, or until biscuits are golden brown. Makes 6 servings.

Dill Biscuits: Combine 2 c. buttermilk baking mix, ⅔ c. milk and 2 tsp. dried dillweed in bowl. Stir until dough forms. Turn out onto lightly floured surface and knead gently 10 times. Roll to 1" thickness and cut with floured 2" cutter.

Chicken Pot Pie

The flavor of this delicious chicken pot pie is enriched
by cooking the giblets together with the chicken and vegetables.

1 (3-lb.) broiler-fryer with giblets, cut up	Water
1 medium onion, quartered	1 (10-oz.) pkg. frozen peas and mushrooms, thawed (2 c.)
1 stalk celery, cut in half	½ tsp. poultry seasoning
3 sprigs fresh parsley	¾ tsp. salt
5 whole peppercorns	1/16 tsp. pepper
1 bay leaf	⅓ c. flour
1½ tsp. salt	½ c. milk
2 c. water	Pastry for 1-crust 9" pie
1½ c. carrot strips, 2" long	1 egg yolk, slightly beaten
5 small onions, quartered	1 tblsp. water

Place chicken, giblets, 1 medium onion, celery, parsley, peppercorns, bay leaf, 1½ tsp. salt and 2 c. water in 4-qt. Dutch oven. Cook over high heat until mixture comes to a boil. Reduce heat to low. Cover and simmer 1 hour, or until chicken is tender.

Strain broth and return to Dutch oven. Cool chicken and giblets slightly. Chop giblets. Remove meat from bones and cut up. Discard skin and bones.

Add carrot strips and 5 small onions to broth. Cook over high heat until mixture comes to a boil. Reduce heat to low. Cover and simmer 15 minutes, or until carrots and onions are tender. Drain carrots and onions in colander, reserving broth.

Add enough water to broth to make 2¼ c. liquid. Return cooking liquid to Dutch oven. Stir in peas and mushrooms, poultry seasoning, ¾ tsp. salt, pepper, chicken, giblets, carrots and onions.

Combine flour and milk in jar. Cover and shake until blended. Stir flour mixture into broth. Cook over medium heat, stirring constantly, until mixture boils and thickens. Pour hot chicken mixture into 2-qt. casserole.

Roll out pastry to 11" circle. Cut slits. Place crust over chicken mixture and trim edge to 1" beyond rim of casserole. Fold under edge of crust and form a ridge. Flute edge. Mix together egg yolk and water in bowl. Brush over crust.

Bake in 400° oven 30 to 35 minutes, or until crust is golden brown and filling is bubbly. Makes 6 servings.

Chicken-Ham Pie with Spinach

Tender chunks of chicken and ham team up with spinach
in a creamy Swiss cheese sauce in this savory double-crust pie.

Pastry for 2-crust 9" pie
3 tblsp. butter or
  regular margarine
¼ c. finely chopped
  onion
3 tblsp. flour
1 tsp. dry mustard
⅛ tsp. pepper

2 c. milk
1½ c. cubed, cooked
  chicken (½" pieces)
1½ c. cubed, fully cooked
  ham (½" pieces)
1 (10-oz.) pkg. frozen chopped
  spinach, thawed and drained
1 c. shredded Swiss cheese

Divide pastry almost in half. Roll out larger half on floured surface to 13" circle. Line 9" pie plate with pastry. Trim edge to ½" beyond rim of pie plate.

Melt butter in 2-qt. saucepan over medium heat. Add onion; sauté until tender. Blend in flour, mustard and pepper. Cook, stirring constantly, 1 minute. Gradually stir in milk. Cook, stirring constantly, until mixture boils and thickens. Cook 1 minute more. Remove from heat. Add chicken, ham, spinach and cheese, stirring until cheese melts. Turn hot mixture into pastry-lined pie plate.

Roll out remaining pastry to 11" circle. Cut slits. Place top crust over filling and trim edge to 1" beyond rim of pie plate. Fold top crust under lower crust and form a ridge. Flute edge.

Bake in 400° oven 35 minutes, or until crust is golden brown. Let stand 10 minutes before serving. Makes 6 to 8 servings.

Chicken-and-Stuffing Pie

A good, easy recipe that combines cooked chicken
and stuffing in an unusual way—the stuffing forms the pie crust.

Stuffing Crust
  (recipe follows)
1 (4-oz.) can sliced
  mushrooms
2 tsp. flour
1 tblsp. butter or
  regular margarine
½ c. chopped onion
1 (10½-oz.) can chicken
  giblet gravy

3 c. cubed, cooked chicken
1 c. frozen peas
2 tblsp. diced pimientos
1 tblsp. dried parsley
  flakes
1 tsp. Worcestershire
  sauce
½ tsp. dried thyme leaves
4 slices pasteurized
  process American cheese

Prepare Stuffing Crust and set aside.

Drain mushrooms, reserving liquid. Stir flour into reserved mushroom liquid; set aside.

Melt butter in 10" skillet over medium heat. Add mushrooms and onion; sauté until onion is tender. Add mushroom liquid mixture, gravy, chicken, peas, pimientos, parsley flakes, Worcestershire sauce and thyme. Heat thoroughly. Remove from heat.

Pour hot filling into Stuffing Crust.

Bake in 375° oven 20 minutes, or until hot and bubbly.

Cut each slice of cheese into 4 strips and place strips on top of pie in a lattice design. Bake 5 minutes more, or until cheese melts. Let stand 10 minutes before serving. Makes 6 to 8 servings.

Stuffing Crust: Combine 1 (8-oz.) pkg. herb-seasoned stuffing mix, ¾ c. chicken broth, ½ c. butter or regular margarine (melted) and 1 egg (beaten) in bowl. Mix until moistened. Press mixture into bottom and up sides of greased 10" pie plate.

Savory Creamed Chicken Pie

An Oregon farm wife treats her family to a nifty hot lunch when she serves this chicken pie with a special biscuit crust.

Savory Biscuit Crust
  (recipe follows)
2 tblsp. butter or
  regular margarine
½ c. finely chopped
  green pepper
½ c. finely chopped
  celery
¼ c. finely chopped
  onion
2 c. cubed, cooked
  chicken (¾" pieces)
1 c. sliced, cooked carrots
1 (10¾-oz.) can condensed
  cream of celery soup
2 tblsp. milk

Prepare Savory Biscuit Crust and bake in 450° oven 10 minutes.

Meanwhile, melt butter in 10" skillet over medium heat. Add green pepper, celery and onion. Sauté until tender. Remove from heat.

Stir chicken, carrots, celery soup and milk into skillet. Spread mixture evenly over partially baked Savory Biscuit Crust.

Bake in 450° oven 10 minutes, or until bubbly. Makes 8 servings.

Savory Biscuit Crust: Combine 2 c. sifted flour, 3 tsp. baking powder, 1 tsp. salt and ½ tsp. dried rubbed sage in bowl. Cut in ½ c. shortening until coarse crumbs form, using a pastry blender. Stir in 1 c. shredded Cheddar cheese. Add ¾ c. milk to crumb mixture stirring with a fork, until soft dough forms. Turn onto floured surface and knead gently 10 times. Roll out dough to 13x9" rectangle. Line bottom of 13x9x2" baking pan with dough.

Chicken Turnovers with Mushroom Sauce

Sour cream and mushrooms are blended into a delicious sauce
to ladle over crisp turnovers plump with chicken and cream cheese.

1 (17¼-oz.) pkg. frozen puff pastry	¼ tsp. salt
1 (3-oz.) pkg. cream cheese, softened	¹⁄₁₆ tsp. pepper
2 tblsp. finely chopped onion	1⅓ c. diced, cooked chicken
2 tblsp. chopped fresh parsley	1 egg yolk, slightly beaten
1 tblsp. milk	1 tblsp. water
	Mushroom Sauce (recipe follows)

Thaw puff pastry according to package directions. Gently unfold thawed pastry. Cut each pastry sheet into 4 squares.

Combine cream cheese, onion, parsley, milk, salt and pepper in bowl. Beat until smooth, using an electric mixer at medium speed. Stir in chicken.

Place one eighth of the chicken mixture on half of each pastry square. Moisten edges with water. Fold each pastry square diagonally in half over filling, forming a triangle. Press edges together to seal, using the tines of a fork. Place turnovers, about 3" apart, on ungreased baking sheets. Mix together egg yolk and water in bowl. Brush over each turnover.

Bake in 350° oven 30 minutes, or until golden brown. Meanwhile, prepare Mushroom Sauce. Serve hot turnovers with Mushroom Sauce. Makes 8 turnovers.

Mushroom Sauce: Combine 1 (10½-oz.) can chicken gravy and 1 (4-oz.) can sliced mushrooms (drained) in small saucepan. Cook over medium heat, stirring occasionally, until hot. Stir a small amount of hot mixture into ½ c. dairy sour cream. Pour sour cream mixture back into remaining hot mixture, blending well. Cook, stirring constantly, until hot. Do not boil. Remove from heat. Stir in 2 tblsp. chopped fresh parsley.

Royal Chicken Pie

Biscuit pinwheels stuffed with chopped green olives
and Cheddar cheese bake on top of the lightly seasoned filling.

¼ c. chopped onion
¼ c. chopped celery
¼ c. chicken fat or butter
  or regular margarine
½ c. chopped pimientos
3 c. diced, cooked chicken
3½ tblsp. flour
½ tsp. soy sauce

¼ tsp. pepper
¼ tsp. garlic salt
2½ c. chicken broth
Cheddar Biscuit Crust
  (recipe follows)
1 tblsp. butter or regular
  margarine, melted

Sauté onion and celery in 2 tblsp. of the chicken fat in 10″ skillet over medium heat until tender, but not brown. Stir in pimientos and chicken. Pour mixture into 2-qt. casserole.

Melt remaining 2 tblsp. chicken fat in same skillet. Blend in flour, soy sauce, pepper and garlic salt. Gradually stir in chicken broth. Cook over medium heat, stirring constantly, until mixture boils and thickens. Pour sauce over chicken in casserole.

Cover and bake in 425° oven 20 minutes, or until bubbly.

Meanwhile, prepare Cheddar Biscuit Crust. Cut Cheddar Biscuit Crust into ½″ slices. Arrange slices on hot chicken mixture. Brush with melted butter.

Bake in 425° oven 12 minutes more, or until crust is lightly browned. Makes 8 servings.

Cheddar Biscuit Crust: Combine 2 c. buttermilk baking mix and ⅔ c. milk in bowl. Stir until dough forms. Turn out onto lightly floured surface and knead gently 10 times. Roll out to 10x9″ rectangle. Sprinkle with ¾ c. shredded Cheddar cheese and ¼ c. finely chopped pimiento-stuffed olives. Roll up like a jelly roll, starting at wide end.

Deviled Turkey Pie

Peas, carrots and tender chunks of turkey in a cream sauce
make a hearty dish, especially when teamed with a corn bread topping.

¼ c. chopped onion	1 (10-oz) pkg. frozen
¼ c. butter or regular	peas and carrots (2 c.)
margarine	2 chicken bouillon cubes
¼ c. flour	1 tblsp. prepared mustard
1 tsp. salt	1 tsp. Worcestershire
⅛ tsp. pepper	sauce
2½ c. milk	Corn Bread Topping
3 c. cubed, cooked turkey	(recipe follows)
(or chicken)	

Cook onion in butter in 3-qt. saucepan over medium heat until tender. Blend in flour, salt and pepper. Gradually stir in milk. Cook, stirring constantly, until mixture comes to a boil. Stir in turkey, peas and carrots, bouillon cubes, mustard and Worcestershire sauce. Cook until bubbly. Pour mixture into greased 3-qt. casserole.

Prepare Corn Bread Topping and spread over turkey mixture.

Bake in 425° oven 30 to 35 minutes, or until corn bread is golden brown. Makes 6 to 8 servings.

Corn Bread Topping: Stir together 1 c. yellow corn meal, 1 c. flour, 2 tblsp. sugar, 4 tsp. baking powder, and ¾ tsp. salt in bowl. Combine 2 eggs (beaten), 1 c. milk and ¼ c. shortening. Add all at once to dry ingredients, stirring just enough to moisten.

Tuna-Cheese Pie

Sure to please tuna-casserole fans, this pie features
tuna, carrots and peas in a Cheddar sauce, all encased in flaky pastry.

Pastry for 2-crust 9″ pie	¼ tsp. salt
1 c. sliced, pared carrots	⅛ tsp. pepper
¼ tsp. salt	1½ c. milk
1 c. frozen peas	1 tsp. Worcestershire sauce
3 tblsp. butter or	1 c. shredded Cheddar
regular margarine	cheese
¼ c. finely chopped	2 (6½-oz.) cans tuna,
onion	drained and broken into
3 tblsp. flour	chunks
½ tsp. dry mustard	

Divide pastry almost in half. Roll out larger half on floured surface to 13″ circle. Line 9″ pie plate with pastry. Trim edge to ½″ beyond rim of pie plate.

Cook sliced carrots with ¼ tsp. salt in small amount of boiling water in 2-qt. saucepan 8 minutes. Add peas; cook 5 minutes more. Rinse vegetables with cold water; drain well. Set aside.

Melt butter in same saucepan over medium heat. Add onion; sauté until tender. Stir in flour, mustard, ¼ tsp. salt and pepper. Cook 1 minute, stirring constantly. Gradually stir in milk and Worcestershire sauce. Cook, stirring constantly, until mixture comes to a boil. Add cheese, stirring until melted. Add tuna and cooked vegetables; mix well. Turn hot mixture into pastry-lined pie plate.

Roll out remaining pastry to 11″ circle. Cut slits. Place top crust over filling and trim edge to 1″ beyond rim of pie plate. Fold top crust under lower crust and form a ridge. Flute edge.

Bake in 400° oven 30 to 35 minutes, or until crust is golden brown. Let stand 10 minutes before serving. Makes 6 to 8 servings.

Microwaved Tuna Pie

Spaghetti, eggs and cheese form the pasta crust
in this quickly prepared supper dish from an Iowa farm wife.

Spaghetti Crust
  (recipe follows)
1 (6½-oz.) can tuna,
  drained and broken into
  chunks

4 c. homemade, meatless
  spaghetti sauce, or
  1 (32-oz.) jar
1 c. shredded mozzarella
  cheese

Prepare Spaghetti Crust and microwave (high setting) 4 minutes, or until center is set.

Combine tuna and 1¾ c. of the spaghetti sauce in glass bowl. Microwave (high setting) 2 minutes. Stir. Microwave 2 minutes more. Spoon mixture into Spaghetti Crust. Cover with waxed paper.

Microwave (high setting) 3 minutes. Rotate plate one-quarter turn. Microwave 3 minutes. Sprinkle with cheese. Microwave 2 minutes more, or until cheese melts. Let stand 10 minutes.

Meanwhile, pour remaining spaghetti sauce into glass bowl. Microwave (high setting) 2 minutes, or until hot. Ladle spaghetti sauce over pie. Makes 6 servings.

Spaghetti Crust: Combine 8 oz. spaghetti (cooked and drained), 2 eggs (beaten), ⅓ c. grated Parmesan cheese and 2 tblsp. butter or regular margarine in bowl; mix well. Turn mixture into greased 9″ glass pie plate. Pat into bottom and up sides, forming a ridge.

Tuna-Egg Pie

A simple pie that's extra-rich in protein because
it's made with mozzarella cheese, tuna and half a dozen eggs.

6 eggs
¼ c. milk
1 (6½-oz.) can tuna,
  drained and flaked
2 c. shredded mozzarella
  cheese
½ tsp. dried oregano
  leaves

½ tsp. dried basil
  leaves
¼ tsp. salt
¼ tsp. pepper
Unbaked 9″ pie shell

Beat together eggs and milk in bowl until blended, using a rotary beater. Stir in tuna, mozzarella cheese, oregano, basil, salt and pepper, blending well. Pour mixture into unbaked pie shell.

Bake in 425° oven 35 to 40 minutes, or until lightly browned and filling is set. Let stand 10 minutes before serving. Makes 6 to 8 servings.

Tuna Pie with Cottage Cheese Biscuits

This pie has it all—tuna, potatoes, vegetables and biscuits.
Just add a tossed salad and dessert to complete the meal.

2 c. cubed, pared potatoes
½ c. chopped celery
½ c. chopped onion
1 (10-oz.) pkg. frozen
  mixed vegetables (2 c.)
Cottage Cheese Biscuits
  (recipe follows)

2 (10¾-oz.) cans
  condensed cream of
  celery soup
1 (9¼-oz.) can tuna,
  drained and flaked
½ tsp. salt
¼ tsp. pepper

Combine potatoes, celery and onion in 3-qt. saucepan in 1″ water.
Cook over high heat until mixture comes to a boil. Reduce heat to low.
Cover and simmer 10 minutes, or until vegetables are just tender.

Add frozen mixed vegetables and cook 5 minutes more, or until vegetables can be separated. Drain, reserving cooking liquid. Add enough
water to cooking liquid to make ½ c.

Prepare Cottage Cheese Biscuits.

Combine celery soup, tuna, salt, pepper, ½ c. cooking liquid and vege-
tables in saucepan. Cook mixture over high heat until it comes to a boil.
Pour into greased 13x9x2″ (3-qt.) baking dish. Arrange Cottage Cheese
Biscuits on top of tuna mixture.

Bake in 400° oven 15 minutes, or until biscuits are golden brown.
Makes 6 servings.

Cottage Cheese Biscuits: Sift together 2 c. sifted flour, 3 tsp. baking powder and ½ tsp. salt into bowl. Stir in 1 tblsp. dried parsley flakes. Cut in ⅓ c. shortening until mixture resembles coarse meal, using a pastry blender. Combine ½ c. creamed small-curd cottage cheese and ½ c. milk in another bowl, blend well. Add to flour mixture, stirring with a fork until soft dough forms. Turn onto lightly floured surface and knead gently 6 to 8 times. Roll to 1″ thickness and cut with floured 2″ cutter.

Salmon Pie in Whole-wheat Crust

This unique and delicious salmon pie won a blue ribbon
for the Washington farm woman who entered it in a local contest.

*Whole-wheat Crumb Crust
  (recipe follows)
1 (15½-oz.) can red
  sockeye salmon
3 eggs
1 c. dairy sour cream
¼ c. mayonnaise or
  salad dressing*

*2 tblsp. finely chopped
  onion
1 tsp. dried dillweed
3 drops Tabasco sauce
½ c. shredded Cheddar
  cheese*

Prepare Whole-wheat Crumb Crust and set aside.

Drain salmon, reserving liquid. Remove skin and bones. Break salmon into chunks and set aside.

Beat eggs in bowl until blended, using a rotary beater. Add sour cream, mayonnaise, onion, dillweed, Tabasco sauce and reserved salmon liquid, blending well. Stir in cheese and salmon. Spoon into Whole-wheat Crumb Crust. Sprinkle with reserved 1 c. crumb mixture.

Bake in 400° oven 30 minutes, or until puffy. Let stand 10 minutes before serving. Makes 6 to 8 servings.

Whole-wheat Crumb Crust: Combine 1½ c. stirred whole-wheat flour, ½ tsp. salt and ½ tsp. paprika in bowl. Cut in ½ c. butter or regular margarine until crumbly, using a pastry blender. Stir in 1 c. shredded Cheddar cheese and ⅓ c. chopped walnuts. Reserve 1 c. crumb mixture for topping. Press remaining crumb mixture into bottom and up sides of 10″ pie plate.

Grilled Cheese Pie

"When you're running low on groceries, this is a recipe
you can put together quickly," an Idaho farm woman told us.

2 eggs	2½ c. milk
1½ c. sifted flour	2 c. shredded Cheddar
1 tsp. salt	cheese
¼ tsp. pepper	

Combine eggs, flour, salt, pepper and milk in bowl. Beat just until smooth, using a rotary beater. Stir in 1 c. of the cheese. Pour into well-greased 10" pie plate.

Bake in 425° oven 35 minutes, or until puffy and brown. Sprinkle with remaining 1 c. cheese.

Bake 2 minutes more, or until cheese melts. Makes 4 to 6 servings.

Cheeseburger Quiche

A Missouri farm mother says that this is an easy dish
that pleases her children just as much as it does her husband.

Onion Pie Shell	¾ c. mayonnaise or
(recipe follows)	salad dressing
1 lb. ground beef	¾ c. milk
¾ c. chopped onion	4 tsp. cornstarch
2 c. shredded Cheddar	½ tsp. salt
cheese	1/16 tsp. pepper
4 eggs	

Prepare Onion Pie Shell and set aside.

Cook ground beef and onion in 10" skillet over medium heat until meat is browned. Drain fat from skillet. Spoon meat mixture into unbaked Onion Pie Shell. Sprinkle with cheese.

Beat eggs in bowl until blended, using a rotary beater. Add mayonnaise, milk, cornstarch, salt and pepper; beat until blended. Pour over meat-cheese mixture in pie shell.

Bake in 425° oven 10 minutes. Reduce temperature to 350° and bake 25 minutes more, or until knife inserted halfway between the center and edge comes out clean. Let stand 10 minutes before serving. Makes 6 to 8 servings.

Onion Pie Shell: Combine 2 c. sifted flour and 1 tsp. onion salt in bowl. Cut in ¾ c. shortening until coarse crumbs form, using a pastry blender. Sprinkle 3 tblsp. iced water over crumb mixture, a little at a time, tossing with a fork until dough forms. Press dough firmly into a ball. Roll out dough on floured surface to 14" circle. Line 10" pie plate with pastry. Trim edge to 1" beyond rim of pie plate. Fold under edge of crust and form a ridge. Flute edge.

Versatile Quiche

Choose the filling variation that appeals most to your
family, and add the ingredients to the basic recipe as directed.

Rich Quiche Pastry Shell	*3 eggs*
(see Index)	*1 c. heavy cream*

Arrange filling ingredients in unbaked Rich Quiche Pastry Shell as directed in one of the following variations.

Beat eggs slightly in bowl, using a rotary beater. Add heavy cream and beat until blended. Blend in seasonings as directed in chosen variation. Pour egg mixture over filling ingredients in quiche shell.

Bake in 425° oven 10 minutes. Reduce temperature to 325° and bake 30 minutes more, or until custard is set. Let stand 10 minutes before serving. Makes 6 servings.

Cheese-Spinach Quiche: Cook 1 (10-oz.) pkg. frozen, chopped spinach according to package directions; drain well. Sauté 4 thinly sliced green onions and their tops in 1 tblsp. butter or regular margarine in 2-qt. saucepan over medium heat. Remove from heat. Stir in drained spinach and 1/4 c. finely chopped fresh parsley. Add spinach mixture, 1/2 tsp. salt, 1/2 tsp. ground sage and 1/8 tsp. pepper to egg mixture; blend well. Pour mixture into quiche shell. Sprinkle with 1/4 c. grated Parmesan cheese. Bake as directed in basic recipe.

Quiche Lorraine: Sprinkle 1 c. shredded Swiss or Gruyère cheese and 8 strips bacon (cooked, drained and crumbled) in bottom of quiche shell. Pour egg mixture over mixture in quiche shell. Sprinkle with nutmeg. Bake as directed in basic recipe.

Ham 'n' Cheese Quiche: Sprinkle 1 c. shredded Cheddar cheese and 3/4 c. finely diced, cooked ham in bottom of quiche shell. Add 1 tsp. Worcestershire sauce, 1/4 tsp. dry mustard and 1/8 tsp. pepper to egg mixture; beat until blended, using a rotary beater. Pour over mixture in shell. Sprinkle with caraway seeds. Bake as directed in basic recipe.

Chicken-Almond Quiche: Sprinkle 1/4 c. grated Parmesan cheese in bottom of quiche shell. Top with 1 c. finely diced, cooked chicken and 2 thinly sliced green onions and tops. Add 1/4 tsp. salt, 1/8 tsp. pepper and 1/8 tsp. dry mustard to egg mixture; beat until blended, using a rotary beater. Pour over mixture in quiche shell. Sprinkle with 1/4 c. sliced almonds and 1/4 c. grated Parmesan cheese. Bake as directed in basic recipe.

Chicken-Mushroom Quiche

The rich flavor of this quiche is a blend of chicken,
mushrooms and two kinds of cheese in a creamy custard filling.

3 tblsp. butter or
  regular margarine
1/4 c. chopped onion
6 oz. fresh mushrooms,
  sliced
1/3 c. grated Romano
  cheese
Quiche Pastry Shell
  (see Index)

1 1/4 c. cubed, cooked
  chicken
1/2 c. shredded Swiss
  cheese
2 eggs
1 c. light cream
3 drops Tabasco sauce
1/4 tsp. salt
1/8 tsp. pepper

Melt butter in 10" skillet over medium heat. Add onion; sauté until tender. Add mushrooms; sauté until tender. Remove from heat.

Sprinkle Romano cheese in bottom of unbaked Quiche Pastry Shell. Then arrange chicken and mushroom-onion mixture in shell and top with Swiss cheese.

Beat eggs in bowl until blended, using a rotary beater. Add light cream, Tabasco sauce, salt and pepper; beat until blended. Pour over mixture in quiche pan.

Bake in 425° oven 10 minutes. Reduce temperature to 325° and bake 15 minutes more, or until a knife inserted near center comes out clean. Let stand 10 minutes before serving. Makes 6 servings.

Broccoli-Mushroom Quiche

Even though there's no meat in this quiche, it's
plenty satisfying, because the custard is made with heavy cream.

3 tblsp. butter or
  regular margarine
1/4 lb. fresh mushrooms,
  sliced
1/3 c. chopped onion
1 c. shredded Swiss cheese
Quiche Pastry Shell
  (see Index)

1 (10-oz) pkg. frozen
  broccoli spears, cooked
  and drained
3 eggs
1 c. heavy cream
1/2 tsp. salt
1/8 tsp. pepper

Melt butter in 10" skillet over medium heat. Add mushrooms and onion; sauté until tender. Remove from heat.

Sprinkle cheese in bottom of unbaked Quiche Pastry Shell. Cut broccoli spears into 1" pieces. Arrange broccoli in shell and top with mushroom-onion mixture.

Beat eggs in bowl until blended, using a rotary beater. Add heavy cream, salt and pepper; beat until blended. Pour over mixture in quiche pan.

Bake in 425° oven 10 minutes. Reduce temperature to 325° and bake 30 minutes more, or until a knife inserted near center comes out clean. Let stand 10 minutes before serving. Makes 6 servings.

Three-Cheese Quiche

"This quiche makes a light, nutritious meal, and it's so elegant to serve when entertaining," writes a California farm woman.

Unbaked 9" pie shell
 with fluted edge
3 tblsp. butter or
 regular margarine
8 oz. fresh mushrooms,
 sliced
½ c. chopped onion
½ c. chopped celery
½ c. chopped green
 pepper
½ c. grated Parmesan
 cheese

1 c. shredded Colby
 cheese
½ c. shredded provolone
 cheese
5 eggs
½ c. milk
1 tsp. dried basil leaves
¼ tsp. salt
⅛ tsp. pepper
⅛ tsp. ground nutmeg

Prick entire surface of unbaked pie shell with a fork.

Bake in 425° oven 6 minutes. Cool on rack while preparing filling.

Melt butter in 10" skillet over medium heat. Add mushrooms, onion, celery and green pepper; sauté until tender. Remove from heat.

Sprinkle Parmesan cheese over bottom of partially baked pie shell. Then spoon mushroom mixture into shell and top with Colby and provolone cheeses.

Beat eggs in bowl until blended, using a rotary beater. Add milk, basil, salt, pepper and nutmeg; beat until blended. Pour over mixture in pie shell.

Bake in 400° oven 10 minutes. Reduce temperature to 350° and bake 20 minutes more, or until set. Let stand 10 minutes before serving. Makes 6 servings.

Golden Onion Quiche

The top of this quiche bakes to a mellow golden brown
because the filling is so rich in eggs and Cheddar cheese.

¼ c. butter or
   regular margarine
3 c. sliced onion
1½ c. shredded
   Cheddar cheese
Quiche Pastry Shell
   (see Index)

3 eggs
1 c. heavy cream
½ tsp. salt
⅛ tsp. Tabasco sauce
Ground nutmeg

Melt butter in 10″ skillet over medium heat. Add onion and sauté until
tender, about 15 minutes. Remove from heat.

Sprinkle ¾ c. of the cheese in bottom of unbaked Quiche Pastry Shell.
Arrange sauteéd onions in shell and top with remaining ¾ c. cheese.

Beat eggs in bowl until blended, using a rotary beater. Add heavy
cream, salt and Tabasco sauce; beat until blended. Pour over cheese-on-
ion mixture in quiche pan and sprinkle with nutmeg.

Bake in 425° oven 10 minutes. Reduce temperature to 325° and
bake 30 minutes more, or until set. Let stand 10 minutes before serving.
Makes 6 servings.

Green Onion Quiche

A mildly seasoned basic quiche with a Swiss cheese custard
flavored with green onions; it's dotted with bacon to add crunch.

6 strips bacon, diced
¼ c. sliced green onions
1 c. shredded Swiss
   cheese
Unbaked 9″ pie shell with
   fluted edge

3 eggs
1 c. milk
¼ tsp. dry mustard
¼ tsp. ground nutmeg

Fry bacon in 10″ skillet over medium heat until crisp. Remove bacon
and drain on paper towels. Drain all but 1 tblsp. drippings from skillet.

Sauté green onions in drippings until tender, but not brown. Remove
from heat.

Sprinkle cheese and bacon in bottom of unbaked pie shell.

Beat eggs in bowl until blended, using a rotary beater. Add milk, mustard, nutmeg and green onions; beat until blended. Pour over cheese-ba-
con mixture in pie shell.

Bake in 425° oven 10 minutes. Reduce temperature to 325° and bake 20 minutes more, or until a knife inserted halfway between the center and edge comes out clean. Let stand 10 minutes before serving. Makes 6 servings.

Spinach-and-Ricotta Quiche

Rich and creamy ricotta cheese teams with spinach
to make this smooth-textured quiche extra-nutritious.

2 tblsp. butter or
  regular margarine
½ c. chopped onion
3 eggs
1 c. half-and-half
1 (10-oz.) pkg. frozen chopped
  spinach, thawed and drained
½ c. ricotta cheese

½ c. grated Parmesan
  cheese
½ tsp. salt
⅛ tsp. pepper
3 drops Tabasco sauce
Quiche Pastry Shell
  (see Index)
Ground nutmeg

Melt butter in 10" skillet over medium heat. Add onion and sauté until tender. Remove from heat.

Beat eggs in bowl until blended, using a rotary beater. Add sautéed onion, half-and-half, spinach, ricotta cheese, Parmesan cheese, salt, pepper and Tabasco sauce; beat until blended. Pour mixture into unbaked Quiche Pastry Shell and sprinkle with nutmeg.

Bake in 425° oven 10 minutes. Reduce temperature to 325° and bake 30 minutes more, or until a knife inserted near center comes out clean. Let stand 10 minutes before serving. Makes 6 servings.

Peanut-Spinach Quiche

An unusual quiche with a pretty ring of sliced tomatoes
over a spinach filling, topped off with a sprinkling of chopped peanuts.

2 tblsp. butter or
   regular margarine
½ c. chopped onion
1 clove garlic, minced
2 (10-oz.) pkg. frozen chopped
   spinach, thawed and drained
3 eggs
¾ c. milk
1 tsp. dried basil leaves
½ tsp. celery salt
1½ c. shredded Cheddar
   cheese

Unbaked 9″ pie shell with
   fluted edge
1 large tomato, thinly
   sliced
½ c. chopped peanuts
1 tblsp. grated Parmesan
   cheese
1 tblsp. bread crumbs,
   packed

Melt butter in 10″ skillet over medium heat. Add onion and garlic;
sauté until tender. Add spinach and cook until excess moisture evaporates. Remove from heat.

Beat eggs in bowl until blended, using a rotary beater. Add milk, basil
and celery salt; beat until blended. Stir in Cheddar cheese and spinach
mixture. Turn mixture into unbaked pie shell. Arrange tomato slices
around edge of crust. Mix together peanuts, Parmesan cheese and bread
crumbs and sprinkle over tomatoes.

Bake in 425° oven 15 minutes. Reduce temperature to 350° and bake
20 to 25 minutes more, or until a knife inserted halfway between the center and edge comes out clean. Let stand 10 minutes before serving.
Makes 6 servings.

Vegetable Confetti Quiche

"I like this recipe because it lets me use up any
leftover vegetables I might have," a Michigan farm woman says.

½ c. sliced, cooked
   carrots
Unbaked 9″ pie shell
   with fluted edge
1 c. shredded Cheddar
   cheese
½ c. cooked peas
1 (8¾-oz.) can whole-
   kernel corn, drained

1 tblsp. chopped pimientos
3 eggs
1½ c. milk
¼ c. shredded green
   pepper
2 tblsp. shredded onion
½ tsp. salt
⅛ tsp. pepper

Arrange carrots in bottom of unbaked pie shell. Top with layers of one third of the cheese, peas, one third of the cheese, corn and remaining cheese. Sprinkle with pimientos.

Beat eggs in bowl until blended, using a rotary beater. Add milk, green pepper, onion, salt and pepper; beat until blended. Pour over cheese-vegetable mixture in pie shell.

Bake in 425° oven 15 minutes. Reduce temperature to 325° and bake 35 minutes more, or until a knife inserted halfway between center and edge comes out clean. Let stand 10 minutes before serving. Makes 6 servings.

Potato-and-Sausage Quiche

An Oklahoma farm woman says this is one of her family's favorite meals. She serves it with homemade applesauce and salad.

1½ lb. all-purpose potatoes, pared and shredded (about 3 c.)	2 eggs
	1 c. milk
	¼ c. finely chopped onion
3 tblsp. cooking oil	½ tsp. salt
½ tsp. salt	⅛ tsp. pepper
1 (8-oz.) pkg. brown-and-serve link pork sausage, cooked and sliced	Paprika
1 c. shredded Cheddar cheese	

Combine shredded potatoes, oil and ½ tsp. salt in bowl; mix well. Press mixture into bottom and up sides of greased 9″ pie plate.

Bake in 425° oven 15 minutes.

Arrange sausage slices in potato shell. Sprinkle with cheese.

Beat eggs in bowl until blended, using a rotary beater. Add milk, onion, ½ tsp. salt and pepper. Pour over sausage-cheese mixture in potato shell. Sprinkle with paprika.

Bake in 425° oven 20 minutes, or until a knife inserted halfway between center and edge comes out clean. Let stand 10 minutes before serving. Makes 6 servings.

Zucchini-Swiss Quiche

Colorful slices of zucchini cover a velvety custard and
Swiss cheese layer in this recipe sent to us by an Iowa farm woman.

1½ c. shredded Swiss
  cheese
1 tblsp. flour
Unbaked 10" pie shell
1 c. sliced, cooked zucchini

⅓ c. minced onion
5 eggs
2 c. half-and-half
1½ tsp. salt

Combine cheese and flour. Sprinkle in bottom of unbaked pie shell.
Arrange zucchini on top and sprinkle with onion.

Beat eggs in bowl until blended, using a rotary beater. Add half-and-half and salt; beat until blended. Pour over vegetable-cheese mixture in pie shell.

Bake in 350° oven 1 hour, or until a knife inserted near center comes out clean. Let stand 10 minutes before serving. Makes 8 servings.

Zucchini-Bacon Quiche

No need to cook the vegetables before adding them
to the custard, because they're finely sliced and chopped.

4 strips bacon
2 eggs
1 c. mayonnaise
¾ c. grated Parmesan
  cheese
1 small zucchini, thinly
  sliced (about 1 c.)

½ c. finely chopped
  green pepper
¼ c. finely chopped
  onion
Quiche Pastry Shell
  (see Index)

Fry bacon in 10" skillet over medium heat until crisp. Remove from skillet and drain on paper towels.

Beat eggs in bowl until blended, using a rotary beater. Add mayonnaise and cheese; beat until blended. Stir in zucchini, green pepper and onion. Crumble bacon and add to egg mixture. Pour egg mixture into unbaked Quiche Pastry Shell.

Bake in 350° oven 35 minutes, or until a knife inserted near center comes out clean. Let stand 10 minutes before serving. Makes 6 servings.

Miniature Bacon Quiches

Great for an open house, these tiny quiches can be prepared before the guests arrive and then reheated as you need them.

Pastry for 2-crust 9" pie	4 eggs
8 strips bacon, diced	1¾ c. milk
½ c. chopped onion	1 tsp. Worcestershire
1½ c. shredded Swiss	sauce
cheese	3 drops Tabasco sauce
¼ c. grated Parmesan	Ground nutmeg
cheese	

Divide pastry in half. Roll out, half at a time, on lightly floured surface to ⅛" thickness. Cut 12 rounds from each half, using floured 3½" round cookie cutter with scalloped edge, rerolling pastry as needed. Line 3" muffin-pan cups with rounds.

Sauté bacon and onion in 10" skillet over medium heat until bacon is browned. Remove bacon and onion; drain on paper towels.

Toss together bacon mixture, Swiss cheese and Parmesan cheese in bowl. Place 1 rounded tblsp. cheese mixture in each pastry-lined muffin-pan cup.

Beat eggs in bowl until blended, using a rotary beater. Add milk, Worcestershire sauce and Tabasco sauce; beat until blended. Spoon 2 tblsp. egg mixture into each shell. Sprinkle each with nutmeg.

Bake in 425° oven 20 minutes, or until set. Cool in pans on racks 5 minutes. Remove from pans and serve immediately. Makes 24 miniature quiches.

Note: If you prefer to make these quiches several hours before serving, cook as recipe directs, cool thoroughly, wrap in aluminum foil and store in refrigerator. To reheat, place on baking sheets in 350° oven 10 minutes, or until hot.

Crustless Bacon Quiche

Here's an easy recipe you can whip up in your blender
at a moment's notice—and it bakes to perfection in half an hour.

8 strips bacon, diced	½ c. butter or regular
3 eggs	margarine, melted
1½ c. milk	Dash of pepper
½ c. buttermilk baking	1 c. shredded Cheddar
mix	cheese

Fry bacon in 10″ skillet over medium heat until crisp. Remove bacon and drain on paper towels.

Combine eggs, milk, baking mix, butter and pepper in blender. Cover and blend 15 seconds, or until smooth. Pour into greased 9″ pie plate. Sprinkle with cheese and bacon. Gently press cheese and bacon below the surface, using the back of a spoon.

Bake in 350° oven 30 minutes, or until a knife inserted halfway between center and edge comes out clean. Let stand 10 minutes before serving. Makes 6 servings.

Extra-Cheesy Hamburger Pizzas

The crusts for these meaty pizzas are easy to make
from hot roll mix: just add water and press the dough into pizza pans.

1 lb. ground beef	Easy Pizza Crusts
1 c. chopped onion	(recipe follows)
1 (15-oz.) can tomato	2 c. shredded mozzarella
sauce	cheese
1 tsp. dried basil leaves	½ c. grated Parmesan
¼ tsp. pepper	cheese

Brown ground beef and onion in 10″ skillet over medium heat. Drain off excess fat. Stir in tomato sauce, basil and pepper; set aside.

Prepare Easy Pizza Crusts.

Spread half of the ground beef mixture over each crust. Sprinkle each with half of the mozzarella and half of the Parmesan cheese.

Bake in 425° oven on lowest rack 18 minutes, or until bottoms of crusts are golden brown. Makes 2 (12″) pizzas or 8 servings.

Easy Pizza Crusts: Remove yeast packet from 1 (13¾-oz.) pkg. hot roll mix. Sprinkle yeast over 1 c. lukewarm water (105° to 115°) in bowl. Stir to dissolve. Add hot roll mix and stir until soft dough forms. With greased fingers, divide dough in half. Press each half into greased 12″ pizza pan, forming ½″ rim around edge.

Hot Dog Pizzas

So simple that even children can make them—and so good
that they'll probably be requested often. Makes two 12″ pizzas.

Biscuit Pizza Crusts
  (recipe follows)
1 (14¾-oz.) can pizza
  sauce
¼ c. chopped onion
1 tsp. Italian herb
  seasoning

¼ tsp. pepper
2 (4-oz.) pkg. shredded
  pizza cheese
5 frankfurters, sliced
½ c. grated Parmesan
  cheese

Prepare Biscuit Pizza Crusts and set aside.

Combine pizza sauce, onion, Italian seasoning and pepper in bowl; mix
well. Spread half of the pizza sauce mixture over each crust. Top each
with half of the pizza cheese, half of the frankfurters and half of the Parmesan cheese.

Bake in 425° oven 18 minutes, or until crusts are golden brown.
Makes 2 (12″) pizzas or 8 servings.

Biscuit Pizza Crusts: Combine 3½ c. buttermilk baking mix and 1 c.
milk in bowl. Stir until soft dough forms. Turn dough onto lightly floured
surface and knead gently 10 times or until smooth. Divide dough in half.
Roll out each half to 13″ circle and fit loosely into greased 12″ pizza pan,
forming ½″ rim around edge.

Sausage Pizza

A basic sausage pizza for the traditionalist, made with just
three ingredients: pizza sauce, pork sausage and mozzarella cheese.

½ lb. pork sausage, cut
  into ½″ chunks
¾ c. Pizza Sauce
  (recipe on p. 269)

1 Freeze-Ahead Pizza Crust
  (recipe on p. 269)
1 c. shredded mozzarella
  cheese

Cook pork sausage in 10″ skillet over medium heat until well
browned. Drain sausage on paper towels.

Spread Pizza Sauce over Freeze-Ahead Pizza Crust. Top with browned
sausage. Sprinkle with cheese. Place pizza directly on rack (not in pan) at
lowest position in oven.

Bake in 500° oven 7 minutes, or until bottom of crust is golden. Remove from oven, using baking sheet as giant spatula. Makes 4 servings.

Hamburger Pizza

If you keep a pizza crust on hand in your freezer, you can assemble and bake this simply delicious pizza in almost no time.

½ lb. ground beef
¾ c. Pizza Sauce
  (recipe on p. 269)
1 Freeze-Ahead Pizza Crust
  (recipe on p. 269)

½ green pepper, cut into
  strips
1 c. shredded mozzarella
  cheese

Cook ground beef in 10″ skillet over medium heat until lightly browned. Drain fat from skillet.

Spread Pizza Sauce over Freeze-Ahead Pizza Crust. Top with browned ground beef and green pepper. Sprinkle with cheese. Place pizza directly on rack (not in pan) at lowest position in oven.

Bake in 500° oven 7 minutes, or until bottom of crust is golden. Remove from oven, using baking sheet as giant spatula. Makes 4 servings.

Pepperoni Pizza

Pepperoni slices, onion rings and lots of gooey mozzarella have made this recipe one of our longtime favorites. Delicious!

¾ c. Pizza Sauce
  (recipe on p. 269)
1 Freeze-Ahead Pizza Crust
  (recipe on p. 269)
1½ oz. sliced pepperoni

2 thin onion slices,
  separated into rings
1 c. shredded mozzarella
  cheese

Spread Pizza Sauce over Freeze-Ahead Pizza Crust. Top with pepperoni and onion rings. Sprinkle with cheese. Place pizza directly on rack (not in pan) at lowest position in oven.

Bake in 500° oven 7 minutes, or until bottom of crust is golden. Remove from oven, using baking sheet as giant spatula. Makes 4 servings.

Freeze-Ahead Pizza Crusts

Use this recipe to stock your freezer with four prebaked crusts— then you'll be ready next time someone at your house craves a pizza.

7 to 8 c. unsifted flour
2 pkg. active dry yeast
1 tsp. salt

2½ c. warm water (110°
  to 115°)

Combine 2½ c. of the flour, yeast and salt in large bowl. Add warm water and beat 30 seconds, using an electric mixer at low speed. Beat at high speed 3 minutes, or until smooth.

Stir in enough remaining flour to make a moderately stiff dough.

Turn dough out onto floured surface and knead until smooth and elastic, 8 to 10 minutes. Place dough in greased bowl; turn over to grease top. Cover and let rise in warm place until doubled, about 45 minutes.

Punch down dough. Divide dough into fourths. Roll out each fourth on floured surface to 12" circle and fit loosely into 12" greased pizza pan. (Or roll out each fourth to 12x10" rectangle and place on baking sheet, building up sides to make rim.)

Bake in 500° oven 6 to 8 minutes, or until crusts begin to brown. Cool on racks. Freeze in pans or on flat surface. Remove from freezer, wrap securely in aluminum foil and return to freezer.

To bake, top with your favorite pizza toppings and bake in 500° oven on lowest rack 7 minutes, or until bottoms of crusts are golden. Remove from oven, using baking sheet as giant spatula. Makes 4 (12") pizza crusts.

Note: If you like, add topping to prebaked, cooled crust and freeze until firm. Wrap securely in aluminum foil and return to freezer. Bake in 500° oven on lowest rack 10 minutes, or until bottom of crust is golden.

Pizza Sauce

Made from tomato paste, this sauce has just the right
amount of garlic, oregano and basil to make any pizza tasty.

2 (6-oz.) cans tomato paste
2 cloves garlic, minced
3 tblsp. dried parsley flakes
4 tsp. instant minced
  onion

1 tsp. dried oregano leaves
1 tsp. dried basil leaves
2 c. water

Combine tomato paste, garlic, parsley flakes, minced onion, oregano, basil and water in 2-qt. saucepan. Cook over high heat until mixture comes to a boil. Reduce heat to low; cover and simmer 10 minutes.

Use to make Sausage Pizza, Hamburger Pizza and Pepperoni Pizza. Makes 3 c.

Sicilian Pizza

A thick-crusted pizza topped with the works—mushrooms, salami, olives, sausage, spicy tomato sauce, and lots of mozzarella!

Sicilian Pizza Dough
(recipe follows)
½ lb. sweet Italian
sausage
1 c. green pepper strips
1 (14 ½-oz.) can stewed
tomatoes, cut up
1 (6-oz.) can tomato paste
½ c. chopped onion
1 clove garlic, minced
1 tsp. dried oregano leaves
⅛ tsp. pepper

2 c. shredded mozzarella
cheese
2 oz. sliced hard salami,
cut up
1 (4-oz.) can mushroom
stems and pieces, drained
¼ c. sliced, pitted black
olives
⅓ c. grated Parmesan
cheese
½ tsp. dried oregano leaves

Prepare Sicilian Pizza Dough and let rise while preparing topping.

Meanwhile, remove sausage from casing. Cook sausage and green pepper in 10" skillet over medium heat until sausage is browned. Remove sausage and green pepper and drain on paper towels. Drain fat from skillet.

Add stewed tomatoes, tomato paste, onion, garlic, 1 tsp. oregano and pepper to same skillet. Cook over high heat until mixture comes to a boil. Reduce heat to low. Cover and simmer 25 minutes.

When Sicilian Pizza Dough has doubled, punch down dough. Pat and stretch dough over bottom and three-quarters of the way up sides of greased 15½x10½x1" jelly-roll pan. Cover and let rise in warm place 15 minutes.

Bake in 500° oven on lowest rack 5 minutes, or until crust begins to brown. Remove from oven. Reduce temperature to 450°.

Spread tomato mixture over partially baked crust. Top with 1 c. of the mozzarella cheese, salami, mushrooms, olives, Parmesan cheese, sausage and green pepper.

Bake in 450° oven on lowest rack 15 minutes, or until topping is hot and crust is browned. Sprinkle with remaining mozzarella cheese and ½ tsp. oregano. Return to oven and bake 1 minute more, or until cheese begins to melt. Makes 8 servings.

Sicilian Pizza Dough: Dissolve 1 pkg. active dry yeast in 1 c. lukewarm water (105° to 110°) in bowl. Stir to dissolve. Add 2 tblsp. shortening, 1½ tsp. salt and 1 tsp. sugar. Stir in 3 c. sifted flour, or enough to make a stiff dough. Turn dough out onto floured surface and knead until smooth, about 5 to 8 minutes. Place dough in greased bowl, turning over to grease top. Cover and let rise in warm place until doubled, about 45 minutes.

Index